UKRAINE

A Warning to the World

Thierry Laurent Pellet

UKRAINE

A Warning to the World

Foreword by General Paul Vallely (Ret)

VINDICTA

Vindicta Publishing

Las Vegas ◆ Chicago ◆ Palm Beach

Published in the United States of America by
Histria Books
7181 N. Hualapai Way, Ste. 130-86
Las Vegas, NV 89166 U.S.A.
HistriaBooks.com

Vindicta Publishing is an imprint of Histria Books and a joint venture of Histria Books and Creative Destruction Media (CDM). Titles published under the imprints of Histria Books are distributed worldwide.

Library of Congress Control Number: 2024933423

ISBN 978-1-59211-496-2 (hardcover)
ISBN 978-1-59211-519-8 (eBook)

Contents

To all the unwavering media...

"When we forget the past history, the story we tell is no longer the history, it is another story."

*"In the **truth**, there is no **mediocrity**."*

— Olivier de Kersauson

*In memory of **Daria Dugina** and of those who fell for **being** and thinking...*

Disclaimer

The content of this book is extremely sensitive because it implicates very active Ukrainian neo-Nazi organizations which use the personal information of citizens and their European representatives referenced in lists of targets to be eliminated on the Myrotvorets.center website.

These groups are responsible for the assassination of a large number of politicians, journalists, and other citizens (especially Ukrainian and Russian). I will therefore not comply with associated authorities and laws stipulating that my address must be included in this work as a self-publisher, for obvious security reasons. This risk is a true case of force majeure.

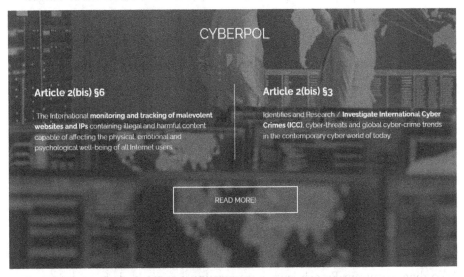

CYBERPOL

Article 2(bis) §6

The International **monitoring and tracking of malevolent websites and IPs** containing illegal and harmful content capable of affecting the physical, emotional and psychological well-being of all Internet users.

Article 2(bis) §3

Identifies and Research / **Investigate International Cyber Crimes (ICC)**, cyber-threats and global cyber-crime trends in the contemporary cyber world of today.

READ MORE!

BLACKLISTED WEBSITES BY CYBERPOL

In terms of the Budapest Convention on cybercrime and organized crime treaty ref# ETS No.185 Art. 3 – Illegal interception, Art. 11 – Attempt, aiding, abetting, Art. 12 – Corporate liability and the first protocol on Xenophobia and Racism ref# ETS No. 189 adopted by CYBERPOL THE INTERNATIONAL CYBER POLICING ORGANIZATION established by Royal Decree WL22/16.595 on 22nd June 2015 with the powers vested under **Article 2(bis) §6** The International **monitoring and tracking of malevolent websites and IPs** containing illegal and harmful content capable of affecting the physical, emotional and psychological well-being of all Internet users of its authorized functions and mandate the following websites are blacklisted and placed under international criminal investigation indefinitely:

...

4) **Myrotvorets[.]center** owned and managed by NGO Myrotvorets Centre Ukraine promoting hatred ideology and assassinations of European citizens and officials.

I personally asked the director of the European entity **Cyberpol**, Mr B.B., to shut down the said site whose owner is none other than the former post-Maïdan president Petro Poroshenko. I have been notified that they are actively working on this very thorny problem. However, I do not believe for a second that any effort whatsoever has been made in this direction. This site has been doing its dirty work for more than eight years now, it has been the subject of several requests to be taken down by European parliamentary committees, **without any results to date.**

This site is managed by an organization **NEO-NAZI called C14**, and not an NGO. This terrorist group has not been banned or subject to an international warrant; it is linked to other extremist groups like Azov, Praviy Sektor, and many others; it cooperates with the SBU (Ukrainian Secret Service), the FBI, the CIA and references a large number of people close to me, some of whom were murdered; no murder perpetrated post-Maïdan has been elucidated, no investigation has been carried out to date. I therefore take note of the criminal nuisance capacity of this group and put in place all the necessary measures to protect myself. All the documents offered in this book have been verified by a group of senior officers of the American armed forces and are also distributed to many of their respective contacts including lawyers, intelligence, geo-politicians and French/European deputies who are or have been part of their respective entities.

The current Ukrainian government's lack of will to denounce the actions linked to these groups makes this country, de facto, a state sponsor of terrorism, and potentially bioterrorism for having allowed biological weapons laboratories to be installed on its territory with absolutely unacceptable levels of security as you will discover.

According to current French laws, not reporting a crime is, de facto, being complicit in this crime. Through this book, I have only applied the law and warned the various French and foreign authorities of the fascist excesses of the criminal regime of post-Maïdan Kiev (*). They ignored it! Let those who have been informed examine their consciences, knowing that their immunity is only linked to a limited time mandate.

To note: the US Republican congressman, **Brad Wenstrup**, heading the **Covid-19 Pandemic Investigation Committee,** has received all the necessary information which is the topic of this book, relating the direct implication of Ukraine in the testing of this virus as well as the death threat from the SBU directed towards Dilyana Gaytandzhieva, the Bulgarian journalist, who initiated the investigation into the laboratories of biological weapons in Europe, which has contributed greatly to our efforts.

(*) And in this specific case we can easily speak of global genocide, you will understand the qualification when reading what follows.

Foreword

Thierry Laurent Pellet is an outstanding intelligence analyst who understands world affairs and articulates those reports in his writings. I have been a recipient of his valued information, particularly the reports on COVID-19 and the Ukraine-Russia conflict.

He is an ultimate professional working with many senior military officers. His reports have been invaluable to the Stand Up America US Foundation. His knowledge is based on an extended time, for example, in Ukraine working with senior officials there. His experience in the Ukraine and Russia crosses social, political, and military areas of interest.

His analysis clarified the different major events regarding the economic impact on the region. As events escalated, Mr. Laurent Pellet warned the West (Europe and America) of the danger of the crisis and the impact on European countries, particularly Ukraine and its people as well as Russia. He clarified the intentions and involvement of the oligarchs and the Azov battalion. The reports on the bioweapon laboratories were very revealing.

I highly recommend this book to everyone to fully understand what has happened to Europe, Russia, the United States, and the world order."

Paul E. Vallely
Major General, U.S. Army (Ret)
Chairman – The Stand Up America US Foundation
and the Legacy National Security Advisory Group

Preface

GLOBAL TREE
PICTURES, Inc.

1925 Century Park East

STE 2140

Los Angeles, CA

Zip 90067

20 of April 2023,

"During the years post Maidan, I had the opportunity to discuss with Thierry Laurent Pellet and exchange our point of view regarding his personal living in Ukraine before and after Maidan. Listening to him I felt the stress he went through and the level of violence he had to witness. Crossing information was useful and comforted us that our production "Ukraine on fire" reflected totally what he experienced.

Thierry point of view is very important, because as a Westerner he was witness of all events in Ukraine on his own. As an expert in that area and author of 4 documentary on the subject of Ukrainian crisis I'm valuing his work pretty high.

Besides, the research Thierry Laurent Pellet and his colleagues conducted regarding the bioweapon labs was compelling. I do recommend reading his book."

CEO of Global Tree Pictures,
Igor Lopatonok

Director, Producer

Igor Lopatonok,
Production Director Global Tree Pictures
Ukraine on Fire - *Oliver Stone Team (*)*

Letter to Ukrainians

Russia is not only your geographical neighbor, but also an integral part of your history because it is your mother. Despite a tumultuous past, conflicting relationships, she will always be a part of your family because during your common history, your families have intertwined, and you cannot divorce your own blood. Your civilization, your culture, your religion are common, forgetting this means forgetting yourself, to the detriment of the essence of your existence. To ignore oneself is equivalent to dying and disappearing in the twists and turns of a pseudo-European culture. It's about to fall into the trap of the USSR (see below).

Not so long ago you were strangled by the shackles of a model of society based on a pure ideological chimera: Bolshevism and Communism. Do not make the mistake of falling into the same trap, because rather than a white dove you will discover a scavenging vulture whose only goal is the submission of populations to satisfy the ego and the interests of a global psychotic oligo-kleptocracy whose sole objective is to enslave the planet. They knew how to exploit your inferiority complex. Don't become the whore of Europe, your women are already in their brothels to survive while your young people are being massacred in combat.

Your elites lied to you; they have deceived, stolen, robbed, manipulated you for decades; they sold your infrastructures, your lands, your forests, your factories, in order to get rich as quickly as possible without risk or effort. Today all of them are all on the Côte d'Azur, in Courchevel, or in Barbados on their Yachts (not subject to sanctions), in their palaces sipping Cristal champagne and eating caviar by the ladle while abusing the opportunities represented by European and American funds, a green color you will never see. They are sending you to get holes in your skin, freezing you in the winter mud while shouting "Slava" from a Ukraine which now belongs to a few US funds, I name BlackRock…

Some idiots made you believe that neo-Nazism is the panacea, the solution. They massacred your brothers, your mothers, your children in Donbass, while the European Union cynically applauded by turning its head away from their heinous crimes, and counted the profits they would make once the Russian-speaking population disappeared. This European Union whose official values are the polar opposite of what these madmen wanted to dust off from the past, did you naively believe in their support? They will let you go when the bill is too heavy to bear, giving you a "Sorry, it's a shame it didn't work out the way we wanted, maybe next time"... But there will be no next time.

Since the beginning of the conflict, the partition of your country was already decided by NATO in high spheres without your acknowledgment. Your awakening will be hard and much worse than a day after being drunk with Pertsovka. Unfortunately, it is far too late to avoid the carnage; your cemeteries are unmistakable proof, and the economic damage is irreversible. Your only solution was to become the Switzerland of Eastern Europe, remaining neutral. Burdened under abysmal and insolvent debts, with your population scattered across the globe, you sawed off the branch you were sitting on.

While you will heal your wounds, cursing Russia for your misfortune and your despair, know that your leaders will relax on deckchairs in the sun aboard their yacht or by their swimming pool, a bit like Rinat Akhmetov does in his luxury hotel in Paris, well sheltered despite the loss of his Azovstal metallurgical complex. I hope that you will understand this message and will be able to forgive yourself for this collective madness and the loss of your own illusions, and that you will be able to become aware of your errors and the horrors that you have accepted as normality, which is what they are not!

Ukrainians, you are SLAVS, do not become EU-slaves!

Comparison of USSR/EUSSR State Structures

Characteristics	USSR	EUSSR
Political structure	President PCUS	President Commission
Parliament	1 PM/ 300K ha/Country	Prorated Pop/Country
Ideology	Communism – Collectivism – Destroyed religion	Wokemunism – Individualism – Destroyed religion
Economy	State-oriented, centralized	Private-oriented, cartelized/Public sounding centralized
Banking system	Centralized GOSBANK Political & economic control tool	Centralized BCE Total economic control tool
Currency	Ruble	Euro
Agriculture	Centralized	Kolkhoze
Police/Security	KGB	EurogenForce/Europol
Army	Red Army	NATO
Language	Multiple but Russian dominant	Multiple but English dominant
Collapsing reason	Against human nature	Ongoing
Difference	Almost none, individual under full control	

A new totalitarianism emerges, it is transnational, it serves an illegitimate and subversive power, it frees itself from nation states by vassalizing them. It is a mixture of Wokism and communism with capitalist appearances which, through media means of false propaganda, has no other aim than to enslave the world population by controlling their mobility, their will, their property... their freedom. Welcome to Hell!

Preamble

I could very well have added many more photos and other layers to this pile: the collaborators, the jokers, the traitors, the puppets…

As some people combine titles, I preferred to simplify to leave readers the choice of attributing to Caesar what would ultimately amount to Caesar. As a serial entrepreneur, having lived in the USA and Ukraine for eight and nine years respectively, quadrilingual, I am part of high-level international networks, and have in particular participated in economic forums from Vienna to Yalta, since the end of February 2015, the date which I left Ukraine definitively. I tried discreetly but in vain to make my interlocutors across the world understand that this country was going to cause serious problems in the near future. Ministers, deputies, senators, monarchs, presidents, advisors, decision-makers from various industries, intelligence services, very high-level military personnel, no hierarchy has escaped my very persistent warnings.

Either ignored, considered lightly, or because my interlocutors felt powerless to act, my admonitions went unheeded. I am not, of course, talking about those who benefit from the present situation, and admit it with smiling cynicism. The elephant remained on the table, watched by everyone while they waited for it to really start breaking the china.

But today my phone rings from morning to evening. My interlocutors seek to understand and find the keys to resolving this infamous mess which will leave an indelible mark in the history of Europe and the USA. It will remain as the biggest unhealthy hypocrisy, the biggest mass manipulation, and the biggest crime ever perpetrated after the Covid crisis, thus destroying all of our credibility and the image of the values that we are supposed to and have claimed to defend.

I affirm with this preliminary declaration that I have absolutely no conflict of interest, that I receive NO money from any entity whatsoever. My testimony is only a reflection of what I experienced and observed directly, and analyzed. All the actions that I have been able to take to avoid the massacre which is taking place at the gates of Europe have to date only cost me, in particular at the personal, professional, and financial levels. I therefore wish to send a very simple message to those who would dare to question my motivations: "F* you…" It's rude, of course, but very appropriate given the situation. Therefore, any search for lice on my scalp will result in a defamation lawsuit. You've been warned, my thanks and greetings. The written records of the email correspondence that I was able to keep to warn of the danger that would strike are available to a judge who could request them.

I did what my conscience, based on my own system of values, dictated to me. The various actors with whom I am in contact today realize to what extent I was right and measure the level of dire consequences the madness of a minority entails, particularly when it benefits from massive support from the directly interested third parties.

Our way of life, our comfort, our security are now threatened. The balance of the world is shifting and we are only a few centimeters from the abyss. The Internet may have abolished physical distances, and accelerated and facilitated communication capabilities between people; but the cultural and geopolitical chasm have widened to a worrying extent. Our passivity, whatever the causes, has directly contributed to the increasing control of the ruling classes to our detriment. The mainstream Western media has contributed decisively to the increase in international tensions and hatred of others instead of playing their initial role of moderator and informer. Regarding that topic I would like to quote John Swinton, former chief of staff of *The New York Times*:

"There is nothing like it, at this date in world history, in America, as an independent press. You know it and I know it. There is not one of you who dares to write your opinions honestly, and if you do, you know in advance that it will never appear in the press. I get paid every week to keep my honest opinion out of the newspaper I work for. Others of you receive salaries for similar things, and any of you who would be foolish enough to write your honest opinions would be out on the streets looking for another job. If I allowed myself to publish my honest opinions in an issue of my newspaper, within twenty-four hours, I would have lost my job. **The job of journalists is to destroy the truth; flat out lie; pervert; defame; flatter the feet of Mammon** (worship of money) **and sell his country and his race to earn his daily bread.** You know it and I know it and what madness is it, toasting an independent press? **We are the tools and vassals of rich men** who remain behind the scenes. We are puppets, they pull the strings and we dance. Our talents, our possibilities and our lives are all the property of other men. **We are intellectual prostitutes.**"

What lucidity and panache, at the precise moment when, as individuals, we can measure what it costs us to dare to think differently! The pack of hyenas of right thinking pull out their labels "conspirator, anti-vaxxer, Putinist..." and pounce on you like a hungry monster to stick one on your forehead. They want to make you outcasts, lock you into a mold and put a padlock on your freedom of thought.

Many have tried this type of alienation, but if they were able to lock up physical individuals, they were never able to lock up their way of thinking, because thought cannot be locked up or controlled. Remember Nelson Mandela, Julien Assange, you, the cockroaches of the press, you, the French publishers, and there are many of them, who refused to publish this book which perhaps made your little collaborators' hearts tremble. With each refusal I saw a new yellow star sewn on a coat, like in 1941 before the Vel d'Hiv roundup.

So you, the distorters of truth and other anti-scribes, be careful, because as Cyrano de Bergerac could have said: "**At the end of this book, the truth hits home.**"

Prologue

Humanity according to Pascal, in his theory of the infinitely small and the infinitely large (the two infinities), oscillates between these extreme spaces which take it between the jaws of a vice, and can apprehend neither one nor the other.

The planets and other celestial bodies of the infinitely large, as well as the atoms and other electrons of the infinitely small, interact with each other, collide, destroy each other, produce energy or absorb it. Human beings do not escape these laws in any way, they act like millions of ping pong balls thrown into a closed box where each one tries to define its own trajectory but finds itself diverted from it due to untimely collisions or just by chance.

This is how our lives go, driven by a desire, a projection, a goal to achieve, a vision of our environment, then a collision changes this well-established course and also our vision of the world. From a comfortable and carefree life where everything goes for the best in the best of all possible worlds (Voltaire), it only takes one event that you were witnessing while unconscious, for all your certainties to collapse.

You begin to look at the world through the prism of this violent reality, an astonished and shocked witness. This is how your new life trajectory imposes itself on you. So you can always turn your head and bury your head in the sand, believing that what you witnessed does not concern you or you can act in order to influence the course of events on which your life has just been shattered.

Maybe you will find the courage. The courage to act, the courage to think freely has become a luxury these days, the same courage that coming out of laundry detergent box leaders fear because it challenges their power. So they do everything possible to prevent it from operating. Freedom of thought cannot be hindered and it is expressed in this book. Only the resulting concrete expression can be hindered.

They are afraid of the powers sitting in place; they are afraid of not conforming to the biased and media-formatted vision of others, the one who judges even if ill-informed. They have the same fear as the European populations in 1941 in front of the Nazis, and they turn their heads to avoid being confronted to reality. One day they will say "We didn't know" to forget their cowardice, and will at the same time be horrified and helpless in the face of the scale of the scandal and the massacre. They are partly responsible because they kept silent.

Einstein said: "**The world is dangerous not because of those who do evil, but because of those who watch and say nothing.**" If he were still alive, he would add "Or because of those who, through their intellectual deviance or their financial enslavement, allowed the lie to transform into truth."

This book is a living testimony. Will it be the ping pong ball that changes the color of light through your prism? It's up to you to judge...

I. From the USA to Ukraine, the Tribulations of an Entrepreneur

It is September 11, 2001. I come out of my shower, ready to go to 909 Las Colinas Boulevard, Irving, TX, where I work at i2 Technologies, and glance absently at my big screen TV, where MSNBC shows in a loop this gaping hole in the North Tower of the World Trade Center in NY, through which thick black smoke escapes. I remain stunned without really understanding what is happening, when I see the second plane hit the second tower live and finally realize the seriousness of the situation. Everything is happening very quickly in my head, I jump into my Corvette C5, rush to my company, and enter the office of my manager, a Frenchman of Syrian origin. We look at each other as if struck by lightning, and I tell him: "The party's over, it's going to be shit for the next 20 years!" We immediately understand the consequences: we are ruined but alive, so for two days instead of going to work, I decide to cycle from morning to evening, to put my life in perspective.

And indeed, Dante's hell begins, three days of a closed stock market. When it opens on Friday, it's a dive. A plunge that never ends, the ENRON affair hits the CEO, Greg Brady, then there are customer problems due to the quality of the software delivered, the NIKE scandal, then that of Ingram Micro, customers fleeing, the digital economy is collapsing, the Internet bubble is exploding in our faces. The cuts in the workforce are enormous, with 500 to 1000 people laid off every month for a year. The stock of i2 goes from $212 to $1.80, no more stock options, in the water. With a strike price of $42, exercising them would be madness and ruin. "Goodbye calf, cow, pig, even brood," Jean de la Fontaine would have exclaimed…

So we have to start again, from scratch. And thinking a little with this incredible number of people in the job market that the internet bubble left on the floor, I analyzed the terribly laborious recruitment processes, and decided to develop an application for scraping recruitment sites which I managed to market at Best Buy, CompUSA. This allowed me to finance a much more ambitious project, "Stream-Jobs", a peer-to-peer system for candidates and recruiters to bypass job boards. But I needed many more development resources, and after meeting Jean François Poncet, at the time vice-president of the Senate, at Mr. Consul of San Francisco, he motivated me to return to France and set up a partnership with a university. That is what I did, heading to Marseille, Luminy, where I met Andrey Bondarenko, a young Ukrainian doing his doctorate in mathematics at the CNRS. The guy was brilliant, way above the crowd, and even went so far as to humiliate one of his lecturers during the defense of his thesis. He developed our multi-criteria matching system and decided that I should go to Kiev to see if the air was fresher at the Kibernetik Institut.

After meeting Igor Shevchuk, the director, I realized how smart were the engineers on site. The atmosphere was still special and, let's say, rustic. The first discussions lasted almost the day, without the offer of a glass of water. Then around 5 p.m., I was invited to the cafeteria where a huge carafe filled with transparent and icy liquid was waiting for us... Thinking it was water, and thirsty after a day of "crossing the desert," I rushed to the large glass, ignoring the very insignificant accompanying shot glass. Under the stunned gaze of my hosts, I greedily swallowed the glass only to realize, too late, that it was vodka and not water. And this was how they showed me around the city which, despite a temperature of -34 and my advanced stage of intoxication (or because of it) pleased me enormously. I felt good about it and after thinking carefully, I recruited a team of engineers to finalize the platform currently under development.

So it was February 2006. I had to return to France because I managed a large potential client there "3 Suisses international" and we still had the training of the various recruiters to put in place before deploying our platform. In June, Andrey had to participate in the Mathematics Olympiad in Odessa in the south of Ukraine and I decided to accompany him. The city is fantastic, I really liked the atmosphere, and I met Olesya.

It was decided, I would settle down to live with her and travel back and forth between France and Ukraine. It was not easy, but this life suited me. I adapted, and learned to trust, even if not always everyone. In these difficult times, fraud and Pinocchio syndrome were everywhere.

I was also surprised by the disparities in living standards and attitudes between city, region, and countryside. To think that Ukraine is this wonderful and idyllic country that the media wants to sell us today is still a lot of nonsense. French people who have lived there for years even go so far as to tell me that it is a white Africa... The statement may shock but it reflects a sacred reality, that of the attitude of foreigners there.

AN "AFRICA" AT THE GATES OF EUROPE

First of all, we quickly understood that the financial resources collected were not redistributed fairly. The infrastructures were in a terrible stage. Comparing Kiev and Odessa would be a bit like comparing Paris and a provincial city in the nineteenth century, in France, a sort of incomprehensible space-time journey. Broken roads, wastewater evacuation systems that overflow during heavy rains, electrical cables in all directions, complicated internet access, huge disparities between city centers and suburbs, dilapidated hospitals... I remember the orphanage in Odessa, in which children slept on the floor in boxes. Which surprised me all the more when I saw the standard of living in Kiev where Porsche Cayennes bloomed like daisies in spring. I don't dare describe life in the villages to you, you would have thought you were in the eighteenth century, no running water (they were forced to collect water from the well), no toilet (a hut at the bottom of the garden, and not the one by Francis Cabrel), no bathroom (water was heated on the stove and mixed with cold water, the toilet in the kitchen stood on a bath towel)... When I visited my step-dad Nik in his village in the west of Odessa, the last kilometers were done on foot because the path was impassable by marshrutka (minibus). I was catapulted into my great-grandmother's way of life in Italy, through terrible winter temperatures.

Who was the prime minister of that time? Yulia Timoshenko, this "poor" political victim of the evil pro-Russian Yanukovich... Who was put in prison when the Kiev prosecutor realized that she had embezzled 2.3 billion dollars by reselling Russian gas to Ukraine at a non-preferential price through her own company while being the representative of the Ukrainian State... A Cahuzac in nitromethane boosted mode. So we can understand how ridiculous the Europeanists were who screamed at the scandal of the persecuted politician while clawing their chest and face.

Her people lived in poverty while she lived in rowdy and insulting luxury, at the expense of the state. Many years earlier, she had served time in prison for tax evasion and then also escaped conviction for the murder of Yevhen Shcherban, CEO of the Donbass Industrial Union, a rival gas company. Murder "never proven," that said, given the sums involved... Life therefore unfolded almost like a long, quiet river. Until... The crisis of 2008 hit me violently! It was a real disaster, my potential clients abandoned the project StreamJobs and to survive, I converted my team to global outsourcing. I looked for projects all over the world and had them developed by my engineering team. As the team grew, I moved to Kiev in the city center, Malaya Zhitomirskaya street, 50 m from Maidan. One of my clients suggested that I set up a startup "KoolDiner" and convert my team which would be dedicated solely to its development. I accepted the deal, a fatal error for which I paid dearly afterwards.

In Kiev, I met Evgeniy P, in his sixties, a very high-level scientist. I discovered his character gradually. A complex guy with tortuous thinking, I quickly understood that he was not only a scientist and that he certainly held a very high position in the KGB during the existence of the USSR. He was evasive when I asked the question directly, a silent laugh betrayed by a look hidden behind rectangular glasses... His son was wanted by Interpol for having hacked and emptied bank accounts all over the world, a slate which would cost dearly to save him from prison. Evgeniy had built the first Geiger counter during the Chernobyl accident, he was in charge of measuring the radioactivity around the power plant and also calculating the optimal time allowing the liquidators (the 860,000 men dedicated to the evacuation of radioactive waste ejected by the explosion of the power plant) to stay alive as "long" as possible, namely six minutes after coming down from the roof of the power plant. This is how I discovered that in the first week 7,800 men had died and that in the first month 62,000 men had perished. Helicopter pilots who were pouring containers of water on the molten reactor to cool it made three rotations and died. Evgeniy's father was the director of the project which consisted of digging a tunnel under the power plant to install a cooling system in order to avoid Chinese syndrome and polluting the entire pan-European water table... He died of cancer. Today there are only 190,000 "living" men left in this group out of almost one million men and the population has dropped by several million due to multiple cancers. There are no young people in Ukraine whose parents do not have cancer. Moreover, you only need to travel to the Kiev Sea region to see the tumors that develop on the jaws of horses grazing on the nearby grass while Pripyat is still 50 km away. On the left bank of the Kiev Sea, Evgeniy showed me an area on a map which was prohibited and unknown to the public. Alluvium is deposited there massively, and the level of radioactivity is enormous, penetrating this area, he told me, is a certain death sentence. If you walk the streets of Kiev, you will see very few elderly people... And for good reason! As a quick aside, I heard an interview with Mr Loïc Le Floch Prigent by Mr Raphaël Mezrahi on Thinkerview, where he said that "a few dozen" firefighters died. I have rarely heard such lies in my life, a shame! Besides my friend Evgeniy, he too left due to the Chernobyl crab, in April 2013.

This is how, little by little, my dear friend Evgeniy began to reveal to me a certain number of juicy anecdotes about his "contacts" in the KGB, espionage techniques, certain information about Ukraine and precisely the frauds and abuses committed by its oligarchs. The extended aperitif evenings were not lacking in interest. From year to year, I learned something new and unripe, notably how Timoshenko, the innocent white dove, stole Russian gas in transit to Europe. Information that I did not fail to transfer to the Russian consul in Marseille when I left Ukraine permanently. I remember a conversation about the 13.6 billion dollars sent by the IMF in the 2010s, former President Chirac had a perfectly adapted formula to describe what had happened... "Pshiiiit!"

Evgeniy and his team had set up a most serious investigation to understand the "evaporation" mechanisms which allowed the funds to disappear, they did not find the shadow of a transfer line, all traces had disappeared completely into the abyss of the oligarchs' offshore accounts. Not seen, not caught! We can, certainly, explain the sumptuous Courchevel chalet that Igor Kolomoisky offered himself with our taxes, but who cares? He is of course a Ukrainian saint who must be forgiven for everything. We will return to this odious character later, he is not lacking in interest. After several years in the country, my very monolithic Western vision of Ukrainian society began to change by observing the behavior of my team, part of which was in Moscow and Krasnodar in Russia, the other in Kiev (but coming from different regions including Donetsk) and in Lviv in Ukraine.

A COMPLEX ETHNIC SOCIETY

Believing that Ukraine is a single, unified society would be a big mistake. First of all, there is a very strong sociological overlap between Russians and Ukrainians, the number of mixed families in Russia as in Ukraine is significant. While Western Ukraine has today slipped towards a "very far-right Ukrainisation" of society (education, language, literature, etc.) at that time, no one around me spoke Ukrainian. In winter I went skiing with a member of my team, Yuri, to Bukovel in the Carpathians, in summer I went to Odessa or Crimea and that's how I was able to understand the ethnicities, culture, and language of this country. In Western Ukraine, people spoke to me and I understood absolutely nothing. My knowledge of Russian was not fantastic, but I got by as best I could, and I only later understood that in this region they spoke a kind of Russo-Polish mixed with Hungarian with an absolutely impenetrable accent. In Crimea, in Odessa, it was different; my friends told me that they were Russian and I didn't really understand why.

This is how my conversations with Evgeniy enlightened me on the divide in this country. Symptomatically, the soccer games between Dynamo Kiev and Spartak Moscow gave a spectacle of desolation, which did not bode well. Ukrainian hooliganism was a worrying phenomenon, the participants in these movements were incredibly violent and against everyone. Russians, Europeans, anyone who didn't have a Yellow and Blue scarf had to take a beating. I remember a Guingamp-

Dynamo Kiev game, during which the French supporters had to leave the central stadium, pursued by a horde of savages armed to the teeth to beat them up.

Ukraine is not, or rather was not simply linked to Russia from a societal but also economic point of view, due to its imbrication in the former USSR structure, in particular its military-industrial complex, which worked almost only for the Russian army (155mm shell in Kiev, ballistic system in Dnepropetrovsk, etc.) and also because of its energy dependence - Ukraine benefited from preferential rates on oil and gas allowing the population to live comfortably heated during harsh and long winters.

But that's not all, Ukraine is a bit like the daughter of Russia, so Mom buys her bonds on the financial markets in order to support her economy and pay her civil servants' bills, and there are also many commercial agreements between companies. This financial package represents hundreds of billions of dollars invested by Russia that a good number of Ukrainians quickly forgot, all due to the siren call of Europe. In the business world, we call this "spitting in the soup." Imagine being a business leader who has taken out a $200 billion loan and hearing your debtor say: "Poka do svidania, I'm going to suck up another pigeon." Personally, this would go badly. In fact, the oligarchs understood that it would be easier to dive into the coffers of their own banks upon receipt of Euro-Atlantic funds than to defraud the issued bank bonds purchased by Russia under the control of financial market authorities...

Pay off the debt owed to the historic creditor, to sell to its rival. Has such situational awareness ever been visible in the history of humanity?

Ergo, Maïdan is on the way!

II. The Beginnings of the Shameful Revolution

Ukraine is a Slavic country, the result of multiple and very particular influences. It is the link between European and Eurasian civilizations. It is an emergence of different peoples, cultures, and religions who were united by a desire to live together, certainly with some small group frictions but insignificant compared to the general trend. The only problem (and what a problem!) was (still is, but no longer the only one) the incredible corruption of its elites, who happily plundered this country to the detriment of the general population kept in a state of appalling poverty for decades. The Ukrainian elite was clever enough to use the general discontent for its own benefit. Whether they are pro-Russian or pro-Ukrainian, the politicians of this country have only one objective: to fill their pockets as quickly as possible without worrying too much about the details. Corruption anyway is a national sport where everyone, from the highest to the lowest, tries to cheat everyone, limited only by a fertile imagination. The whole of society complains about it with remarkable candor, but everyone practices this sport and enjoys it as much as possible. Get stopped on the road, 20 Grivna (1.6€) in the driving license and thank you. You want a driving license or a visa for Europe, it's $100. It gets a lot more expensive at higher levels. During my stay the black-market estimates represented 50% of GDP. Nobody wanted to pay his taxes, and it continued to get worse.

I was meeting a group of French people in Kiev who had come to set up the headquarters of their airport security consulting activity with European funding. The team leader, Louis G, quite a man with a lot of talent because he lived in Russia for several decades, seemed very friendly to me. I helped them find apartments and that's how a great friendship was born. A Supaéro engineer, speaking English and Russian fluently, he is responsible for accepting the project to secure Borispol Airport with a view to increasing traffic for Euro 2012. I warned Louis that here in Kiev without a good briefcase garrisoned, getting a Ukrainian minister to accept such a project risked being a very difficult task. A few hours after his meeting with the Minister of Transport Youshenko (pro EU), we met in a restaurant in the center of Khreschiatik, "Shato," to taste Pertsovka, an extraordinary chili-honey vodka. Louis arrived disappointed and said to me: "What the hell is this country! You were right, the first thing he said to me was: 'Where is my money!' Dobro pozhalovat' v Ukraine, brat!

Thus Louis realized that most Ukrainian politicians first made a career in banditry and crime, the famous Poroshenko "became" or rather parachuted into post-Maïdan president, cut his teeth in drugs and prostitution and much worse before trading his Glock for a suit and the "Roshen" chocolate factory, part of whose turnover is still made in Russia today. Money has no taste or smell!

THE CONTEXT

2010 was a pivotal year which marked the changeover of Ukraine, the election of Yanukovich (pro-Russian) triggered the indictment of former Prime Minister Timoshenko in June 2011 for abuse of power and embezzlement of funds by prevarication thanks to the lucrative gas contracts signed with Russia, which we talked about in the previous chapter.

The tents of demonstrators who came to support Timoshenko were springing up like mushrooms on Maïdan. It was actually quite surprising because there were crazy people throughout the weeks, and the first question that arose for me was: "But who pays these people to do nothing from morning to evening for months? Living in Kiev is very expensive; we are not in Chernivtsi or Rivne."

Kiev is a trompe-l'oeil mirage; foreigners arrive in the capital and think they are in Paris; on the other hand, you only need to go 50 km out of the city to experience a San Diego-Tijuana style shock. Kiev is a cosmopolitan city where money flows. Embassies and IT companies have developed significantly thanks to the efforts of the Tigipko family, the husband Sergey being deputy prime minister and Viktoria his wife, at the head of a forum investment for startup, IDCEE in which I participated thanks to my friend Evgeniy. The IT industry had gone from $200M to $2B in a few years, Globallogic, Cyklum, Microsoft, Google, Facebook, Oracle, all the big guys from Silicon Valley rushed to Kiev to recruit from the best universities and business schools. Engineers like the famous Kiev Polytechnic Institute (KPI). Wages thus exploded and personal services were able to develop and create a middle class, however limited.

In certain circles that I frequented, notably "Internations," I began to appreciate the increasingly pressing European influence, of the ambassadors who came to evenings for a rather young crowd, what were they doing there? Little did I know what was being prepared right under my nose.

When Yanukovich wanted to break the demonstration in support of Timoshenko, he banned tents on Maïdan, but accepted them on the top of Khreschatyk near Arena and sent the tent to Kharkov to avoid any uprising, while remaining very accommodating.

During Euro 2012, all European leaders boycotted the matches and did not go to Kiev to celebrate this event, despite colossal efforts to build infrastructure (stadium, roads, bridges, etc.). There was a political desire to humiliate Yanukovich by snubbing him, to support a criminal. One wonders if the various European leaders were still able to distinguish between the position that Timoshenko occupied and what she really did to enrich herself, a blank check for corruption and fraud. Perhaps they simply did not care - anything that could be used to weaken Russia in Ukraine suddenly became legitimate.

Besides, during Euro 2012, a funny mishap happened to me. Having to meet my team lead, Roman, to invite him to lunch, I found myself on Kreschatik opposite the Shato restaurant in the middle of a fan zone, a crazy crowd, with noise that prevents me from hearing him on the phone. I feel at home in this famous restaurant which serves as my canteen and "team gathering" location on Saturdays when I invited my team for a nice brunch outside of a work session. When I was going up the stairs to shelter from the noise, a nasty guy with a face that would scare you at night (during the day too...) stood in the way and barred me from entering in a very pronounced British accent. I explained to him that I only had a few minutes and he began to act extremely vindictively; his tone rose and two of his acolytes came down and began to threaten me in a violent manner. Given their behavior and their appearance, in hindsight, there was absolutely no doubt that these guys were not only not football supporters, but that they were most certainly in recognition of the events to come.

It should be noted in this regard that the CEO of the largest marketing company in Kiev, the Pulse Agency, was a former member of the marketing services information at British MI6, which, in retrospect, could explain the presence of these individuals who were so un-Ukrainian. He was very well introduced into post-Maïdan Ukrainian society, at a very high level.

In one night in October 2013 everything went crazy: 4 m high barricades, barbed wire, entry control gantry on Maïdan with more than dubious guys in military fatigues doing "face checks" (some hiding guns in their hands under their jackets), flags in all directions with Nazi symbols, all the streets adjacent to Maïdan blocked with masses of sandbags, a political podium at the foot of the Hotel Ukraina on the other side of Globus. A real war zone organized and designed to channel the Berkuts (Ukrainian CRS), whose barracks are in my street, along a single axis towards the top of Maïdan, a real mousetrap. It screamed until 2 a.m. every day, life becomes a real hell which can very quickly get out of control at the sight of the behavior of certain people... A real "muscular vest-jaundice." The considerable cost of this "spontaneous" demonstration is certainly part of the $5 billion that US "diplomat" Victoria Nuland so elegantly boasted about.

I didn't think I was saying that well since I subsequently discovered that the hot tea distributed free of charge on Maïdan was loaded with captagon, a Table B amphetamine that DAESH fighters used to avoid feeling fatigue, pain, and fear in Syria, manufactured in clandestine CIA laboratories in Bulgaria. Years before I had spoken with a young ranger in Las Vegas, who was returning from Syria; he told me that he had to fire several rounds into a jihadist before seeing him fall. He had the impression of fighting against invincible zombies. So, this was how a peaceful population went crazy in Kiev and set fire to hundreds of Berkuts... Many people who participated in this terrible charade ended up in rehabilitation clinics for withdrawal, Doctor Jekyll and babushka Volk.

Maïdan atmosphere, Nazi flag when leaving my apartment!

III. Why Shoot Down Ukraine?
The Real Issues!

Let's take a step back from the unfolding events of Maïdan in order to understand the underlying plan. Consequences always have causes and uncontrollable side effects! The USA has been at war since its creation, the American military-industrial complex represents more than 3.5% of America's GDP, which represents the largest global expenditure.

Since 2001, the USA has continued to push manufacturing outside towards Asia and mainly China; the only thing they can sell today that has high added value is weaponry. They therefore need to fuel conflicts all over the world to survive. In 2008, the real estate crisis was aggravated by exorbitant oil prices. These two factors combined almost defeated Uncle Sam. From then on, they developed the extraction of shale gas and oil to free themselves from the threat of external energy shortage. But this shale gas is only profitable if the barrel is above around $45. If demand collapses as during the Covid crisis then all the companies involved in this type of very expensive CAPEX project collapse.

This is what happened between 2020 and 2021 when lockdowns paralyzed the global economy... It even happened that the barrel went into negative prices because the refineries could not be stopped. The quantities refined were such that they exceeded storage capacities and the oil companies were prepared to pay to get rid of a bulky stock that could lead to production stoppages of terrible complexity. This was a terrible blow to the companies which had invested enormous capital, and brought them to the brink of bankruptcy. The post-Covid recovery was crucial for these companies.

In 1994, an article in the NYT related an interview with Colin Powell, the man with the "silver vial" sent to the UN to "prove" that Iraq was a producer of anthrax and other weapons of mass destruction (never actually found). By the way, if the vial contained any it would have put all the diplomats on the planet at risk... Ridiculous!

He also has declared: "We must bring Ukraine into our portfolio to control Russia." First attempt, the Orange Revolution of November 2004 which ended with a terrible flop and the election of Yushchenko. Did this solve the corruption problem in Ukraine? No. The oligarchs are bandits whatever their political side, and they are diving into the fund under the benevolent gaze of the USA.

But why focus on Ukraine in this way with 42% of Russians and Russophones in the country... It's not an easy thing. The real goal is of course to destabilize Russia, to balkanize it in order to get their hands on all its agricultural, gas, oil, and mining wealth (Wheat, Barley, Potash, Zinc, Aluminum, Uranium, Gold, Platinum, Titanium, etc.). Strong power in the Kremlin is a significant obstacle. Natural resources are limited on earth, they will run out sooner or later, so appropriation ex nihilo will always be welcome, and we still have to tear the bear's claws out, which is no easy task. What could be more suitable than destabilizing Ukraine because in this country everything can be bought without any moral limits.

As General Miller said: "$50 billion to bring down this country was a gift compared to the humiliation of the $1.5 trillion ejection from Afghanistan by guys riding mopeds, AK-47s slung over their shoulders."

THE SOCIOLOGICAL REASON OF THE CONFLICT

Once the big piece is swallowed, only China would remain to control the world and set up a world government dominated by the USA (under the control of the Democrats, precision is important, we will see later), and this thanks to transversal organizations such as the Atlantic Council, the World Economic Forum (WEF), Bilderberg and Soros' "Open Society." The sheep slaves at work, the privileged is above ground and free at the beach! I can well imagine the reaction of some here, who must say to themselves... That's it, the author is slipping, he's a conspiracy theorist!

Statement from Sarkozy (Elysée): https://tinyurl.com/ESARKO

Attali's statement: https://tinyurl.com/EATTALI

Statement from Macron (Elysée): https://tinyurl.com/EMACRON

Statement by Klaus Schwab, chairman of the WEF in his book *The Great Reset*: "They will own nothing and will be happy to own nothing."

Not having cognitive dissonance, I read in the sixth paragraph, the last line of Macron's speech, at the APEC 2022 forum: "**We need a single world order. Unique!**" This is not a conspiracy but an established fact that cannot be hidden! You will find the same type of statement from Soros, Schwab, Gates and other dangerous and very deranged benefactors of humanity.

Such a megalomaniacal and psychotic worldview implies terrible things like the unification of thought and conformity to a pre-established mold. This goes against the nature of populations, cultures, religions and above all their differences. These crazy people want you to accept the diversity of the biosphere but you as a population or individual must not exceed the limits that they have defined by ensuring that our differences as a population or individual are no longer acceptable and by making us accept the unacceptable. **Wokism** is born, you are no longer a man or a woman, a father or a mother, you are what you decide to be (non-binary, zombie, extra-terrestrial, woman with a man's genitals or the opposite, and why not a floor lamp, if you wear bulbs as earrings…). More differences to erase the differences; the loss of meaning and reference points, cultivated in the most total chaos (chaos was also praised by George Soros as a necessary condition for making real profits). A real openair hospital serving as an electoral base on clientelism, twenty years ago those were ending in psychiatry.

You will be parent instead of father and mother because we want to allow you from a legislative point of view what nature does not allow - we have (yet) never seen a lion giving birth. You no longer have the right to be Catholic, to wish a Merry Christmas because the republic is secular but, we can wish Eid el Kebir in public. By erasing Christianity, we can make room for other types of religions,

"Greta Thumbergism." That girl explains to you that CO_2 is a scourge while without it, no plant grows. We replace the real scientists who de facto become conspirator-dissidents with Ayatollahs painted green (we also speak of the "Khmer Greens," in homage to their great tolerance). You will be told that an FFP2 mask is useless and then you will be forced to wear one outdoors on a beach in a square drawn on the sand of a minimum of 4 m2.

We are witnessing the establishment of mental alienation based on sending contradictory signals, sociological and psychological conditioning, and a lowering of educational levels in order to submit (this is in the Maastricht agreements). All to break free will, only strong minds resist. Add to this the planned organization of essentially African migration in Europe in order to kill indigenous cultural identity and voila. This is the "philanthropic" goal of Georges Soros through the Open Society organization thanks to funds from the European Union financed in part by our taxes, thank you Jean Claude Juncker who gave him a check for €1 billion… Conspiracy? Soros in an interview on CNN boasts of having financed the Maïdan coup. He and his "NGOs" have since been persona non grata in Russia and Hungary. The globalist diaspora wants to project its pure schizophrenic madness onto entire populations. We want to make your references disappear and transform you into a production tool or consumption machine, the being of light dies out, you become a uniform malleable object at its disposal. Welcome to the "progressive-leftists" ideal imaginary land where they tell you that a cherry is a little red melon and everyone must believe it…

Who refuses this type of deviant behavioral governance and opposes it with cultural, traditional, and family respect? Vladimir Putin!

THE FUTURE COLLAPSE OF THE EUSSR

To understand this extremely serious and complex Ukrainian crisis, it is necessary to distinguish between supranational global goals and the more directly mercantile national interests of specific individuals and entities.

The overall goals involve: "**The total destruction of the European economy in order to restore US hegemony in Europe as well as the introduction of electronic currencies as an international currency reserve and population control.**"

The link between Russia and Germany is the constituent basis of the Eurasian union which would sound the death knell for the dominant Anglo-Saxon empire. This goal would be largely achieved by hitting Germany's energy capabilities. This strategy imposed by the USA at the head of the Euro-Globalist organization, thanks to the suggested sanctions, completely escapes the understanding of the European Union executives due to their mediocrity, corruption, and/or personal interest. They are piloted by the CIA, the WEF, Soros, and the lobbying agencies, they obscure the real European interests without jailing anybody.

The total overhaul of this institution is essential. This involves a redefinition of its mandate, oriented towards global infrastructure projects to support the common interest. Certainly not to legislate according to a copy of the USSR model as well as total control of the financial flows of these administrators by a specialized, independent cabinet, that could be commissioned by third parties without the possibility of self-control. Without this new approach, its collapse will resemble that of the USSR in 1992, in extreme pain.

The German economy had become too threatening due to its global footprint and its ties to Russia. Together, they thus became the pivot of the Eurasian union and a critical complement to the Chinese Belt & Road Initiative (BRI or new Silk Road). The BRI project is financed by China thanks to the Asian Infrastructure Investment Bank (AIIB) founded by three Chinese multi-billionaires, a serious competitor to the World Bank and the International Monetary Fund. A double "Kiss Kool" effect would have followed. The bringing of Russia to its knees was therefore necessary, with the destruction of Europe to better vassalize it, in order to reestablish American economic power... This was without taking into account the fact that today's Russia is not the USSR of the 90s as the brilliant Bruno Lemaire wanted us to believe. This French professor catapulted to minister of the economy after an obscure stint at the ENA, the school for administrative donkeys. Remember that during an interview, he still did not know that 1 hectare = 10 thousand m2 (which more modest people learned in 5th grade in the 70s).

Let's look at the world from a little higher point and see what the reasons are for Uncle Sam to fear the forces involved. Europe, a producer of advanced technology due to its industrial past, but experiencing the threat of decline through its intellectual collapse (for example, the average IQ of the French has fallen below the barrier of 100), Russia, the leading producer of natural resources and advanced scientific discoveries (50% of the world's fundamental discoveries in mathematics and physics), China the reservoir of global manufacturing production and a country in full technological emergence, the union of such forces would be a major unprecedented threat for the Anglo-Saxon world, and the US-UK axis since its financial power could no longer face the Eurasian bloc. This could also explain the real reason for BREXIT, such as the desire to get closer to the USA. The UK always had a propensity to manage its own interests before thinking about those of the community. Moreover, London today controls global finance since all the EU stock exchanges are located in the suburbs of London's city; the stock exchanges of Madrid, Milan, Paris, and Frankfurt have been relocated. This is a fact and a major loss of control, what would happen in the event of a serious disagreement between London and the EU? We also measure through the deployment of such a financial infrastructure, the specter of globalists. This is how the UK, under the benevolent eye of the USA, did not hesitate to blow up the Russian North Stream pipelines and plunge Germany and Europe into unprecedented energy chaos, under the orders of the USA. Surprising because they too suffer from this sabotage.

In 2021, the EU consumed 450 billion cubic meters of gas. Around 35% of natural gas imports come from Russia, i.e. 155 billion m3. Our sanctions geniuses are busy finding new sources of gas supplies around the world. However, which are the largest producers, Qatar (26%), Australia (20%), or Malaysia (9%)? Given the distance to be covered, only Qatar is in the running to allow a rapid supply, but its production capacity is limited to 240 million m3 per year. They also forget an important detail: its delivery, which planned to use the black magic of "Let's Do It" (certainly dear to our Bruno Le Maire).

There are 640 LNG tankers in the world, with a capacity of less than 150K m3. Assuming that they can make three annual rotations from Qatar or US supply points, and ignoring the maximum production constraints of the refineries and mobilizing most of the tankers (which is not the case), it would be necessary to build further "a few thousand" boats to reach the necessary count, which would take hundreds of years... After the destruction of the North Stream pipelines, Germany faces a 30% supply deficit.

The consequences are terrible, the lack of gas leads to a fall in electricity production, the shutdown of two BASF factories, the largest producer of products derived from oil and gas (epoxy resin, plastic, fertilizers, etc.) leads to the paralysis of several industries such as automobiles, aeronautics, construction, cereal production. Hundreds of thousands of jobs are threatened because a large number of companies are moving their production to countries where energy costs are lower (in China and the USA)... Putting an embargo on Russian oil is completely stupid since the European governments obtain their supplies from China and India who refine Russian oil and resell it to the same very intelligent boycotters, after adding their modest remuneration. Which of course also pushes the cost of transport and production of any manufactured products higher. When we know that the final cost of all goods produced includes 33% transport, we quickly understand where inflation comes from. And yet in her statements, Christine Lagarde, chairwoman of the ECB, was surprised not to understand why prices continued to skyrocket despite an increase in key rates. (It is true that this topic has nothing to do with the promotion of a more equitable Europe, her only real expertise, interest, and competence). A simple formula that we apply when the economy is overheating due to overconsumption... And no Christine, inflation is not cyclical but external to consumption mechanisms. Perhaps she knows but nevertheless pretends to ignore it. The consequence is the same - she comes across as an incompetent person who has no place at the head of the ECB. Meanwhile, the bakers are closing because they cannot pay their electricity bill, while the elites are still supplied with bread because they are the only ones who can afford the baguette at an exorbitant price with our tax expenses. During this time, no car chassis will leave Slovak factories, since aluminum production has stopped due to lack of electricity, workers will become unemployed, and the world will be surprised by this industrial disaster.

So of course, in France we try to tinker, we are asked to turn down the heaters, wear pullovers, they (the government) have to hold the people by the hand, we are so "irresponsible" (forgive my humor). Great hero Macron asks the Germans to produce electricity traded for gas in goodwill because Ukraine's Zaporozhye power station went off the grid. The principal, which supplied electricity to Germany, the largest power plant in Europe, unfortunately is at a complete standstill **because of the bombings carried out by Kiev.** They want to blame Russia for a nuclear accident to push NATO into this conflict, while this family affair only concerns these protagonists: Ukraine and Russia, its mother. That said, ironically, all these great theorists of global warming are starting to open coal-fired power stations again while in Switzerland they are banning the recharging of electric cars. (France and Germany, the main suppliers, can no longer suffice for their own needs). Worse still, Macron travels to South Africa to give them a paycheck for €1 billion so that they stop coal extraction, and orders some from them sometimes after the reopening of this type of power plant in France... We are sinking in the tragicomic, Macron could single-handedly fill an insane asylum.

So the Russian economy, which was supposed to sink faster than the Titanic, is absolutely thriving, with a minimal projected contraction of 2.3% in 2022 and surpassing the EU in 2024 according to the IMF. Russia climbs in the world GDP ranking from 15th to 5th place. Foreign currency income flows into the volts of the Russian central bank, the army is allocated unexpected budgets, the minimum wage has just been increased, as well as family allowances to encourage the birth of a third child. Of course, there were some adaptations to put in place. But from the discussions I can have with my friends in Moscow, no one suffers from lack of anything, and the temperature in the apartments is 25 degrees (C) during the winter, enough to make Air France executives turn pale with rage. They are working wearing coats in Paris. A large number of companies have left Russia, which has turned into a colossal opportunity for some. An example is McDonald's abandoning its 850 distribution points: the "M" of MacDonald is transformed into "B" (in Russian the "B" is pronounced "V") and a new brand is born "Vkusno i Tochka" (Delicious and there you have it), all for a cost of a measly symbolic Ruble, or €2 cts. The laws of Antoine Laurent de Lavoisier are well respected in Russia, "Nothing is lost, nothing is created, everything gets transformed." This made Russians realize their need for independence from the West. China being the manufacturing neighbor next door through Kazakhstan, the order book of AliExpress is always full, satellite companies have set up in abundance in Dubai to allow Russia to operate. This flexible world whose doors had to be closed due to this conflict highlighted a capacity for rapid and agile adaptation by Russian society. When I heard Von der Leyen proclaim in the European Parliament that Russia could no longer continue to build missiles due to a shortage of electronic components and that they were dismantling household appliances to recover used components, I imagined with an admiring smile washing machine drums raining down on Ukrainian electrical infrastructure, to replace missiles that have become unavailable. This is a poor understanding of the Russian military-industrial complex; they have had their own foundry for microprocessors and other components for many years. When in 2015, the European Union applied the first economic sanctions, the backlash was immediate and it was French farmers who paid the price: the Russians set up a porcine industry in Crimea with one of the largest livestock farms in Europe, the Breton breeders remained with their noses in the water or rather in the sausage... Hollande resold the Mistral helicopter carriers to Egypt thanks to a French bank loan (which may never be repaid...), and Egypt today joins the BRICS and opposes the sanctions applied to Russia. Who paid? The French, thank you François Hollande! Thanks boss!

THE ESSENTIAL RUSSIA

Westerners cannot measure the resilience of the Russian people, who are intelligent and adaptable. At the Yalta Economic Forum in 2019, I had the opportunity to listen to and discuss with Sergei Glazyev, who successively held the positions of economic advisor to Vladimir Putin, then minister of transport, and subsequently minister of the commission Eurasian. The railway dynamic put in place by Russia to connect China and old Europe through UTLC, a consortium of trains between Kazakhstan, Russia, and Belarus, is a stroke of genius that we owe to Xi Jinping. That is to say the economic support of the BRI project which we spoke about previously.

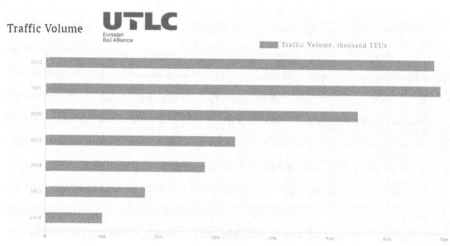

A few months earlier, in October 2018, I attended a meeting behind closed doors dealing with optimization of supply chains between Europe and China using the different existing vectors, rail, maritime, air to the holy of holies: the Austrian central bank with the vice president. Mr. Grom (CEO of UTLC) exposed the exponential growth of his traffic while the maritime freight players pretended to doubt it, so sure of the importance of having marginally lower costs.

The stock/cash flow/supply frequency effect is indeed becoming increasingly important. The train was perhaps 20% more expensive than (this is no longer the case due to the explosion in the cost of diesel). But that is nothing compared to the stock cost of 35 additional days on board of a container carrier crossing oceans with a risk linked to navigation hazards during which your merchandise is immobilized without touching the shelves of your distributors. Decathlon is a big beneficiary of BRI, well it was, because today freight forwarders, due to sanctions, are seeing their prices skyrocketing.

The China-Europe route involves a change of rail at the China-Kazakhstan border. Because sanctions force them to avoid Russia, from Kazakhstan, they go through the Caspian Sea by boat, reload on train in Azerbaijan, cross Georgia, reload on boat, and cross part of the Black Sea to Constanta in Romania to reload on train to truck dispatch points. The next step should go through Saturn or the moon (thanks to Elon Musk), and who knows how much a tennis racket will cost... Great call EU! As for air freight from Asia, the costs have become prohibitive because having to avoid Russian airspace increases kerosene consumption. The Covid crisis has devastated this industrial sector, the cost of oil due to the geopolitical context risks finishing them off if European governance does not recognize their errors (I really want to call them their crimes).

UKRAINE MISSES A UNIQUE OPPORTUNITY

Let's summarize: the reason why the BRI project is so important is that it allows all European companies to increase freight frequencies, while optimizing their inventory and cash flow. This is significant supply chain optimization. This project is based on an investment of around 3 trillion dollars (AIIB).

The Chinese are acquiring/building transportation infrastructures or signing partnerships with those who wish to remain independent. This was the case for Blagnac Airport in France, the Port of Athena in Greece, and the Port of Zadar in Croatia. But be careful, if you do not repay financial loans in China it can cost you dearly. Partners, yes, but be careful. This project aims to bring continents closer together, from Africa to South America. As Dr. Ho said during the Danube region economic forum in 2017, "Asia has 4 billion inhabitants, a population to feed which will double within two generations." Africa will produce what is needed and

Europe will become a hub of capital importance. This is how China financed in Africa the construction of 100 ports, 1000 bridges, 10,000 km of rail, 100,000 km of highway, highlighting the importance of the interconnectivity of these infrastructures to link the continent to Europe, as quickly as possible. Ukraine could have played an essential role in this set of infrastructures because passing through Kiev by land constituted the central corridor to Europe via Vienna in Austria. Doubling transfer capacity is vital for everyone. The USA understood this, so they torpedoed this country partly for this reason, unless the conflict is only a pretext to insert itself into the loop. This infrastructure belt supports a formidable global commercial development strategy that is necessary for the best of all of us.

This is how, on a magnificent sunny day in October 2018, during the EEDF economic forum in Vienna, I questioned the vice president of the European Investment Bank (EIB), Mr. Hudak, on the merits of a (modest) investment of €48 million to upgrade Ukrainian railway infrastructure while their minister the day before, Vladimir Omelian, wanted to declare war on Russia and had ensured that no more trains coming from Moscow would cross Ukraine. You can imagine the discomfort caused and the dead silence that followed, while the Ukrainian infrastructure investment director, Vitaly Kondrativ, looked at his shoes when the moderator wanted to hear his answer.

What followed was a terse sentence from the moderator: "It seems that we are not going to solve the problems of geopolitics today." My response then rocketed like an Iskander missile at the training camp of the foreign mercenary legion in Lviv: "It will still cost us dearly in Porsche Cayenne..." In an audience of 400 European supply chain leaders and other politicians, only two burst out laughing: the representatives of UTLC Russia who did not fail to thank me for this memorable and unforgettable hit.

Email sent on October 15, 2018, to the Austrian Economic Senate:

Request to bann Ukraine of EEDF » inbox ×

thierry laurent   Oct 15, 2018, 10:45 AM   ☆   ↩   ⋮
to

Dear

I raised the legitimacy/relevancy of railway investment in Ukraine during the discussion (EEDF morning session of the 9/10/2018) due to the fact their minister of transport Vladimir Omelian came out with a worrisome statment (8th of August on 1+1 TV Chanel) calling for disrupting any railroad link with Russia and therefore destroying completely the Belt and Roads Initiative our community support with so much energy. Two weeks ago, the president of Rada, Andriy Parubiy, but also former founder of the first neo Nazi party UNO (now Svoboda) in Ukraine and known for having managed the snippers in Ukraina hotel to murder the protestors and the berkut (Shouldn't he be in jail for those facts instead of running the Ukrainian parliament?), came out with an astonishing statment on TV that outraged the full Jewish community, by saying: "Hitler was the greatest democrat of the XX century". Yesterday, right after the EEDF presentation of Vitaly Kondrativ director of infrastructure investment representing the ministry of infrastructure of Ukraine, the minister shooted on TV that the only way Ukrainian men should travel to Moscow was in a military outfit with gun in hands. I do not want to emphase what their president Poroshenko is trying to do by splitting the Ukrainian society over religious problems, it goes to a new level of psychotic behavior.

We, the business community of EEDF, could not accept that members and partners of our group could have their lives threatened that way (I am thinking of the representant of UTLC, Vladimir Remizovich and Alexey Grom who are from Russia). Lately I heard my name was on a list managed by the neo Nazi organization called C14 who works closely with SBU (Secret Services of Ukraine), they are responsible of the assassination of several journalists (Oles Buzina, Olga Moroz...), deputy of Rada (Irina Berezhnaya...) and act of torture (my good friend and member of the Ukrainian free diving team Spartak Golovachev...). I do believe the ambassador of Ukraine should be convoked by the Austrian MFA to get warned over the derives the Ukrainian government and their representants are taking. I suggest Ukraine should be banned of EEDF until minister of transport and president of Rada present their public appologies upon their outrageous declarations.

I notified   of my thinking and I was thinking appropriate to suggest what could be done in that matter. The situation has drifted to new level of public verbal xenophobic violence, this is not the representation of Europe neither its conception of international relationship. It is time for the international community to tell them that enought is enought and we could not work with people with such a mindset.

Best regards. Thierry

The following year I was kicked out of the forum, but today its founder calls me every week telling me that I was right and that they should have listened to me and banged their fists on the table. Very often visionaries and those who anticipate problems are not always understood in their time, only history proves them right, and that is a shame. The xenophobic anti-Russian madness of a minority part of the Ukrainian population, but especially of their leaders, is today costing our economies hundreds of billions of Euros. European leaders, all categories combined, are guilty not only of their inaction but of their direct involvement in the coup d'état in Kiev and the organization of this conflict which brings absolutely nothing good. Former Chancellor Merkel spilled the beans by admitting that the Minsk agreements were just a bunch of lies so that Ukraine could prepare for a major conflict. The intention was announced clearly and unambiguously. The icing on the cake is that these leaders are asking their respective populations to pay the bill. By tightening our belts and freezing, I believe above all that we must hold them to account in an international tribunal, and certainly not that of The Hague, which is controlled by Soros in person.

THE FATAL MISTAKE OF THE USA

The USA made a monumental mistake with Ukraine. This has always been marked in red ink by the various security and foreign affairs authorities, notably by Henry Kissinger who was not known to be tender towards Russia. They have always firmly vetoed the idea of any military/either destabilization operations in this territory, exposing the unfortunate consequences that direct confrontation with Russia could entail. And yet the Obama/Biden administration took the bait in 2014, which may be its death knell.

After the Second World War, the USA developed the Bretton Wood agreements to impose the dollar as the transactional support for all raw materials in the world, gold, wheat, oil, gas, uranium... Becoming an international reserve currency, the dollar guarantees their economic growth through the issuance of debt (bonds), but above all because any international transaction amounts to buying American debt. 3-cushion billiards.

When you want to understand the political power of an entity or a conflict problem, you have to follow the money, my manager in the USA told me. By analyzing the US debt we can understand the power games taking place in the world. Of the $33 trillion in US debt, 7.3 trillion are owned with the breakdown described below... The entities represented are broken down into different creditor countries as follows:

Link: https://tinyurl.com/FOREIGNUSDEBTS

EUROPE: UK, Belgium, Luxembourg, Switzerland, Ireland, France, Norway, Germany, Netherlands, Sweden, Poland, Italy, Spain

TAX HAVENS: Cayman Islands, Singapore, Bermuda, Bahamas

AMERICA: Canada, Mexico, Colombia, Chile, Peru

SOUTH EAST ASIA - PACIFIC: Japan, Taiwan, Hong Kong, Korea, Australia, Philippines, Thailand, Vietnam

MIDDLE EAST: Israel, Kuwait, Iraq, Saudi Arabia, UAE

BRICS: China, Brazil, India (excluding Russia, South Africa)

Several forms of power emerge from the graph below. It shows quite surprising results, especially when we zoom in on some of these entities, particularly in the distribution of ownership of US debt within the entity known as Europe. We observe that the United Kingdom owns the majority of US debt because it hosts most of the European stock exchanges, and capital is fleeing massively from old Europe to London. What is very surprising is to see very small countries, outside Switzerland (whose banking past is historic), such as Ireland, Belgium, or Luxembourg now having such financial capacity. The last two being the headquarters of the European Union, it is safe to assume that enormous tax optimization mechanisms have been put in place to allow such a capacity at the highest level which would more closely resemble tax fraud.

World distribution of US debt excluding BRICS

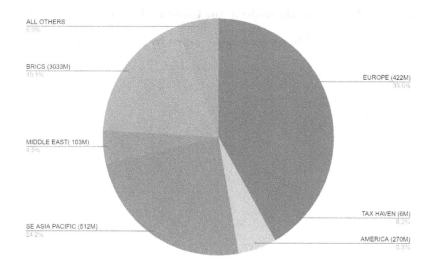

European distribution of US debt

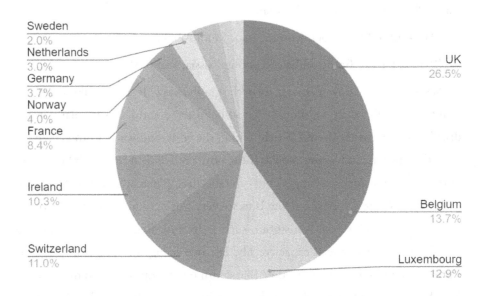

It is the per capita ratio of debt ownership which best demonstrates the first conclusion. Noting that Luxembourg, a city of 640K inhabitants, is able to buy $313 billion in US bonds seems surreal, even more incredible to see its **GDP/inhabitant grow by 23%, in the midst of the Covid crisis (from 2019 to 2021).**

Distribution of US debt ownership per capita by European countries

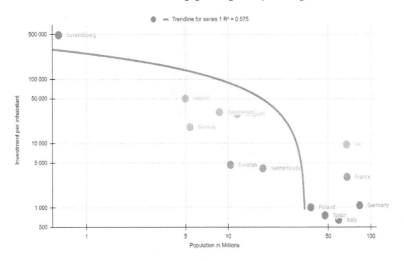

We thus understand that the Brussels parliament has every interest in going in the direction of the USA if we refer to their investments. This is a very bad calculation in the long term. Letting the US manage our economy internally is worse than a Trojan horse, we will see that later. How can we explain to the French people to work hard until the age of 64 when the profits of the French economy go into hiding without paying their share in the functioning of the country?

In Brussels, we should perhaps look into the identity of the companies hosted, the origin of the funds allowing such transactions, the hosting of the head offices of large groups, and the impact that this has on the taxation of Europeans... That said, such investments are double-edged because when rates rise, the nominal value can easily collapse, which can lead to sovereign bankruptcies with formidable consequences.

Intertrust Group, 6 rue Eugène Rupper, Luxembourg, hosts more than 1,800 companies... Mailbox, note that they operate all over the world, particularly in the tax havens of the Caribbean (Bahamas, BVI, Caymans, Belgium, Cyprus, Jersey and Guernsey, Luxembourg...). The biggest tax fraud is orchestrated by those who dare to tighten your belt.

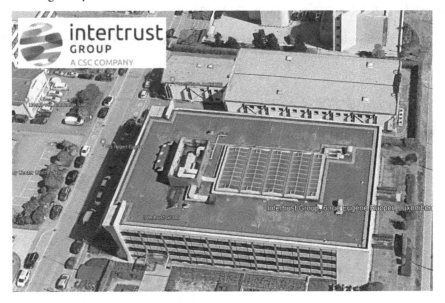

Note the small size of the building for so many companies housed. How many employees work in this building? Several questions emerge:

- Could this be why Uncle Sam turns a blind eye to tax evasion?
- Isn't that the main reason for Europe's alignment with the USA, to put its eggs in the same basket?
- How come the Cayman Islands are not on the blacklist of tax havens, and who decided on this exemption at the European Commission level?
- Are we dealing with a state kleptocracy?

The graphic below is shocking, it highlights that tax havens in the Caribbean are the landing sites for all the fraud on the planet. It is impossible to explain from an economic standpoint that the Cayman Islands or Bermuda can have such monetary capacity with less than 70K inhabitants and whose respective PBIs are $2 and $5 billion (i.e. an asset 142 and 17 times greater to their respective GDPs). On the other hand, if we refer to the link that these entities maintain with the United Kingdom, only one conclusion is evident: capital from the old continent migrates explicitly. A gigantic fraud which fuels the US debt and which allows fraudsters to be paid in the long term without working or being worried.

Distribution of US bonds per capita in Europe and Tax Havens

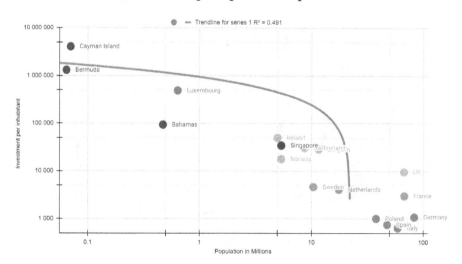

We thus understand why the dissidents of the Bretton Wood agreements have in the past paid very dearly for their challenge to the diktat of the greenback, as the two events described below suggest:

On May 14, 2011 just before the future presidential elections, **Dominique Strauss-Khan** collided with a chambermaid abnormally quickly in the Sofitel Hotel, Manhattan, NY… We could stop at this dark story of buttocks if we did not know that a few weeks before the "collision", DSK had the brilliant idea to annoy the CIA by disseminating within the IMF a white paper stipulating that it was necessary to put an end to the Bretton Woods agreements by introducing a common electronic currency to support trade which would aim to avoid purchases of dollar currency to streamline transactions and therefore abandon the dollar. From a slip of a pen, he moved to a slip on a bar of soap in a bathroom of a New York hotel, without going through the Elysée box and ending up in prison. Sad end of Monopoly party! (I can't quote my solid sources here).

The CEO of Total, **Christophe de Margerie,** has paid cash for his independence of thought by signing an agreement to purchase Russian oil and gas in Euros with D. Medvedev and V. Putin on the afternoon of October 20, 2014, right after the neo-Nazi coup of Maïdan and the shooting down of MH17. His private jet crashed into a snow plow on the runway at Vnukovo Airport, Moscow, even though there was no snow that day. It's still strange! Who decided to send several snow plows onto the runway at that time? My source told me that the two tower controllers in charge of traffic are chilling towards Irkutsk and that they will have to enjoy the sunrises over Lake Baikal for some time to come. Christophe De Margerie was a great friend of Vladimir Putin, and the latter will not forgive those who orchestrated his assassination. The Bretton Woods agreements are definitely just a matter of unfortunate collisions.

THE BRICS ARE EMERGING, THE WEST IS COLLAPSING

The USA cannot act with states the way it acts with individuals; it's more complicated and dangerous. The US debt can also be seen as a double-edged sword that Xi Jinping wields masterfully.

March 2023: China has told state banks to prepare for a massive dollar collapse and yuan buying frenzy as Beijing's previous interventions failed to stem its currency's worst year since 1994. The move could stem the yuan's fall, as it remains on track for its biggest annual fall. In a context of freezing US debt, the dollar may be threatened and its collapse would cause hyperinflation in the USA but above all a global financial cataclysm.

China has started liquidating US debt

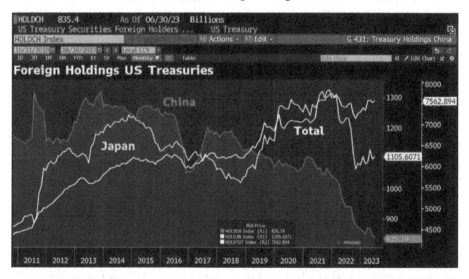

The Sino-Russian alliance can do considerable damage because the interconnection of the world shows the limits of such aggressive geopolitics led by the USA. Not to mention the fact that, while Indo-Russian relations were in good shape within the BRICS, India's purchase of Russian oil is going well and is increasing significantly by doing without the dollar (in light blue).

Oil suppliers to India since 2011

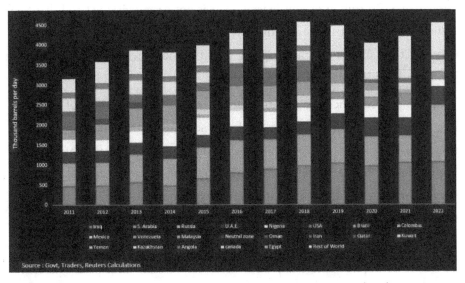

According to data from the Indian Ministry of Commerce and Industry, Russia moved from 18th place in terms of imports to 4th and therefore became one of India's main partners. This is due to a sharp increase in trade between the two countries.

If during the 2021-22 period, trade only amounted to $13.1 billion, during the 2022-23 period, the sum of trade reached $39.8 billion. India exported goods to Russia worth $2.5 billion and imported goods worth $37.3 billion. Furthermore, in January, Moscow became New Delhi's largest supplier of raw materials for the third consecutive month. IMF Deputy Managing Director Gita Gopinath said that **sanctions on Russia could undermine dollar dominance by encouraging the creation of small trading blocs using other currencies...**

"Small," really? If they are accepted (Saudi Arabia, UAE, Iran, Thailand, Mexico, Egypt, Venezuela, Algeria, Turkey, Indonesia, Malaysia, etc.), the BRICS will represent a group whose GDP would be 30% higher than that of the United States; more than 50% of the world's population would control 60% of total gas reserves, and this group would abandon the dollar as the sole currency. The US debts, now carried with serious difficulties, would therefore no longer be supported. When we know that $170 trillion of non-federal debts is not yet provisioned and that $33 trillion worth of bonds have already been issued, we wonder how the USA will be able to get out of this without dragging the world down with it! When denial of reality leads to destruction...

The financial sanctions and the various excessive declarations of our dear elected and non-elected representatives from the Elysée to the European Commission, pressured by the Biden administration, have triggered events which will be unprecedented in the restructuring of the world of tomorrow. Russia therefore pegged the ruble to gold in order to support its price and to make it even stronger and more credible and stipulated that from now on the purchase of its raw materials would be made in rubles, or the sale would no longer be made.

It is an earthquake whose impact certainly very few can anticipate. This sent a very clear signal to the whole world: the dollar party is over. Thus a large number of countries have followed in Russia's wake to free themselves from this shackles of systematic and systemic threats.

The USA has put in place legal mechanisms for the externalization of American jurisdiction through its currency. Any dispute related to dollar transactions is resolved under American law. This constraint on international affairs is exploding. Ukraine will therefore have allowed what many would never have dared: attack the dollar and blow up the US debt support tool. The cocaine puppet Zelensky, the USA's greatest ally, managed to torpedo Uncle Sam thanks to a handful of psychotic little Nazillons like Parubiy, Yarosh, Thiagnibok, Turchinov, Avakov, Biletsky, Lyashko. What a remarkable feat!

Certainly, the real goal to be achieved was to cause an unprecedented energy crisis in order to weaken the European economies and regain control thanks to the sale of GLN and US oil overpriced (x4) by making the industries of the old continent uncompetitive and killing the purchasing power of Europeans. **But it is also a huge error of assessment.** Let's take the example of B2B software companies from Silicon Valley. In 60% of cases, the opening of a branch in Europe is linked to the objective of sales growth. On average, the European market represents 30%

of their global turnover. American companies are eyeing the European market of 740 million people and a higher GDP than the United States. The European market is the largest software market abroad and a considerable growth lever. However, the software industry only works if the secondary sector works well. If the purchasing power of European households collapses, the mechanism stops. So because European companies:

- Go into technical unemployment due to a lack of cheap energy (Saint Gobain, Duralex, William Saurin, ArcelorMittal, etc.) or go abroad where energy is cheaper (BASF, etc.)

- Have their order books melting in the sun. (Airplane manufacturers like Airbus are slowing down because the travel industry is grounded, in any case, they also have difficulty supplying materials from... Russia).

- Close their doors (bakeries, craftsmen, etc.) because they can no longer cope with the cost of energy and raw materials or semi-finished materials.

- Or push the price of their products and services high due to the impact of energy (ski resorts, food, etc.) and therefore put a stop to consumption...

The music stops now. The turnover of American companies no longer corresponds to the expectations of investors, capital flows back to other, more secure targets, and the financial markets collapse, an infernal spiral which leads to more layoffs, unemployment, etc.

In conclusion, in a system where everyone is held together by links of energy, commercial and financial dependence, it is better to pursue balanced policies without excess. In the configuration that is developing, the long-term consequences are beginning to be seen explicitly. Several significant events show the crumbling influence of the Atlanticist bloc which is suffering this crisis against a backdrop of internal dissension due to divergent personal interests:

- President Biden rushed to Saudi Arabia to request an increase in the production of barrels of oil and faced a total refusal from Bin Salman. OPEC, backed by Russia, is closing the door in his face. So the US/Saudi axis is in trouble. Asia and the Middle East no longer want to have their geopolitical lines dictated to them by the USA (nor their social choices for that matter). It's a stinging setback. This is how the BRICS are expanding their club with the aim of seeing many oil & gas producing countries join it. Emboldened by Russia's frontal clash with the USA, they aligned themselves with the Eurasian bloc and took advantage of the opportunity to free themselves from Western grip.

- Macron suffered a slap in the face from Biden with a refusal to deal on the GLN, and from Scholz who will defend his interests with Xi Jinping.

- Hungary and Croatia are distancing themselves from the warlike mood of the Baltic countries and Poland. The European Union is in fact just a puzzle ready to fall apart.

While the Russia-China rapprochement strengthens and their economic ties are cemented, last quarter the level of exchange between the two protagonists amounted to the equivalent of $400 billion, the Western partners are separating and playing their personal card.

A war is maybe won on a battlefield (and you still need to have the logistical capacity and be able to supply this battlefield, especially in a high-intensity conflict), but it is mainly won from an economic standpoint. When we are facing a military giant which has a phenomenal arsenal and all the raw materials necessary for the proper functioning of its economy, which is also allied to the largest manufacturer in the world [China] whose production is essential for any protagonist, I don't think it's a very good idea to provoke him in his garden.

It's a case that ends very badly. And it's not the so-called TV set experts who will change anything. The words on continuous news channels will end up in the dustbin of history with their speakers, while the Russian flag will fly over the Odessa Opera House for centuries.

Bankruptcy rate in Europe

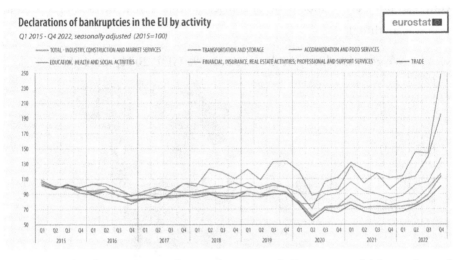

Declarations of bankruptcies in the EU by activity

eurostat

Q1 2015 - Q4 2022, seasonally adjusted (2015=100)

TOTAL - INDUSTRY, CONSTRUCTION AND MARKET SERVICES — TRANSPORTATION AND STORAGE — ACCOMMODATION AND FOOD SERVICES

EDUCATION, HEALTH AND SOCIAL ACTIVITIES — FINANCIAL, INSURANCE, REAL ESTATE ACTIVITIES; PROFESSIONAL AND SUPPORT SERVICES — TRADE

Worse: the deterioration of our relations with Russia on which we depend without wanting to recognize it, will not be repaired with the snap of our fingers. Restoring our ways of life will be a long and painful road. This will be all the more difficult because when economic policies are established by real leaders like Vladimir Putin or Xi Jinping, the rollbacks are far from explicit. It is the European populations who will pay the price. The results of this suicidal policy were not long in coming, with the bankruptcy rate across all industries combined. And it's only just beginning.

It is sufficient to observe what is the rate of industrialization versus GDP of each European country to understand the energy needs of Europe are substantial in its center (Germany, Poland, Czech Republic, Slovakia, Austria, Hungary), although above average and this is one of the reasons why they suffer much more than France (and also because of the climate during the winter when the temperatures are much less comfortable). The map below shows that we (France) have become a country of tertiary sector and tourism. It should be noted that France is now the 3rd least industrialized country in Europe, ahead of Greece and Belgium.

If 7% below the European average is the French exception, then France has become exceptionally mediocre (or, of course, so brilliant that we no longer need to produce anything).

Weight of industry in the economy (% GDP 2021, source WB)

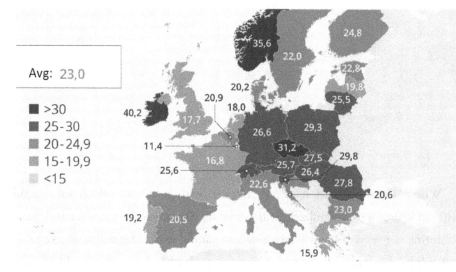

After the various governments since Sarkozy have sold off our industrial infrastructures to foreign entities, we hear Bruno Le Maire proclaiming that we must reindustrialize France even though he participated largely in its downgrading, and his current master very directly. That being said, Poland is becoming the strong pillar of Europe thanks to a gas pipeline established with Norway through Denmark which provides them with 50% of their energy needs estimated at 20 billion m3 annually. But also, thanks to Le Maire's zealous and fierce desire to become the best student of frenzied Atlanticism, seeing himself as the spearhead of anti-Russian Europe. Clearly, the ghosts of the past continue to shape what becomes of our future.

Russia has turned its attention completely to China and has no motivation to repair the two North Stream pipelines. The gas flow is now directed towards the East. In 2022, Gazprom has exported gas to China in excess of daily contracted quantities and exceeded its annual obligations. This brought the company to a fundamentally new level of deliveries to the Celestial Empire, said the head of the holding, Alexey Miller. "This, of course, positions Gazprom as a responsible supplier and reliable partner. Supply through the Russian gas pipeline is of the greatest interest to China and represents the most promising market," he said.

Moreover, the development of the Chinese direction is associated with two promising routes: from the Far East and through Mongolia. In total, Gazprom could supply around 100 billion m3 of blue fuel per year via three routes. In 2022, the holding company produced 412.6 billion m3 of gas and exported 100.9 billion m3 to non-CIS countries. The company paid more than ₽5 billion to budgets at all levels.

In a previous chapter we talked about the impact of the Belt & Road Initiative on European supply chains. The Covid crisis was destructive for the maritime sector, ports were closed, container ships remained docked, and all this made rail routes very advantageous for charterers in terms of cash flow (Three times faster by train at the peak of the crisis).

The post-Covid reorganization was slow because cleaning the containers and reassigning them empty to loading points took time and cost a fortune. The drastic drop in consumption due to the energy crisis[*] (*) has even impacted the filling times of container ships and therefore the attractiveness of this mode of transport. The return to activity of businesses after China's zero-Covid policy has been long, and global trade speeds are struggling to return to their pre-Covid levels despite an accelerating trend in (albeit eye - the worst is ahead of us). We note a downward trend from December 2022, then a violent reversal to go back to an increase in November 2023 (remaining well above the pre-Covid levels).

---

[*] which makes the filling of super container ships slower before departure because these monsters must be 95% full to be profitable.

The period from the date of freight preparation to the departure journey to the port of origin is increasing again, which weakens the cash flow of exporting companies, forcing them to increase their stocks to avoid shortages…

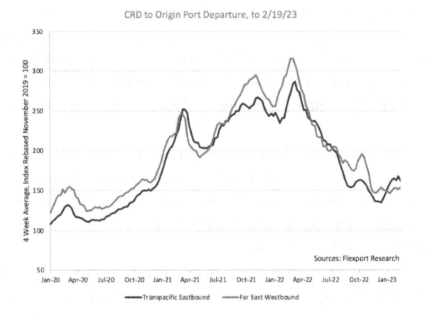

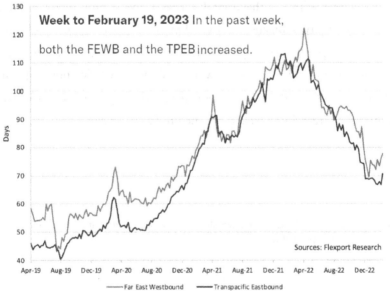

If you are wondering why you can't find Solupred for your asthmatic child in pharmacies, the answer is in the graphs above... Minister of Health Véran's excuse pointing out the fault of the relocation of the production centers of active molecules is just nonsense. Until now this mechanism has worked well and supplies have never been lacking. He is just trying to clear the government of its inability to have a balanced diplomatic approach that would have avoided this terrible maelstrom.

We see that before the Covid crisis, between the moment you placed an order and the moment the goods were delivered to their destination, an average of 160 days passed (China to East or West transfer); and today the average is 220 days, or two months more. The consequences for Western companies are enormous.

Let's focus on the main economic indicators to better understand the situation. Generally before any major crisis the manufacturing index collapses. In the current configuration, its significant fall is linked to the collapse in consumption due to the costs of raw materials and energy (exogenous inflation), as well as to the delay in transfer times of goods or raw materials coming from foreign suppliers, mostly Chinese (which creates situations of technical unemployment among importers).

Evolution of the US Manufacturing Index (ISM)

The impact is all the more violent as the Covid crisis has had a very harsh impact on the global economy, and the time interval between the two crises and the conflict is very short. The financial, production, and supply chain system suffered enormously for two years and did not have time to recover. They suffer a new shock significantly increased by an anxiety-provoking climate. When the manufacturing sector (including capital goods) is not doing well, all real estate is in crisis. The analysis of this sector can be summarized in a few graphics, the main one being purchases of goods. The Covid crisis has triggered an isolation reflex almost everywhere in the world which has manifested itself in the desire to move away from big cities. As much in Europe, this phenomenon has proven to be relative because populations are very attached to their place of life and the cost of real estate (including rental) is rather unaffordable, just as in the USA this phenomenon has been remarkable.

A million people left New York and roughly the equivalent left California heading to Texas, which is why the post-Covid period saw a huge boom in this sector. If demand suddenly collapsed, it was due to the significant impact of the Russo-Ukrainian conflict on the American economy. The population is suffering from the cost of energy, shortages of a large number of foodstuffs, and the credit crunch preventing access to property. Observation of the consumer index of the University of Michigan allows us to evaluate the psychology of confidence in the economy, we see that it is not at its best, furthermore, caused by major crises in close succession. We still note a slight improvement in the downside but still at the level equivalent to the Subprime crisis. In the kingdom of the blind, the one-eyed are kings... Still, they only see with one eye.

Evolution of the University of Michigan consumption index

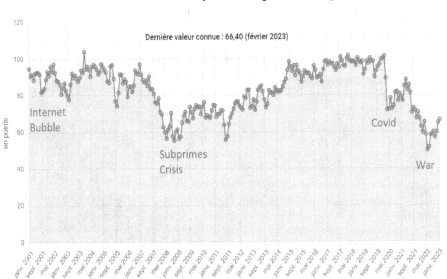

Dernière valeur connue : 66,40 (février 2023)

Evolution of the purchase of US real estate

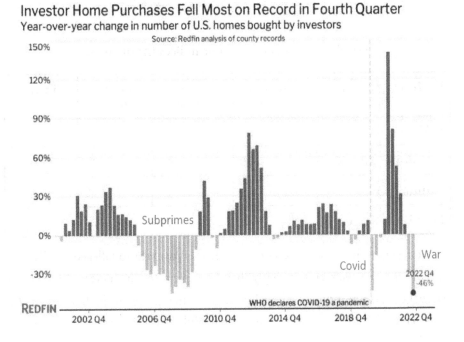

Investor Home Purchases Fell Most on Record in Fourth Quarter
Year-over-year change in number of U.S. homes bought by investors

Source: Redfin analysis of county records

Global debt is more than 3.5 times global the GDP (i.e. wealth created). The levers of central banks are completely paralyzed because issuing even more money means devaluing purchasing capacity and generating even more inflation (the purchase of raw materials or consumer products purchased in other currencies).

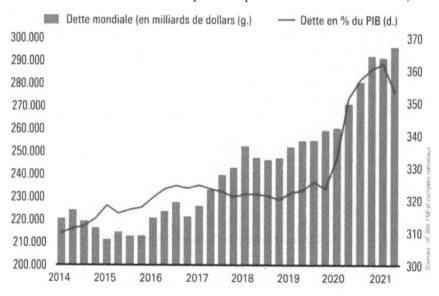

Dashboard of main economic indices (April 2023)

US Index/Crisis	Internet 2001	Subprime 2008	Covid 19 2020	Ukraine Jan 2023
ISM (%)	-29	-42	-28	-18
Consumer Index	80	58	75	55
Immo (%)	3	-42	-38	-46
FED Dettes ($T)	7	10	24	33

Interest rates have increased considerably this past year to (allegedly) "Tam inflation" and we have seen previously that the reasons for the increase in prices are external to consumption, which makes this rate-increase policy ineffective. On the other hand, this had several particularly harmful effects; for example, when rates rise, the value of bonds already issued collapse, investors prefer high return; thus, the market for previous bonds value collapses, exposed banks may be subject to "margin calls" and/or sudden recapitalization obligations (Basel III agreement), interest on saving account deposits is impossible to afford and/or customer repayment defaults. Leading to a fall in basic capitalization...

This causes a liquidity problem because savers are fleeing this type of institution. (In March 2023, bank deposits collapsed to the level of 1934). This creates not only a liquidity risk for exposed banks, but also a systemic risk, where the difficulties of a bank are transmitted to its own banking partners and correspondents, as we saw with the bankruptcy of Silicon Valley Bank SVB.[*] SVB faced one of the biggest bank runs in banking history with $42 billion in 24 hours (fintechs are more sensitive to this mechanism). Banks begin to reduce their outstanding loans to limit their exposure to debt default, and the machine spirals into an infernal spiral when households and companies can no longer refinance their debts and/or when they can, find themselves in a situation of over-indebtedness with deadlines that they can no longer meet...

Last year US banks lost 20% of their investments in 10-year bonds while the S&P 500 (Dow Jones stock index) only lost 15%. Most of them issued variable rate loans whose initial value at 1% was very attractive. When rates rose to 3.5%, borrowers found themselves in a situation of inability to repay (called "credit crunch"). We note that the number of companies with a market capitalization greater than $50M, which have declared bankruptcy, is 70 in the 1st quarter of 2023.

Losses in five days of fourteen US regional banks (03/13/23): $111 billion

Bank Name	Symbol	Market Cap ($B)	Share Max ($) 5 days ago	Share Today ($)	Share losses last week ($)	Losse Ratio	Cap loses ($B)	Market cap % Loss	Net debt Dec 2020 ($B)	Ratio Debt / Cap	Status
Bank of NY Mellon Corp	BK	35.282	51.1	44.12	-6.98	1.16	-5.58	13.66%	n/a		
U.S. Bancorp	USB	55.972	46.58	36.54	-10.04	1.27	-15.38	21.55%	15.846	0.28	Warning
M&T Bank Corp	MTB	21.36	149.12	127.11	-22.01	1.17	-3.70	14.76%	n/a		
Zion	Zion	4.446	47.94	29.97	-17.97	1.60	-2.87	37.48%	5.75	1.29	Bankrupt
Fifth Third Bancorp	FITB	17.878	34.44	26.25	-8.19	1.31	-5.58	23.78%	15	0.84	Warning
Western Alliance	WAL	2.291	71.56	19.86	-51.7	3.60	-5.96	72.25%	5.5	2.40	Bankrupt
First Horizon Corp	FHN	8.389	21.54	15.62	-5.92	1.38	-3.17	27.48%	1.658	0.20	
Charles Schwabs Corp	SCHW	96.515	75.94	52.24	-23.8	1.45	-43.15	31.12%	n/a		
First Republic Bank	FRB	6.337	119.92	29.1	-90.82	4.12	-16.66	75.73%	10.996	2.06	Bankrupt
Region Financial Corp	RF	17.453	23.19	18.69	-4.5	1.24	-4.20	19.40%	n/a		
Comerica Inc	CMA	6.921	68.53	45	-23.53	1.52	-3.10	34.34%	n/a		
Atlantic Union Bankshares Corp	AUB	2.724	39.89	36.31	-3.38	1.09	-0.25	8.52%	1.087	0.40	Warning
Bank of Hawaii Corporation	BOH	2.038	73.36	51	-22.36	1.44	-0.89	30.48%	0.089	0.04	
Customers Bancorp, Inc	CUBI	0.4936	29.76	15.68	-14.1	1.90	-0.44	47.35%	0.6497	1.32	Bankrupt
TOTAL		275.08					-110.73				
% CAP LOSSE TOTAL		-48.26									@Demories ©

---

[*] whose CFO is none other than the former CFO of Lehman Brothers

We have to go back to 2009, post-subprime crisis, to observe such figures. In March 2023, the Federal Deposit Insurance Corporation (FDIC) asked the Federal Reserve (FED) to inject $468 billion in panic mode to avoid the systemic collapse that was experienced in 2008 while US banks found themselves in a situation of unrealized losses of $1.8 trillion on total assets of $2.2 trillion. Suffice it to say that in the month of June, the month during which the banks will have to publish their balance sheets, or in October/November (the stock market crash season), it may not be a pretty sight.

4-Week Moving Average of U.S. Bankruptcy Filings

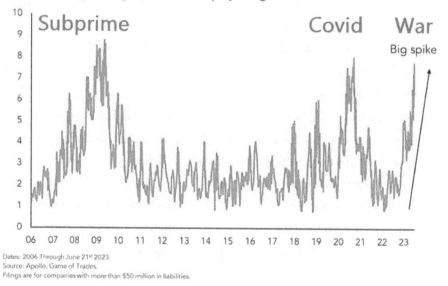

Dates: 2006 Through June 21ˢᵗ 2023.
Source: Apollo, Game of Trades.
Filings are for companies with more than $50 million in liabilities.

We are beginning to measure the impact of banking monetary policies on the real economy while Wall Street continues to ignore the signals from Main Street (the "street," or the real activity of real operators, i.e. non-financial).

The icing on the cake is that consumers in the USA have an unfortunate tendency to borrow from account to account by playing interbank cavalry trading, this works when rates are low without a risky context. But if one of their banks collapses then they can no longer pay the monthly payments on the "previous" bank, and it's a cascade of dominoes! Financial markets are bullish today because companies have managed to raise prices and margins, major assets shifted from the

EU to the US, but it will be a rude awakening as consumers cut back on purchases to adapt to what is effectively a decline in their power purchase.

This is what we observe in the curves below. Households are having difficulty repaying their monthly consumer credit (credit card) and monthly car loan payments, due to the tightening of credit conditions (blue and orange curve). What is worrying is to see the beginning of a collapse in student loan borrowing, which would mean that university registrations are not doing well, with American youth refusing to go into debt in the face of the looming economic slump on the horizon and preferring to wait for a more favorable period for study.

US household debts

Auto loan ■ Credit card ▦ Student loan

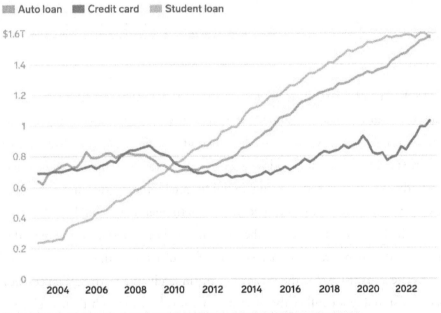

Chart: Madison Hoff/Insider • Source: Federal Reserve Bank of New York's Center for Microeconomic Data

INSIDER

The USA does not have a problem with layoffs while the credit crunch is putting households in difficulty due to rising rates. What will happen when the banking system collapses?

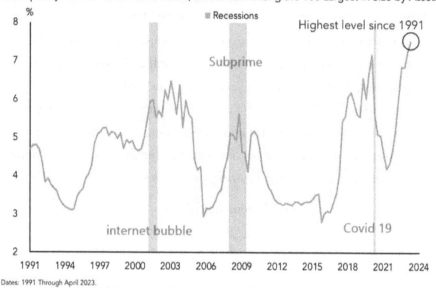

Delinquency Rate on Credit Card Loans, Banks Not Among the 100 Largest in Size by Assets

Dates: 1991 Through April 2023.
Source: Bureau of Economic Analysis, National Bureau of Economic Research, Game of Trades.

In the case of France, it is the state itself which risks debt default with a rise in exorbitant rates because the ratio of external debts versus GDP rose to 289%. This, due to the madness of "whatever it takes" instead of curing and letting live. Macron preferred to kill the hospital and write bogus checks for €600 billion, while listening to the real doctors and investing in our hospital infrastructure and staff would have saved us €580 billion and two years of retirement. We could reach a stage where the loan would not cover the repayment of the interest on the debt thus constituted, leaving the State naked in the face of its operating needs. You will appreciate at its true value the capacity of the individuals governing France, incapable of stopping a conflict (because they are involved through their negligence and ideological lies aligned with the Democrats) which costs us security and financial stability. And finally, they showered money (free from others) on a bankrupt and corrupt state, perhaps thoughtlessly, and fueled a war leading to more instability and risk. Real world champions!

CONCLUSION: All the factors announcing a financial and economic crisis are correlated, delays in production, transport, collapsed consumer and manufacturing indices, real estate and vehicle sales plunging in an unprecedented way, large cascading bankruptcies, a level of debt never reached, 170 trillion in un-funded debt in the USA, the issuance of US debt suspended, emerging countries abandoning the dollar, stratospheric inflation due to energy costs out of control and central banks which will no longer be able to play quantitative easing in fear of devaluing their respective currencies...

This is the worst of the worst scenarios, and we continue to hear all the political classes of the West singing together that everything is fine... Both feet in deep shit! A cataclysmic financial crisis, in an inflationary context, awaits us. The year 2024 will be spotty. Covid has done a lot of harm to the financial balance, the Ukrainian die-hard murderous madness will bring us to our knees because of incompetent, manipulative, and criminal leaders. *The Perfect Storm* by W. Petersen will end in *The Day After Tomorrow* by R. Emmerich, Georges Clooney and Dennis Quaid, sitting on a pile of ruins and it is not the *Oceans 11*, *12,* or *13* team that will save them, nor us for that matter.

IV. The Real Face of Euro Maïdan

I experience the Ukrainian crisis as a real personal trauma. This gratuitous and abominable violence that one part of the population was able to practice on another, which transformed even people with whom I lived into monsters, is impossible to understand and even more so to accept.

I remember one of my engineers, Roman C., telling me "If a few babushkas are killed in Donbass and I can travel to Europe without a visa, I don't see the problem." He didn't mind that my assistant Katia F.'s family, living in Donetsk, was being bombed every day. Working with guys who behaved like this became impossible. How could I accept that Marusha, our marketing advisor based in Moscow, was called Moskal (a terrible insult for a Russian of Belo-Ukrainian origin) by another of my developers, Andrey R., who came from Lviv. What I experienced in my own professional environment happened in hundreds of thousands of mixed families. It must be strongly emphasized that, above all, Maïdan is an unprecedented social drama that has given rise to terrible internal family divisions, men beating their wives, divorces, inter-family fights, and worse.

Russia and Ukraine are not only the same people, they are the same family. My young Russian teacher in Odessa, disgusted by the behavior of the fascists in her city, left lately to Moscow to apply for Russian nationality, while her mother is devastated by the departure for the front of her new husband. For a Ukrainian, not really voluntary refusal to fight ends with a bullet in the back of the neck in the middle of the night while sleeping, shot by the enthusiastic nationalists who's roles are to "frame" the conscripts. Understand my anger and my frustration when I see a bunch of idiots screaming in our streets, waving their little yellow and blue flag. They all look like the sheep of Nazism in 1936, like brainless morons under the orders of Duce Makrona.

MAÏDAN'S NEO-NAZI SCAM

The big excuse for the Maïdan slaughter was the corruption of a pro-Russian regime, and joining the European Union to allow Ukrainians to travel freely when they already did. It only cost a small ticket for the embassy attachés to ride in a Jaguar. And yes, corruption did not simply come from where we believed, in this new libertarian El Dorado with a democratic character. Let's see what it really was. After reading the document proposed by the European Union, I understood deception:

- The EU certainly offered a reduction in customs taxes on exports, but only for products conforming to European technical standards, which de facto excluded Ukrainian products. What did Ukraine have to gain? Nothing!

- They would benefit from the free visa regime and a tax reduction on luxury goods. But who would purchase these products? A small, privileged part of the population (which we now find in Courchevel rather than in a trench in Donetsk).

- There was a financial aid package (€600 million) but it was very weak compared to the real need for the functioning of the administrations.

- The energy component necessary for the well-being of the population was completely ignored and makes the (unreasonable) hypothesis that the spoiled Russian interests will continue to agree to conditions derogatory to cousins who spit in the soup.

A high-level scam without any interest because the main Ukrainian necessity is energy for heating in winter. Russia offered a much more advantageous deal including the purchase of bonds worth several billion dollars and of course gas galore at a preferential rate. They even went so far as to propose a tripartite agreement which would have been absolutely fabulous for Ukraine, but refused for reasons of geopolitical ego, angering the Kremlin, knowing that the debt contracted with

Russia in the 27 years of existence of this ersatz country was counted in several hundred billion dollars.

February 2014. The pressure from the street was increasingly out of control, the Berkuts were burned alive by massive jets of Molotov cocktails and a large number died (more than 200). The European agreement was signed on the 19th. Note that on that day, shaking the hand of Oleg Tiagnibok, co-founder of the 1st Ukrainian neo-Nazi party UNO-UPA, did not at all bother our national Fabius, socialist minister of foreign affairs (who was going to shortly after declare that Al Qaeda was doing "good work" in Syria - we have the neo-Nazis we can afford).

Yanukovich agrees to hold new elections and resign, but that is not enough. Now we have to make the population mad, hysterical, and anti-Russian. On this afternoon of February 20, 2014 the butchery begins, the snipers come on stage, they are located on the 8th floor of the Ukraina Hotel at the top of Maïdan on the hill to the left of the cinema. Ironically, it is in this hotel and on this floor that I spent my first night in Ukraine years ago. The snipers (interviewed by Italian journalists) claimed to have been recruited by former Georgian President Saakashvili to carry out the dirty work; not having been paid, they threw out the sponsors).

Tiagnibok, Klitschko, Yatseniuk (left) in front of Fabius (right), social-fascism gathered to sign the association agreement.

They killed everything that moved, Berkuts (CRS) and protestors. Two years later, I met the Bosnian Minister of Tourism and Environment in Sarajevo; he told me about the massacre that he himself experienced in 1995 (Maïdan is only a remake orchestrated by the CIA whose main agent is none other than the infamous A. Parubiy, co-founder of UNO-UPA).

Parubiy is a fan of the Stepan Bandera and Sushkevich club, two nationalists that emerged from WWII after having collaborated with the SS Das Reich division. They were so violent that they scared even the SS. They have to their credit the massacres of Babi Yar (+33,000 Jews, Russians, Gypsies), and also Kharkov, Krivoy Rog, Nikolaev, Mariupol, Simferopol, and many others, and the supply of humans to the camp, extermination of Treblinka in Poland... In total 1.4 million people were murdered (source Simone Veil, former French minister). When younger, Parubiy was interned in a psychiatric hospital, escaped, and later founded the first Ukrainian neo-Nazi party UNO-UPA, transformed into Svoboda. (Freedom, it's more palatable it's a bit like marketing Nazis - Orwell didn't invent anything). He loved walking the streets of Lviv in SS division uniform while sporting a Luger pistol on his belt. Later, he shared the management of UNO-UPA with Oleg Thiagnibok, whom I often saw on Maïdan with "right-arm tendonitis" (a greeting immortalized in the 20th century, inherited from "Nordic traditions") to say hello, accompanied by Arseniye Yatsenyuk, the post-Maïdan prime minister (whose grandfather favored a certain type of uniform during WWII). He was rewarded by being promoted president of the Verkhovna Rada, the Ukrainian parliament. Moreover, we were able to collect a video where we see Parubiy, the day after the Maïdan butchery, chatting with the snipers outside the Europa hotel where they spent the night before disappearing by bus. Igor Lopatonok, production director of Oliver Stone with whom I have been in contact for years, illustrates the scene well in one of his films *Ukraine on Fire*. Igor is of Ukrainian origin on his mother's side, and no one can question his motives. The full video of the scene where we see the snipers leaving the hotel and chatting with Parubiy is systematically deleted from YouTube and other social networks. How so? Who decides this?

Hundreds of dead people littered the ground. That day Olga Bogomolets, the Maïdan doctor, declared: "The bullets that kill the Berkuts and the protestors are exactly the same." She was in the lobby of the Ukraina Hotel (headquarters of the Maïdaners). The shots came from the 8th floor of the hotel, the protestors were shot in the back while they cornered the Berkuts (CRS) against the central post office of Kiev on the opposite side of Khreschatyk, who themselves had injuries in the chest.

Later it was the former head of the Ukrainian secret service, Igor Smeshko (pro-Europe, his two sons are on Maïdan) who exclaimed: "If we want to arrest the murderers, all we have to do is go to the Verkhovna Rada." His silence was purchased since he returned to the bosom of Poroshenko, the post-Maïdan president chosen by Victoria Nuland, American secretary of state. (His grandparents who immigrated to the USA are of Moldovan-Ukrainian origin). It should be noted that the American-Canadian diaspora of Ukrainian origin comes from post-WWII immigration and that these people all came to the new continent to be treated for this epidemic of tendinitis of the strained right arm which Parubiy and many others suffer from without complaining (a condition that has become chronic). At the head of parliament, Parubiy constitutionally established the famous war criminal Bandera as a national hero. Streets, avenues, and boulevards flourish in his name in all Ukrainian cities. A real rehabilitation of Nazism, just wondering how G. Patton would have reacted seeing this infamy. The loop is closed, Ukraine plunges back into the most fetid hours of its history, the USA congratulates itself on a good move, and the victims of the Babi Yar massacre are twisting in unison in their common grave to the delighted applause of the European Union.

Oye Oye, good people, come out and demonstrate in support of a neo-Nazi regime, and wave your little yellow and blue flags. The Covid pandemic is unfortunately over (or almost), and we are lacking entertainment shows.

Ask Parisian elected officials (Photos below) to rename a few streets, parks, and other places in memory of our national "heroes" and I name: Maréchal Pétain, Maurice Papon, Pierre Laval, and the best of them Klaus Barbie, this benefactor of humanity. It's ironic of course, I hope you understand that. We clearly see Rachida Dati, Yannik Jadeau, Anne Hidalgo, displayed with in the background, the flag of the Ukrainian Praviy Sektor, the neo-Nazi armed paramilitary branch which distinguished itself in the Donbass with ugly crimes against the populations, crimes which we believed Europe was protected from, since the Yugoslav wars. Let us imagine the faces of General de Gaulle and Jean Moulin if they were to contemplate this terrible spectacle. It's so "Republican" isn't it?

Shortcut: https://tinyurl.com/BFMPSKT

Note the banner "Info Alert", where the post-Maïdan mayor complains of "ruthless" attacks on the neo-Nazi group Azov who previously committed the worst abuses for years, in particular against the residents of Mariupol... the ridiculous, flirting with the grotesque!

Streets and avenues named after Stepan Bandera are flourishing in Ukraine; long live European values! IKEA and Metro in Kiev are thus associated with this Nazi butcher from WWII. A fitting return to its roots for IKEA, since its founder Ingvar Kamprad was a great admirer of Hitler. He was an active member of the

Swedish version of Hitler Youth and regularly attended meetings with pro-Nazi extremist groups...

METRO & IKEA, next door neighbors, Stepan Bandera Avenue, Kiev

So the European Commission would have expressed itself like Voltaire in *Le Tartuffe*: "Cover these Nazis that I cannot see, by such monsters the souls of Jean Moulin and other resistance fighters are injured."

A LONG-PLANNED NEO-NAZI COUP

Trying to make people believe in the Ukrainian democratic movement on BFMTV or CNN is one thing; witnessing the real facts of an unnamed butchery is another matter. It's a bit like swallowing the red pill in *The Matrix*. Every time you hear the manipulative villains of these 24/7 news channels, you turn into Neo, and the only thing that comes to your mind is to beat up Agent Smith. I'm tired of their lies, I'm tired of their hypocrisy, I'm tired of their manipulations of little losers, tired of these guys who have never set foot in this country, who are inventing bullshit from morning to evening, who do not speak a word of Russian (or Ukrainian…) and who transform the facts in order to satisfy their masters, like the little lackeys they are. Journalistic ethics have lived on and remain an exercise in fiction for apprentice stooges.

"No, there are no Nazis in Ukraine," "It's Russia that is invading," "The Russians are self-bombing at the Zaporizhia nuclear power plant," "The Russians are murdering and raping women in the Donbass." It also seems that if it is raining frogs in the Sahara, it is because of Vladimir Putin… All this is not serious, these pseudo-journalists have no credibility! They are confusing journalism and propaganda.

An old German proverb says **"You never believe someone who has lied once;"** in this specific case they go so far that it becomes grotesque.

Let's go back to the events in their chronology to understand the dynamics put in place. On February 20, 2014, eight buses of Crimeans (mainly families) fled Kiev. They fell into a nationalist trap from Pravy Sektor to Korsun (located 150

km from Kiev, detail of great importance), in the trees across from the road, they are beaten all day, and their buses are burned. After their testimonies, the governor of Crimea, Natalia Poklonskaya, called the Kremlin, and the decision to secede was made by referendum. Much later I learned from someone close to White House advisors that Obama had given no guarantee to Vladimir Putin that a NATO base would not be installed in Crimea... The last straw to break the camel's back, Crimea joins Russia. A little historical reminder is still necessary to clarify an important political point:

On February 19, 1954, the Presidium of the Supreme Soviet of the Soviet Union issued a decree transferring the Crimean Oblast from the Russian Soviet Federative Socialist Republic to the Ukrainian SSR. According to the Soviet Constitution (Art. 18), the borders of a republic within the Soviet Union cannot be redrawn without the agreement of the republic in question.

The transfer was approved by the Presidium of the Supreme Soviet Union however, according to Article 33 of the constitution, the Presidium did not have the authority to do so. The constitutional modification (Artt. 22 and 23) to take the transfer into account was made several days after the decree issued by the Presidium of the Supreme Soviet, therefore it is illegal and obsolete.

This administrative transfer was made for management convenience. At the time, traveling to Moscow required crossing the Kerch Strait by boat and then taking the train to Moscow, which took more than a week round trip. In addition, the amenities (water, electricity, gas) were from Ukrainian sources, Zaporozhye region, so this transfer seemed better suited to everyday life. This is how the Crimean parliament was born, administered at the time of Maïdan by Natalia Poklonskaya, we must not forget that it had total operating autonomy.

What the Korsun attack teaches us is explicit: the organization of Maïdan was planned months in advance, and throughout Ukraine these fascist groups from hooligan football clubs were ready to act on orders. Certain leaders with no capacity (the useful idiots) of these groups distinguished themselves in actions that went beyond the limits and had assumed political ambitions. These leaders were eliminated.

This is the case of Alexandr Muzishenko, known as Sasha the white man, who was doing "facies control" at the corner of Zara - Khreschiatyk. I took a discreet photo of the individual and Google informed me about this guy with disturbing information: wanted by Interpol for war crimes in Chechnya, banned in Russia... Everywhere in Ukraine, notably in Kharkov and Dnipropetrovsk, actions of this type were carried out. At the beginning of April, the cities of Lugansk and Donetsk rose up and declared their independence after noting that a band of neo-fascist weirdos had begun to control the streets in all the cities. The Azov group with its symbolic SS butcher's hook was not hiding at all.

When Eastern Ukraine, did not yet accept the Kalashnikov AK-47 as a democratic and consensual tool of negotiation or vote, Kiev sent all its neo-Nazi reprisal battalions for arbitrary executions, headed by Oleg Liashko, Andriy Biletsky, Dmitry Yarosh, the butchers of Pravy Sektor and Azov. This is how a large number of administrative executives were kidnapped, sequestered, tortured, and sometimes also purely and simply eliminated. Many were paying the price in Mariupol, Melitopol, Zaporozhye, Kharkov, Odessa, and Kiev... The website Mirotvorets.center was born, its owner is none other than the criminal Poroshenko, now elected president. It is a neo-Nazi organization called "C14" which is responsible for feeding it; they refer to "enemies of Ukraine;" they also display the CIA logo to legitimize themselves. That such an institution could be associated with a Nazi criminal organization is disturbing to say the least. The European Union has been very frequently asked to legislate on the banning of this site which goes against the security of some of their members, in vain, the murderous organization is excused since it is Ukrainian. The "Ukrainian" status is de facto a blank check for the whitewashing of any crime despite the unequivocal condemnation of Cyberpol, which declares explicitly on their site that Ukraine supports a terrorist organization endangering citizens and representatives of the European Union.

The list below is not exhaustive but explicitly shows that opposition of thought can end badly. I even wrote to Yaroslav Yodin, an attaché at the Ministry of Foreign Affairs in Kiev, to free Spartak Golovachev, a member of the Ukrainian Olympic freediving team who had been tortured in the most terrible way possible. After his release he told me what was happening in the illegal SBU jails: cigarette burns, broken limbs with hammers, food deprivation, forced ingestion of urine and excrement... Since his release, we are still in contact, and he is ready to testify in due time. Ukrainian-style democracy more closely resembles the regime of the Tonton Macoutes of Haiti under the Duvallier presidency in the 1960s. When all this madness is over, some will have to be held accountable, notably for the assassination of Daria Dugina, with whom I had the opportunity to speak during the Chisinau economic forum, December 2017 in Moldova. A brilliant young woman speaking several languages (including ours), with an unparalleled capacity for analysis and reflection. I presented her to the management of France Soir for an interview, which did not take place, and for good reason. The following is just a small excerpt. During the post-Maïdan period, Ukraine is experiencing an "epidemic of far-right Democrats" (including the most visible symptom, which is this tendinitis mentioned above), a disease more fatal than Covid.

Non-exhaustive list of my contacts on Myrotvorets.info

First Name	Last Name	Function	Nationality	Status
Thierry	Mariani	Minister	French	Target
Yves	P. Di Borgo	Senator	French	Target
Hervé	Juvin	EU Deputy	French	Target *
Henry	Kissinger	Sec. State	USA	Target **

Elon	Musk	Entrepreneur	USA	Target
Oles	Buzina	Journalist	Ukraine	Killed
Olga	Moroz	Editor	Ukraine	Killed
Irina	Berezhnaya	Deputy	Ukraine	Killed
Daria	Dugina	Journalist	Russia	Killed
Alexandr	Dugin	Geo-politolog	Russia	Target
Faïna	Savenkova	Journalist	Russia	Target ***
Christelle	Nean	Journalist	France	Attempt
Laurent	Briard	Journalist	France	Target
Xavier	Moreau	Geo-politolog	France	Target
Spartak	Golovachev	Athlete	Ukraine	Tortured
Valentina	Samsonenko	Politician	Ukraine	Killed
Mikola	Sergiyenko	Administrator	Ukraine	Killed
Sergiy	Walter	Mayor	Ukraine	Killed
Olexandr	Bordyuh	Lawyer	Ukraine	Killed

Segey	Sukhobok	Journalist	Ukraine	Killed
Dimitry	Malinovsky	Procuror	Ukraine	Killed
Etc…				

(*) During the Davos Economic Forum (WEF) at the end of May 2022, Henry Kissinger, former American Secretary of State for Foreign Affairs, stated that Ukraine should cede the Russian-speaking part of its territories to Russia if it does not want to disappear, the next day he was registered on Myrotvorets.

(**) When Elon Musk decided to stop Starlink for free which cost him hundreds of millions of dollars, he got immediately registered on Myrotvorets. Was he pressured by the Biden administration to restore this service?

(***) Faina is 14, a bit young to be assassinated for political reasons!

Илон Рив Маск / Ілон Рів Маск / Elon Reeve Musk

Дата рождения: 28.06.1971
Страна:США

Покушение на территориальную целостность Украины.

Участие в попытках легализации аннексии Крыма россией.

Дата рождения: 28.06.1971

Американский предприниматель, миллиардер 14.10.2022 компания Илона Маска SpaceX отказалась оплачивать услуги спутниковой связи Starlink для Украины, тем самым нанесла удар по критической инфраструктуре страны. Также Илон Маск неоднократно содействовал российской пропаганде, например, публикуя «план урегулирования конфликта», в котором призывал признать Крым российским

Центр «Миротворец» просит правоохранительные органы рассматривать данную публикацию на сайте как заявление о совершении этим гражданином осознанных деяний против национальной безопасности Украины, мира, безопасности человечества и международного правопорядка, а также иных правонарушений.

14.10.2022 10:36   SBU   Поскаржитись

The header of the site is explicit, our politicians are considered terrorists, mercenaries, war criminals, and murderers… This indicates cognitive deviance which leads to the conclusion of the advanced state of dementia of the Kievan junta which no longer makes the difference between free will and totalitarianism, it recalls a dark period in German history.

Link: https://myrotvorets.center/ registered in Thailand, since 06-11-2015, belonging to Poroshenko, former post-Maïdan president.

Much later we learned that it was the Biden administration that banned Europeans from talking about the neo-Nazi problem in Ukraine because it would compromise their entire communication plan... Is this the reason why Baretsky, director of Cyberpol, did not have the right to prevent this site from operating? The Soros Nebula appears again. Indeed Myrotvorets refers on their site to a content protection license developed by **Creative Commons (CC), a Californian NGO**, to avoid lawsuits over usage of personal information... when in fact, they do not have authorization from the owners of these contents, if we consider a photo or an address being the property of the person represented by these informational materials.

Link: https://photoidentite.eu/glossaire/legislation/photo-identite-vie-privee/

Personal protection legislation. The right to privacy is set out in several international treaties:

– **No one should be subjected to arbitrary or unlawful interference with their privacy,** his family life, his home and his correspondence, or illegally affect his honor and good reputation.

– **Everyone has the right to protection by law against such interference or invasion...** and a fortiori if the invasion is characterized by the physical elimination of the person represented by the said identity photo.

Confidentiality of an identity photo. Someone's picture or ID card is special data about someone's race. An identity card is covered by privacy legislation. In 2008, a judge ruled that a photo with an image of someone or a photo ID is exceptional personal data with respect to a person's race. see the French Senate website

https://www.senat.fr/lc/lc62/lc62_mono.html

Conditions of use of the customizable license **CC** are explicit: exhibitable materials may be subject to additional authorizations concerning, which is certainly not the case with regard to the legislation on the protection of identity photos.

Link: https://creativecommons.org/licenses/by/4.0/

Shortcut: https://tinyurl.com/CCLicense4

Notices:

You do not have to comply with the license for elements of the material in the public domain or where your use is permitted by an applicable exception or limitation.

No warranties are given. The license may not give you all of the permissions necessary for your intended use. For example, other rights such as publicity, privacy, or moral rights may limit how you use the material.

The rights of users under exceptions and limitations, such as fair use and fair dealing, are not affected by the CC licenses.
More info.

You may need to get additional permissions before using the material as you intend.
More info.

https://tinyurl.com/CC-FAQWARN

What happens if someone applies a Creative Commons license to my work without my knowledge or authorization?
CC alerts prospective licensors they need to have all necessary rights before applying a CC license to a work. If that is not the case and someone has marked your work with a CC license without your authorization, you should contact that person and tell them to remove the license from your work. You may also wish to contact a lawyer. Creative Commons is not a law firm and cannot represent you or give you legal advice, but there are lawyers who have identified themselves as interested in representing people in CC-related matters.

CC therefore exempts itself from the prevention of use of materials when it would be very simple to establish rules excluding the use of licenses in support of criminal activity.

Conclusion: Myrotvorets operates completely illegally without being worried, uses legal **CC** licenses fraudulently because it does not respect the rules defined for its use. There are certainly grounds for legal action...

Let's highlight the donation request button... Since when can we sponsor murders with complete impunity? But what does the ECHR do (see below)?

Note the reference to Langley, CIA address in West Virginia

Organizational diagram of another arm of the Soros octopus

THE ODESSA BUTCHERY

This marked a serious turning point in the Ukrainian crisis. After the separatist announcements from cities in the Donbass region, the Kiev regime was in panic mode and must face growing protest movements in Ukraine, particularly in the Odessa region, which is a strategic port for supporting its economy. Without this port for transit of raw materials (oil, gas but especially cereals), Ukraine's economy was collapsing. To break up the protests against the coup d'état, on May 2, 2014, Kiev sent the factions of Praviy Sektor from the Dnepropetrovsk region with the complicity of the police and the SBU to eliminate the protestors, all financed by the oligarch Kolomoisky who wants to keep control of all traffic. We witnessed the worst massacre of this pseudo-democratic masquerade. Early in the morning a horde of these savages armed with baseball bats and other delicate objects descended on the protestors who were camped in front of the union building. They set fire to the tents and chased their occupants into the building. The killing began. The protestors were literally massacred, their hands and faces burned so that they could not be identified. They even went so far as to strangle a pregnant woman.

The attackers set fire to the building in order to cover up their crimes. The protestors who had escaped the first massacre tried to escape the flames by jumping out of the windows and were shot down by the police or finished with baseball bats and sledgehammers. The Ukrainian media said that there was a fire and that people died without talking too much about the subject of the various discussions I had with all my contacts. This was without counting on the relationships that I was able to establish in this country since I was in direct contact with the lawyer in charge of the investigation who took all the photos of the victims inside the building. For security reasons I will not name him because he was convinced to abandon the investigation unless he wanted his own family murdered - a cruelly credible threat. He now resides in a country that I will not disclose.

During one of our conversations he said to me: "It feels like we were during the Nazi occupation of 1942." The families of the victims were received by Thierry Mariani in the French parliament to explain the ordeal they were experiencing.

When they returned to Ukraine, they were convicted of treason, and many ended up in prison or worse. Odessa, built by the Duke of Richelieu in 1794, allowed its builder to escape French revolutionary madness after Louis XVI lost his head, and thus sees itself caught up by history. So Odessa acquired its letters of revolutionary blood that its creator had fled, post mortem...

Photos of the murders provided by my Odessa lawyer contact

What an irony of historical fate, here is the famous democratic Ukraine that the media boasts of to us and the beautiful reasons for our financial sacrifices, it makes us dream! Of course, all the news channels were careful not to show you these images **because it would have been difficult to sell you the white dove Ukraine which is in fact just a common fascist vulture.**

If they had done so you might have heard their columnists proclaim that this woman choked on a piece of candy sent by Russia during her yoga break while the building was under construction and her son had left his sports gear behind, carelessly accompanying him on a motorbike in the morning. Audiard, the famous French movie maker said: "Idiots always dare to do or say anything, that's how we recognize them." Gérard Collomb, minister of internal affairs, can be proud of his Ukrainian creature counterpart, Arsen Avakov, with whom he held a wedding in the cozy salons of Place Beauvau (https://tinyurl.com/COLLAVAK). This is called murderer complicity. His colon cancer serves as divine justice, what an irony with such a name!

Murdering a pregnant woman? But where were Marlène Schiappa (minister of social affairs), Anne Hidalgo (mayor of Paris), and Sandrine Rousseau (deputy "Escrologist") to scream against Ukrainian femicides? That said, this woman spoke Russian so "it didn't count," right?

Accepting such crimes unpunished in the name of the sacrosanct concept of democracy opens a door, the one opened by the Nazis in 1936 and through which all the collaborators rushed!

UKRAINIAN PANDORA'S BOX, A SWORD OF DAMOCLES

The constitution of any country in the world is supposed to guarantee the security and integrity as well as the fair treatment of its citizens. The result is a civil and penal code describing a number of rules/laws, pillars of a social system allowing a population to function in the best possible conditions. This is what we call "representative democracy" here, a system in which our representatives are elected by popular vote, and this representation sets political orientations in order to theoretically ensure the well-being of the population.

It turns out that in the West the systems put in place have largely become misguided because they allow an elite corrupted to the bone to keep populations in slavery under unbearable fiscal or health pressures, policies carried out by pirates leading to the collapse of the economy, programmed to better control them, crushed by the stress of their uncertain future. But that's not the subject here.

Is Ukraine a democratic entity?

- A government overthrown in violence and murder by neo-Nazi organizations.

- Elections organized excluding the eastern regions concerned.

- A president chosen by Victoria Nuland, American secretary of state with a more than sulphureous family past.

- Ethnic cleansing, torture of citizens, serial political murders without conviction.

-

- Control of the media by eliminating vectors of opposition physically and legally.

- A perverted and criminal legal system inciting murders, arbitrary arrests, and massive institutional corruption.

- Ban on religious freedom.

- Constitutional bodies massively infiltrated by neo-Nazi organizations (Police, Army, Security Services), which organize the elimination of political and religious opposition.

- An unimaginable level of corruption for the benefit of oligarchs and politicians, which leaves the population in a state of total misery and without hope.

Ukrainians are effectively free to live in poverty as long as they keep quiet and obey with average salaries already divided by three since the Maïdan massacre: "Slava Ukraina." **Endorsing this type of governance therefore means accepting it as a possibility in one's own country.** How can Western governments allow themselves to demonize their own opposition who do not approve of the official discourse, whether in Ukraine or elsewhere?

How dare we say that a movement like the "Yellow Vests" is unconstitutional when they accept population behavior a thousand times worse (particularly in terms of violence) in Ukraine... A double standard that will not last long when we see the constraints that these same governments impose on European populations. For example, by imposing on them the consequences of the sanctions dear to our Minister Bruno Le Maire, and also of sanctions proven to be unnecessary and for many illegal, affecting individuals, such as the seizure of their property. The immutable right to property is no longer respected, and the confidence of foreign investors is completely collapsing. This is a major precedent in the history of law, and one that scares away investments, including foreign ones.

Let's do a little science fiction transposition:

Let's imagine this brave Jean Luc Mélenchon, LFI far-left party (alias Oleg Lyashko), entering the office of Robert Ménard, (alias Samsonov), mayor of Béziers (alias Slaviansk), accompanied by a few LFI thugs (alias Azov) armed to the teeth, forcing that Rober dude to sign a rag dictated under threat (of death) to announce one's resignation. We can already imagine the entire French Republican right party screaming about left-wing fascism, the media repeatedly seizing a state affair, the city S.W.A.T mobilized in emergency intervention mode to prevent a townhouse coup d'état under the amazed eyes of the population crying scandal!

However in Ukraine, Slavyansk, in 2015, it was completely normal since this poor guy was not a supporter of a brutal federal coup orchestrated by all the neo-Nazi factions in the country. And the whole world welcomes this very original "libertarian" impulse that Ukraine has gained thanks to ballot papers on which is written: "You get out or you die." We will not fail to hear David Pujadas on LCI channel talking to us about morality and the law to protect Ukraine. Hilarious David, you rock, what a funny guy!

Shortcut: https://tinyurl.com/Liashko

HYPOCRISY AND COMPLICITY OF THE RULING CLASS

Initially I found that the rapprochement between Ukraine and Europe was a good idea, if it was integrating the strong existing ties between Ukraine and Russia, especially from a social point of view because a breakup would fracture loads of families, until I was confronted with the horrors being perpetrated.

That was the moment I turned against this abomination of Maïdan. At that time I did not fail to inform Thierry Mariani, deputy for French people living abroad in the CIS region, of what I was observing from my window. He welcomed me in his office at the parliament upon my final return at the beginning of March 2015 because things almost went wrong regarding my physical integrity in this country that had gone crazy!

From 2015, I did not fail to express my feelings regarding the dangerous Nazification which was spreading in this country in particular to Gérard Larcher, president of the Senate, Philippe Bas, his vice-president, as well as Bruno Le Maire, former Minister of Agriculture (now reconverted and famous rival of the Oracle of Delphi). I keep the traces of these correspondences safe for possible confrontations, including legal ones. All these little people were well aware of all the xenophobic crimes and tortures that were being perpetrated in every city, but they were careful not to brag about it.

I also had on the phone a certain Pierre Person, a socialist deputy, who after a few minutes of conversation said to me: "We know about it, don't get involved in this!" We couldn't be clearer, but it's the kind of sentence that provokes (at least in me) the opposite reaction! When the Macron Leaks are released on Wikileaks, I rush to search through all the documents offered. What was my surprise to see that this Pierre Person attended meetings organized by a certain Quentin Guille-main, founder of the NGO "**Cosmopolitan Project Foundation**" (**CPF**) certainly financed by George Soros according to Google's cash, and who went back and forth from Paris to Kiev to organize the mess on Maïdan. He was dating a Ukrain-ian woman whose father was an SBU colonel. Person was subsequently Macron's campaign chief, and there is no doubt that the latter was aware of what was hap-pening and who was doing what. Here are the old email ID references but the file has been deleted from the platform. To believe that the content was more than compromising and dangerous for the protagonists!

From December 2013 the fine team was in place on Maïdan, so a French so-cialist deputy came to meetings to organize a neo-Nazi coup d'état... Curious mix of genres! Who has something to hide? **The references to the following emails have curiously disappeared, the why seems to be blatantly obvious.**

https://wikileaks.org/macron-emails/emailid/8736,23067,40030, 24146, 9918

Below is the only saved screenshot of the "Macron Leaks"

WikiLeaks Leaks News About Partners Search

This email has also been verified by Google DKIM 2048-bit RSA key

nous suivre à Kiev

Data in this email come from pierrperson@gmail.com archive

From:qguillemain@gmail.com
To: depassernosfrontieres@googlegroups.com
Date: 2013-12-07 01:04
Subject: nous suivre à Kiev

Chers amis,

Ca y est, nous sommes à kiev !
Vous pouvez nous suire via ukraine-euromaidan.tumbl.com

A bientot,

Quentin GUILLEMAIN
*Tel *: 06.11.20.59.98
E-mail : qguillemain@gmail.com
*Facebook *: http://www.facebook.com/quentin.guillemain
Twitter : http://twitter.com/qguillemain

Below the foundation's website has also curiously disappeared but the yellow pages have a good memory. Who could pay rent of €1500 per month for six years? or 108,000 Euros to support an NGO in a neighborhood 500 m from Paris town hall... We have no doubts about the origin of the patron!

Fortunately they kept their Facebook page:

https://www.facebook.com/CosmopolitanProjectFoundation/about_details

The general secretary of **CPF** is none other than Nicolas Furet, **a friend of Stéphane Séjourné, secretary general of Macron's Renaissance party**. We see explicitly that **CPF** worked with the Polish NGO **Open Dialog Foundation (ODF)**, directly involved with the financing of Maïdan paramilitary operations and the financing of the Ukrainian neo-Nazi factions Praviy Sektor, Ydar, Azov, Kiev 1/2, etc. referenced in the following online document:

Link: https://odfoundation.eu/content/uploads/i/fmfiles/pdf/podsumowanie-finansowe-dzialan-pomocowych-odf-na-rzecz-ukrainy-2013-14-en-new.pdf

Shortcut: https://tinyurl.com/ODFPLUANAZI

The funds of **ODF** are from obscure foreign sources not described but with regard to the chosen name, which is strangely close to the **Open Society** of Soros, their offices being located a stone's throw from each other in Brussels, doubt is still difficult to maintain. However, a court decision would be required to request details of their source of funding. The same goes for the **Cosmopolitan Project Foundation** whose site has also disappeared as if by magic.

Brussels, Open Society, Open Dialogue, and the European Parliament

The small world of Don Camillo-Soros on the same page

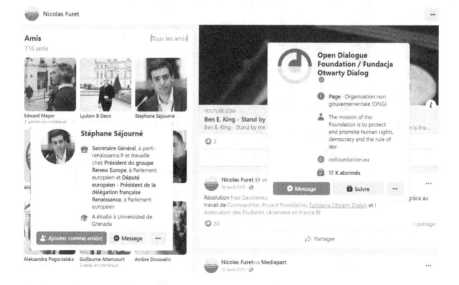

In one of Furet's publications, Colline Aymard appears, she works at Change.org whose CEO is none other than Ben Rattray, a former Democratic banker, who raised $15 million from the Omidyar Network in May 2013. Change.org is responsible for all leftist petitions in the world (immigration, etc.) and of course also supports the Ukrainian nationalist Savshenko imprisoned for the murder of two journalists. The circle is complete.

 Nicolas Furet
25 juin 2015 · 🌐

cc Coline Aymard, Jean Barrau, Bertrand de Franqueville, Aurore Biarnes, Serge Bléhoua, Nadège Buquet, Eléonore De La Varde, **Wendy Duvignau**, Anastasia Fomitchova, Boris Garcia, Blaise Gonda, Quentin Guillemain, **Eliott Khayat**, Irina Kogutyak Volodymyr Kogutyak, Alberto Iturralde, Manon Laroucau,....
Et bien sur Nathalie Pasternak et Nagy Navarro Balazs!

Omidyar works closely with the **Open Society et Google.** On February 18, 2008, in New York, the trio announced a new $17 million small and medium business investment company... It turns out that ODS would subsequently benefit from funding from Google, to promote the articles of resistance of Ukrainian society against… We don't know who since in 2013, Ukraine has no enemy but itself. Were they already considering Russia as the enemy with no war declaration?

Shortcut: https://tinyurl.com/SOROS-OMYDIAR

And of course, the conspiratorial bonus of the day: the mayor of Paris Anne Hidalgo… Clearly, in a photo in front of the flag of the Ukrainian neo-Nazis of Praviy Sektor, and another with their financiers… That's a lot for a socialist who respects human rights! **#JeSuisCharlie** except when the murdered journalists are Russian speakers, these are not taken into account in the charter of human rights. We note the presence of Quentin Guillemain (**CPF**) in the company of the financial manager of **ODF**, all these beautiful people to support Nadia Savchenko, the Ukrainian murderer.

Cosmopolitan Project Foundation ·3 se sent déterminé avec **Anastasia Fomitchova** et **5 autres personnes** à **Paris**.
30 juin 2015 · ✪

Ce matin, suite à la venue de Vira Savchenko en avril dernier à Paris et à l'action de Cosmopolitan Project Foundation avec Fundacja Otwarty Dialog , l'
Association des Etudiants Ukrainiens en France et le CRCUF / РКУГФ, Paris a manifesté son soutien à la libération de Nadia Savchenko par le vote d'une résolution à l'unanimité demandant sa libération immédiate et sans condition !
#FreeSavchenko Free Savchenko
Anne Hidalgo rejoint le Comité international de soutien à la députée ukrainienne.

https://fr.wikipedia.org/wiki/Nadia_Savtchenko

Social-leftism from Holland to Macron, hand in hand supporting butchery and massacres of all kinds, which tries to lecture the whole world, very touching, isn't it? The sad reality is quite different since, whatever their actions, they were de facto accomplices in sordid murders, and I almost want to add that they encouraged them. They pushed an entire population into the most infamous abyss in human history. Their Kievan accomplices masked all their misdeeds by controlling the media completely and forgetting the fundamental principles of all forms of civility.

The **Neo-Nazi Andriy Parubiy** appearing in an **EXPLICIT** manner associated with the purchase of paramilitary equipment well **BEFORE** the Maïdan clash, **This is irrefutable proof that this coup was premeditated.** Below are details of all funding for Maïdan by the Polish NGO ODF.

Link: https://odfoundation.eu/content/uploads/i/fmfiles/pdf/podsumowanie-finansowe-dzialan-pomocowych-odf-na-rzecz-ukrainy-2013-14-en-new.pdf

Shortcut: https://tinyurl.com/PnLODF/

OPEN DIALOG

Open Dialog Foundation
11a Szucha Avenue, office 21
00-580 Warsaw, Poland
T: +48 22 307 11 22

No.	FINANCIAL RESOURCES				
1	Maidan Self-defence (Andrij Parubij)	12,179.60	N/A	10-Feb-2014	N/A
2	Maidan Self-defence (Andrij Parubij)	12,192.40	N/A	26-Feb-2014	N/A
3	Organisation Rabiv do Rayu ne Puskayut for the soldiers whom they provide with resources and who fight in the ATO zone (inter alia, purchase of a car)	24,000.00	N/A	20-Jun-2014	N/A
		48,372.00			

SUMMARY	
Protective equipment	476,727.20
Financial resources	48,372.00
Total	565,246.00

Let us summarize a tiny part of the Soros nebula linked to Ukraine. **LREM** Macron's party renamed **Renaissance** like the NGO financing Ukraine "**International Renaissance Foundation**" ($230 M)... Coincidence or an explicit branding desire?

The Soros Nebula - NGO - Public

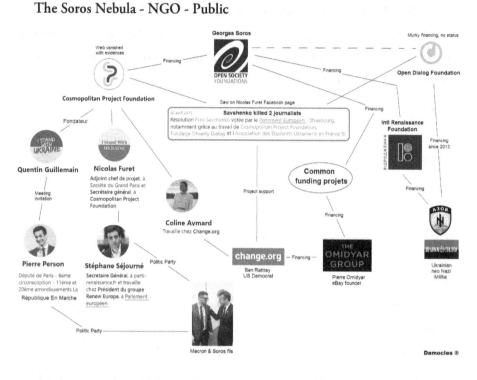

THE DRIFT OF A FASCIST REGIME

To illustrate this, Kiev refusing any form of diplomacy and thus bringing this country into the abyss of extremism under the benevolent gaze of the Western community, I must include the following anecdote. In 2016, after a short discussion with Dr. Andrey Kortunov, director general of the Russian International Affairs Council, he told me he had a diplomatic mission in Kiev and was due to meet the Minister of Foreign Affairs, Pavlo Klimkin. It turns out that the minister's secretary was a friend of mine. We had known each other since my three-year stint in Odessa, years before. At that time, he worked for the governor of this region. The ethno-political purge had started in Ukraine since Maïdan, and I told myself that Andrey could risk his life. So I called Dima and asked him if he could provide security for Andrey on his way out of the airport to the minister's office, which was located at the top of the street I lived in for years. Dima therefore assured me that he would take care of this overriding concern. Then, no more news from Andrey for several days.

I called Dima, asked him what's going on, he told me that Andrey never made it to the minister's office, to my complete amazement... And this without any other form of explanation. When Andrey contacted me again on his return to Moscow, stunned, he told me that some "zealous" and totally crazy henchmen had prevented him from entering the country when going through customs. In anger, I posted a message on Dima's Facebook page regarding this episode, and that's how a week later he contacted me telling me that this little message had cost him 48 hours of "custody" by the SBU and that he had seen himself at the bottom of a hole in a dark forest. In Ukraine, having friends who don't have the same democratic notions as yours can lead you to eat dandelions by the root, without olive oil of course. Since this episode, he hasn't spoken to me anymore and I can't blame him.

This episode may be trivial but nevertheless indicative of the way in which this country has fallen into the most basic extremism and which shows the incapacity of these people to set up a balanced negotiation between intelligent people and in good faith.

Moreover, after the first negotiation which took place on March 5, 2022 which would have put an end to the emerging conflict, according to sources from Ukrainska Pravda, a member of the Ukrainian negotiating delegation which met the Russian side, was shot dead by security agents as they attempted to arrest him. The man was allegedly Denys Kirieiev, former vice-president of Oschadbank. When we know which groups have infiltrated the SBU we are not surprised at all by what can happen to a member of the diplomatic corps. This is certainly one of the reasons why Zelensky is scared to death of putting in place a stop to the fighting. He knows full well that his life is in the crosshairs of the nationalists. He may be an accomplice, but he is certainly a hostage. The story of this conflict will end in a settling of scores between a group of neo-Nazis and those who want to stop the carnage.

V. From MH17 to Butcha, the MSM Wallows in Propaganda

"Sometimes people don't want to hear the truth because they don't want their illusions destroyed."

— F. Nietzsche.

You might believe that my judgment is indeed pro-Russian when in fact it is only oriented from a strict legal point of view, which amounts to the same thing in these circumstances. My lived experience and my knowledge of the rule of law shape my opinion and I will never accept that the propagandistic delusions of a few journalists addicted to God-knows-what can affect my way of thinking because, after all, facts are facts. We can avert our eyes from reality when it is too violent or cruel, and this privilege is reserved for the weak and the manipulators. But when we have been educated in a certain way we refuse the easy way because it would be a denial of intelligence and values. I don't live in a parallel world, my perception of the world has simply changed. Like Neo in *The Matrix*, I can see the hypocrisy, the lies, the manipulations and like a Don Quixote I try to fight against my own windmills with means of infinite weakness, without wanting to give up, because if I do so then my existence as a being of light would eventually end. I constantly think of these people who live in fear of dying every day throughout Ukraine and particularly in Donbass because of madmen exhumed from the past. Because yes, a large part of the population lives under the influence of these Banderist patients related to psychiatry (opinion given by a psychologist from western Ukraine). When a population eliminates its history, it tends to disappear and dies. This is how the education system was completely rewritten and a new history of Ukraine invented. You only need to look at the school textbooks to realize the chimerical madness into which this population is immersed. But it is much worse... Nazism is trivialized in the West!

THE COGNITIVE DISSONANCE OF THE MEDIA

Of course, the media will tell you that it is an epiphenomenon, bla bla bla... In 2016, the American Senate, horrified by the crimes perpetrated in Donbass, declared the following organizations terrorists: White Hammer, C14, Pravy Sektor, Azov, Aydar, Tornado, Kiev 1 /2, to then rehabilitate them under Biden.

The Tornado battalion had even been imprisoned in Kiev for absolutely abominable and "original" crimes: the rape of infants. The Azov battalion distinguished itself by burying DNR soldiers alive or by crucifixion and immolation... As the former colonel of the Swiss intelligence services, Jacques Baud, said on Sud Radio: "these groups operate with incredible uninhibited violence," comments subsequently confirmed by the founder of the US mercenary company "PMC Mozart," and former colonel of the US Marine Corps: "I am not a fan of Ukraine... The Ukrainian society is completely rotten and corrupt as are their leaders... Their soldiers do not respect the Geneva Convention and execute prisoners of war, this is unacceptable. If a US Army soldier behaved like this, he would be court-martialed immediately." What a thunderous statement for someone who fought alongside them. He adds at the end of the interview: "Vladimir Putin's fight is fair!" Check & mate for the French media!

You have certainly heard on TV that the fabricated Jewish marketing cover "Zelensky" is proof that Nazism does not exist in Ukraine, or it is an epiphenomenon. However, the Jewish neo-Nazi association signed its letters of nobility in March 2015, when Kolomoisky, the godfather of the said Zelensky, very curiously sponsored the Azov group, which also allowed him to carry out a raid within the state company UkrTransnafta, Kalashnikov on his shoulder, in order to appropriate the gas company's certificates of possession. Certainly to the amazement of readers, but this is the way business is done in Ukraine. We don't acquire legally, we just take over by force... At the risk and peril of those who would be bothered by the method of course! This is how you become a multi-billionaire in this country. Why bother asking the ECB to issue bonds to merge LVMH and Tiffany as Bernard Arnault did, Ukrainian methods avoid paperwork and they would be very wrong to deprive themselves of it.

During Maïdan, the flags of Praviy Sektor and Svoboda adorned the streets, en masse, processions armed with torches roamed the streets. These groups were formed from football hooligan groups known to be extremely violent and racist. During my meeting with Rosine G., Tea Party supporter, in October 2016 before the American presidential elections, in the presence of two European deputies including Pierre Seillac (who died a few months later), she confirmed to me all the information that I had gleaned from my contacts in Ukraine and my own observations. During the pre-election information transfer meetings, Senator McCain (not at all appreciated among the Pentagon military for his frequent lies about his military exploits in Vietnam) explained to them how these groups were trained by the CIA at their training camp in Arizona. She was even shocked by the youth of these participants and their capacity for limitless violence. She asked me to be careful because people around the Clintons were dying in strange ways and in epidemic proportions.

Training camps for these groups are set up throughout Ukraine around cities, and even in the city center of Kiev, Andriy Puskiy district. This is what Senator Nathalie Goulet, whose grandfather of Jewish origin ran a shop in the center of Kiev before the Second World War, was able to see first-hand. Since 2015, Ukrainian society has dangerously slipped towards nationalism. TV channels, education programs, bans on political opposition, the Nazi group Azov has even set up training camps for young people and even very young people in the format of Hitler Youth, draining en masse towards a morbid ideology. Every year for eight years, thousands of young people have passed through the Azov brainwasher from the age of six to eighteen years old. How many thousands of these young people are sent to the front today after being formatted by shameful propaganda?

From 2008, all the major IT groups in Silicon Valley have set offices everywhere in Ukraine and salaries jumped, a project manager was paid $3,500, a software developer $2,500 at all the heavyweights in this sector (Globallogic, Cyklum, Google, etc.), in Kiev in 2010. IT resources were being fought over on the market, it was a real war being waged to attract talent from this sector, to the point that two years later salaries had increased by more than 50 %. Having contributed to the book by the former Chief Technology Officer of IBM in New York *6 Billion minds* by Mark Minevich, I relate the explosion of global outsourcing in CIS countries, which contributed to the creation of a middle class with a huge delay compared to Russia. However, this has allowed Ukrainian society to take a leap forward as IT populations begin to consume and accelerate the underlying dependent sectors. All of this, thanks to the Tigipko family, whose husband Sergei was deputy prime minister, from the Regions Party supposedly opposed to the Maïdan ideology. The propaganda argument of extremist groups justifying political violence completely collapses, they justify their existence with shameful lies (Video below). This is what Obama, Hollande, Merkel, Macron, Von der Leyen sold you:

A FASCIST LIE

THE GUARDIAN: https://tinyurl.com/GUARDIANAZOV

NBC: https://tinyurl.com/AZOVNBC

because they can't make good money in our country.

Only nationalists can give something to this country.

Ukraine's far-right children's camp: 'I want to bring up a warrior'
The Guardian
2.06M subscribers   Subscribe

The **president of the Verkovka Rada** (Ukrainian parliament), is none other than the sulphureous founder of the first Nazi party UNO-UPA, **Andriy Parubiy**. In 2018, he proclaimed on a TV channel: "Hitler was the greatest democrat of the 20th century." He was supported by the CIA.

The advisor to the minister of the armed forces is **Dmitry Yarosh**, founder of **Praviy Sektor**, an armed far-right neo-Nazi militia, which has distinguished itself by its war crimes for eight years.

The **police director in Kiev** is none other than one of the leaders of the neo-Nazi group **Azov, Vadim Troyan**. He recruits into the police mainly individuals from Azov. This group is integrated directly into the regular army to avoid bad press and its leader **Andriy Biletsky**, distinguished himself in a masterly manner in the operation of massacres and torture of all kinds in Donbass.

Oleg Liachko, part radical, **deputy of the Rada**, an extremely violent individual with a serious and tortuous criminal past, does not hesitate to torture and execute political opponents, in the regions of Zaporozhye, Mariupol and Melitopol. Etc…

Let's summarize the situation, the tandem Democrats Obama/Biden, Wokists denouncing Trump as a fascist, formed and trained neo-Nazi groups to overthrow Yanukovich in October 2013. The Republican Trump administration declared these groups terrorists in October 2019, for the Biden administration to subsequently rehabilitate them in February 2022…

So we live in a truly crazy world where white is black and black is white - it's all about the direction of the wind and not the explicit facts.

A bit like hydroxychloroquine which kills, according to a study published in *The Lancet*, one of the largest medical journals in the world financed by Bill Gates, a call girl (Anglo-Saxon marketing term for a luxury whore) in Las Vegas; a story that a "great" French minister of health, Olivier Véran, followed without blinking an eye in order to eliminate a real scientific rival, Professor Didier Raoult. For your information, I had plaquenil delivered to me from Russia by a friend during the Covid crisis, I took it for two years every day to check and I still can't die, what an embarrassment. Thus, nowadays, an eminent professor like Didier Raoult has no right to be credible since it is the journalists who are practicing medicine and who format the information as it fits their perception or rather as they see fit in the Elysée…

What is surprising is that a large number of these bartending doctors, a new species that is rife in the upper echelons of government and television, have come to consult this great "charlatan"* to be cured of the Covid-19. During my last online conference with Professor McCullough, I learned that the number of cancers and heart attacks in the USA have multiplied by five and eight in the last 12 months after the end of the vaccination period and that the aging of the population in America was not due to the deaths of seniors but of the 20-40 year old group…This parallel semantic parenthesis closed, let's return to the subject of Ukraine…

January 7, 2015, the Charlie Hebdo attacks. The entire planet is shocked by the assassination of satirical journalists. The whole world converges on Paris for a march against Islamic terrorism. Hollande (who as usual seems totally absent) invites one of the butchers of Maïdan, Poroshenko who also seems very preoccupied. Perhaps due to the uneasiness of the situation compared to what is happening in his own country? Indeed, Oles Alexeïevitch Bouzina, one of the greatest journalists and a Ukrainian historian, born July 13, 1969 in Kiev (USSR) was murdered on April 16, 2015 in Kiev by two bullets in the head as he left his left bank home by neo-nationalist C14 Nazis.

---

* I am only quoting the qualifier used on continuous news channels by these famous experts of all kinds. I have far too much respect for this man to allow myself any criticism whatsoever.

Who cares, who talks about it in France? Nobody! Logically, he does not accept the coup d'état and is very critical of Poroshenko when he endorses the erection of the Nazi Bandera as a national hero by having streets and avenues renamed in after this war criminal.

I then learned that on i-Télé, Laurence Ferrari was going to give an interview with Poroshenko on April 22, 2015. I called her communications director and told her to ask him some embarrassing questions concerning the crimes perpetrated since Maïdan. She looked down on me and I heard myself retort in a somewhat dry tone: "But who do you think you are, we're not going to change the plan of our interview because an ordinary citizen asks us to, moreover we will stick to the plan of the Elysée and there is no question of changing it."

Everything is said, I leave you free to assess the situation. Above all, no scandal possible, the parrots are at work, let's make sure not to inconvenience the power in place, behaving like a real little collaborator of the 1940s. This is how in Ukraine we can now assassinate anyone without being worried as long as it is satisfying its masters. Human rights? In your face, Mr. Lambda citizen.

https://tinyurl.com/iTVPoroshenko

I would still like to point out that citizen Lambda has been and is contacted very frequently by deputies, very high-ranking servicemen (see the recommendations of General Paul Vallely), presidents of international forums, people from intelligence, certain ministries from foreign affairs to Oliver Stone's team with whom I have long-standing links concerning the post-Maïdan period.

The media treatment of this crisis is completely biased because it gives no alternative vision of the situation. The dissenting voices from the already decided narrative are completely destroyed. It is enough to say one wrong word against Ukraine to be cut off and immediately blacklisted, says Eric Denécé, co-founder of the French Center for Intelligence Research (CF2R) with whom I had the opportunity to speak on the phone several times.

State censorship on foreign channels (RT, Sputnik) and internet broadcast channels (YouTube, Twitter, Rumble, etc.) was extremely effective in containing information that disturbed the propaganda narrative. Daring to say that France is not a dictatorship is almost ridiculous. Have you heard about the stele erected in

Donbass for the 180 children who died in the bombing of Kiev during the period before Operation Z? This information was well hidden from you, they were Russian-speaking children, so from an ICC point of view, they did not exist.

Quite surprisingly, Anglo-Saxon media control is not as sectarian as in Europe, you just have to listen to Tucker Carlson on Fox News (and now on X) to hear a sound that stands out from that of the Biden administration, and which would surprise more than one French parrot. Even if European political powers try to channel information by emitting a single musical note, the French are not fooled and this veneer will crack with surprising consequences.

We live in an era where instant communication has become king, the first to speak and make the most noise is right, whatever the facts. Goebbels, Hitler's Nazi propaganda minister, was an early practitioner of this widely used technique. The USA, under Obama, showed us during the episode of the shooting down of MH17 on July 17, 2014 at the very beginning of the conflict between Kiev and Donbass that they had mastered this art of persuasion.

> *"Take a lie, repeat it loud and clear as much as possible until people think it's the truth."*

> — Joseph Goebbels

MH17 THE FACTS

MH17, a Malaysia Airline Boeing 777 airliner flying from Amsterdam to Malaysia Kuala Lumpur, is shot down over Donbass. Moment of amazement! Less than twenty minutes later, at a press conference at the White House, spokesperson Jen Psakis announced in front of an audience of sworn journalists: "The Russians did it, we got the proof on Twitter and Facebook,"* a very impressive way to prove a war crime... The Russians therefore become Kennedy's "Lee Harvey Oswald" in

---

* It's a move by the Russians, we have proof of it on Facebook and Twitter.

real time, same technique, immediacy! We might have expected a radar trace or to be presented with recordings from the Dnepropetrovsk tower, a satellite view because the area was extremely monitored... No... It's thanks to Super Zuckerberg that we will solve all war crimes live, including those of September 11, without a prosecutor, without a judge, without evidence, and without an investigation. Justice 2.0 is Facebook! It should be noted that the video of July 19, 2014 has disappeared from YouTube. (https://www.youtube.com/watch?v=oQRvlNebeok).

My friend and neighbor in Kiev, Louis G, who has certified the safety of most airports in CIS countries for a decade, sent me a big pdf file: MH17 pre-report of the Dutch Safety Board and asked me to take a look, knowing my critical mind, he thought that I would see things that an expert distorted by routine would not note. In addition, being in contact with French and English journalists living in Donbass, I could collect testimonies and videos. The report contained surprising gray areas and posed many questions (I subsequently handed it in person to Thierry Mariani in his office at parliament on March 8, 2015, upon my tumultuous return from Dnepropetrovsk):

- Why were the black boxes, recording flight parameters, cockpit and passenger conversations, handed over to MI6, the British secret service, when the plane belonged to Malaysia?

- Why did the USA force all parties (including the nations from which the passengers come) to sign an NDA to refrain from transmitting information regarding the crash even though it was a commercial flight?

- Why were the conversation recording boxes silent, since we found passengers with oxygen masks on their faces (which means that after being hit, the passengers were still alive)? Remember that black box recording the voices on the German Wing flight which disintegrated when hitting a Vercor mountain revealed the screams of the passengers before the crash while it was in a terrible state. In the case of MH17, the boxes were intact.

- These boxes did not reveal information (although they were intact), but a trajectory map was established, how so?

Figure 4: Cockpit voice recorder. (Source: AAIB)   Figure 5: Flight data recorder. (Source: AAIB)

- And if the recordings had not disappeared then how could this trajectory be established?

- Why was Nataliya Petrenko, controller of the Dnepropetrovsk tower, changing the flight parameters of MH17, directing it towards combat zones and lowering its altitude? Who gave her the order? Why did recordings from the Dnepropetrovsk control tower disappear?

- Why did MH17 not vaporize in flight and still hover for more than 8 km before crashing? It was full of kerosene and had only been flying for two hours, a BUK SA 11 missile has an explosive charge of 70 kg. Here is what Justin Bronk, an aeronautics expert at the Royal United Services Institute, said, a statement that ran counter to what happened:

"The missile is programmed using a tracker to approach within a meter of the target, then releases a ring of shrapnel, which enters the aircraft at different points. The shrapnel would have hit the wings, engines, and fuel tanks, **It should have exploded in flight instantly**." https://tinyurl.com/MH17Expert

- Why did Nataliya Petrenko disappear without being questioned? (One of my contacts found her in Dubai living in a luxury apartment, three years later. Who paid for it?)

- We could observe 30 mm round impacts (caliber of an SU25 cannon) coming out of the cockpit. Very curious shape for missile fragments. Outgoing impacts as the missile explodes externally? Why did some photos disappear from the final report?

- **View of the left side cockpit annotated by me.**

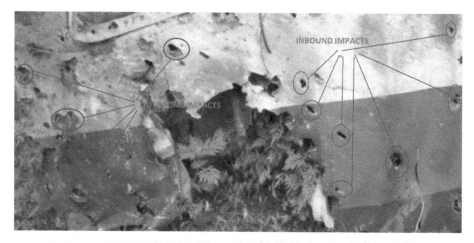

- Witnesses saw two SU-25 fighter jets flying in the area on the same day, at the same time; the separatists did not have a fighter plane. A name emerged, that of Vladislav Voloshin who returned to the Dnepropetrovsk base with two missing M60 type missiles. Voloshin is found to have "committed suicide" in Nikolaev with two bullets in the chest (curious way to proceed). Why didn't the Joint Investigation Team interview these witnesses?

- The JIT notified in the final report that the shrapnel (missile fragments) which hit MH17 were of the butterfly type, but this is confidential information that the Russians only disclosed between the pre-report and the final report. The pre-report only mentioned round impacts. In the final report they became butterflies. Why were there no butterfly impacts in the cockpit?

When I put all these questions to Louis, he was stunned by their common sense and triviality... No need to be an aviation expert, you just need to open your eyes. But the only question that must be answered and which will name the culprit as in all investigations (B.A.BA of the little detective): **Who benefits from the crime, Doctor Watson?** Information that you will not find anywhere else: these were all the European HIV specialists who were going to Kuala Lumpur for a conference on the subject. That's twenty years of international research on AIDS that disappeared in a crash!

Below is the breakdown of the different elements of the plane. Loss of certain elements of the cockpit at the time of the attack then the plane deviated from its course, towards the north-east, hovered for several kilometers (seen by several inhabitants of the region) to crash in Hrabove...

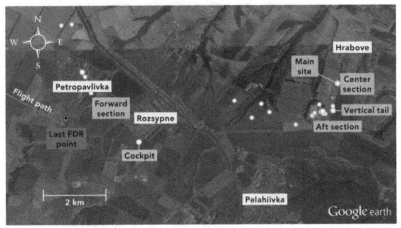

Figure 6: The last location of the aircraft in flight taken from the FDR. Wreckage distribution is grouped per section of the aircraft (Source: Google Earth, wreckage information Dutch Safety Board).

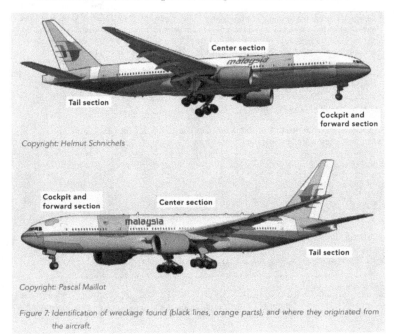

Figure 7: Identification of wreckage found (black lines, orange parts), and where they originated from the aircraft.

Letter issued by the Australian government confirming the signing of an ILLEGAL NDA (a commercial flight is subject to transparency).

Australian Government

Department of Foreign Affairs and Trade

15 October 2014

Dear

Thank you for your letter dated 11 September 2014 to the Minister for Infrastructure and Regional Development, Mr Warren Truss, regarding the non-disclosure agreement signed by the parties to the criminal investigation into the downing of Malaysian Airlines flight MH17. Your letter was subsequently referred to the Minister for Foreign Affairs, Ms Julie Bishop. I have been asked to reply on behalf of the Minister for Foreign Affairs.

Australia, along with the Netherlands, Belgium and Ukraine, is a party to the criminal investigation into the downing of Malaysian Airlines flight MH17. All parties to the criminal investigation have signed a non-disclosure agreement, which requires consensus among the parties before information regarding the investigation will be released. I regret that as the document is classified, the Department cannot provide you with a copy of the agreement.

As with all criminal investigations, the non-disclosure of information is important to avoid jeopardising the investigation or prejudicing a future judicial proceeding arising from the investigation. The government remains focused on finding, prosecuting and punishing the perpetrators of this cowardly attack.

We appreciate your interest in this issue and thank you for bringing your query to the attention of the Australian Government.

Yours sincerely

Melissa Stenfors
A/g Director
Crisis Management & Contingency Planning Section

R G Casey Building   John McEwen Cres   Barton   0221
Telephone:02 6261 1111   Facsimile:02 6261 3111

A GETAWAY TO DNEPROPETROVSK

Being in Ukraine, I thought that taking a trip to Dnepropetrovsk might be a good idea to collect some additional information to get to the bottom of it. On February 15, 2015, I left Kiev, around the so-called ATO zone, therefore "a little sensitive," despite the risk involved. Arriving there, I detected a certain tension even though we were still 200 km from the front line. I found that for a city in Ukraine there was a lot of English spoken in uniform...

On the morning of the 17th I left my room to have my coffee around 5:30 am at the Smart Hotel Dnipro, and I found myself surrounded by five guys with not very Catholic faces, guns in hand, who asked me to follow them immediately. Knowing the context of the assassination of journalists and other recalcitrants, I refused with all the confidence I could muster, to destabilize them. It's a bit of a game of prey and predator, if you run... you trigger predation; if you confront them, you put the predator in a position of doubt. Looking back, knowing what happened to a large number of people, like Dasha Dugina, doing what I did required a huge dose of recklessness (or courage?), and insane risk-taking. Despite the time that has passed, I still have trouble evaluating it, but I think it was more of a survival reflex.

So I told them with great arrogance that they had to show me identification, the administration they represented, and the reason for such a deployment of force. Then of course, I called Louis in Kiev to warn him of my misadventure by asking him to contact Thierry Mariani at the parliament as well as the French embassy in Kiev to notify them of what was happening in case something went wrong. A Jason Bourne, Slavic version, who was given a Glock certainly less than six months ago, judging by his young age, started to stamp his feet. I asked him to sit down while I had my coffee in great silence. Then, looking him in the eye, I said the following to him in a mixture of Russian and English to test his intellectual capacity:

"I know who you are and who you work for, don't give me lapsha (bullshit). I prefer to warn you that my CIS deputy and former minister Mr. Mariani knows that I am here, I must send him a report on the situation in a few days. So if you have the very bad idea of damaging a single hair of mine, because I know your methods well, don't forget that his former colleague in President Sarkozy's government is Ms. Lagarde, head of the IMF. This woman sends a check to your puppet president to pay your salaries every month." I almost had the bad idea of adding: "You little punk m*therf*cker," but they were armed and I wasn't! It was important not to push the song of arrogance too far, but he understood that I spoke Russian well enough that he wouldn't try to fool me. So I brought him into the field of a foreign language that I had mastered better than him in order to dominate him. The guy didn't know how to handle the situation anymore. At the end of breakfast, I was taken for a drive for an interrogation at the regional SBU headquarters, escorted by several cars. Perhaps they mistook me for a Russian GRU general. It was ridiculous! I was placed in a room facing the same guy and I had three dome-shaped cameras moving above my head, so I understood that all my gestures would be analyzed. Questions started to arise, "What are you doing in Ukraine and why this and that…" I rushed unto this breach and told him that he should be better trained since if he had asked for my passport he would have been able to see the large number of customs stamps printed to deduce that I had lived in this country for almost ten years, and I worked there. My destabilization technique had worked, he had forgotten the main point. Annoyed, he confiscated my phone and my iPad which he entrusted to a third party to go through all my data. This lasted for hours. He therefore informed me that for reasons of suspicion of terrorism, they would keep me as long as necessary. Of course, I burst out laughing and took the opportunity to make fun of him. I unpacked my backpack completely on the table, which he had not searched (another failure that I pointed out to him), grabbed a pair of underwear and retorted that it was a formidable biological weapon and that it was better not to put his nose into it. The guy was red as a peony. Obviously, he was a beginner; the more he asked, the more I ridiculed him. The interrogation became hell for our operetta James Bond. I told myself that this was a good opportunity to pressure him with increasingly embarrassing questions;

observing his behavior would certainly say more than what he would tell me. I looked him straight in the eyes to make him very uncomfortable and began:

Me: "How come you annoy me instead of arresting the murderers of the Maïdan and Odessa protesters? What is this mess? What are you doing in this country? Do you know your job? Why is nothing being done?"

Him: "Sir, it's political…" He stammered uncomfortably (I had my guy by the throat, it was time to reverse the roles).

Me: "Are you kidding me? Murder is murder! You want names, Parubiy, does that mean something to you? Do you want evidence? Call the Kiev prosecutor and ask him to make me testify in court, I have what it takes."

Him: Livid, he lowered his eyes and was quiet, then said, "I can't do that…" And for good reason, the previous prosecutor was assassinated before the trial!

Me: "Why are you afraid? Can you look at yourself in the mirror in the morning? You have no shame? Do you think we don't know what you're doing?" Dead silence! The guy was just paralyzed. "Tell me about Captain Vladislav Voloshin and MH17, your rotten government corrupted to the bones, that has been lying to us for months. That's enough! Do you think we don't know that you shot down this plane?"

Him: As if struck by lightning, cowardly: "I'm coming back, I have to talk to my chief." He saw that he was no longer in control of the situation in the face of my outraged anger.

He left me alone for two hours in this freezing room without heating, outside it was Siberian cold. I told myself that I might have been like swearing in a church and I risked ending up at the bottom of a hole in a forest in the form of humus, the end of my career as an eco-friendly entrepreneur! Either way, it was too late to walk back. I embarked on a path of no return and I had to go all out. It was 3pm, the puppets had been getting me drunk off stupidity for ten hours playing a Pinder circus KGB. I had only one thing in mind, which was to go back to Kiev and go out with my friends for my birthday on February 19th. At the same time, I had started to realize that this country was plummeting toward the abyss, and that it really didn't bode well. Although I had seen abominable things, it was certainly nothing compared to what must be happening underground. It was high time for a change of scenery - you can't play with matches for too long while sitting on a barrel of TNT.

Our budding James Bond came back, and I decided to crush him with no remorse. I yelled at him, telling him that this charade must stop, I ordered him to ask one of his henchmen with the head of a killer to lead me to the Dnipro station, he refused by asking me to take a taxi. It was so harsh for him that to stop me he agreed on the condition of signing a letter stipulating that I must leave the territory and could no longer return to Ukraine. As I left, I shook his hand and told him that I had no grievance against him but that their government was pushing towards a major conflict with Russia and when that happened, they would find themselves facing an angry bear because no one in Europe would come to die for Ukraine. A nation that, out of control, was sliding towards fascism, their approach would scare away all investors and sink the country's economy. Today he could call me Nostradamus.

The security bulldog accompanied me in the car to the station and troubles started flying in squadrons, our dear former President Chirac would say. You should know that in Ukraine, at least in this bygone era, the SBU delegated the dirty work to gunslingers (the very enthusiastic neo-Nazi groups already mentioned) because they did not want to bear direct legal responsibility for a "slip." Plausible deniability. I was on the bus, we'd been driving for 30 to 40 minutes in the open countryside, a car overtook us in a curious way, braked in front, turning on its indicator to let the driver know to stop. I was on the left side, window and when she passed , I could see a huge sticker on the hood in the colors of Praviy Sektor. In a second, I realize that everything could go very wrong very quickly. I took out my taser loaded the day before (compact, with a flashlight so as not to attract attention), ready to grill one of these madmen if necessary. I tried the 50K volt once, I'm not about to do it again, it feels nasty.

Two guys entered the bus and headed directly to the back just behind me even though there were free seats everywhere. As they passed I noticed that one of them had a sort of huge machete knife on his belt and the other a Glock. Discreetly I took a photo of myself at an angle that allowed one to be identified and which I send to my embassy contact in Moscow, with my mother's telephone number, telling him to report that I would certainly have big problems.

The two crazy people took out a tablet, played neo-Nazi propaganda videos and stuck it above my head while having fun with their respective toys. I was on guard, turning three quarters to make sure I saw a bad move coming. I had an impossible knot in my stomach. Their fuss lasted for a very long 90 minutes, an incredible noise to the point that people turned around, but no one moved because their appearance was frightening... Crazy faces!

Arriving in Kiev, at a traffic light I got up like a devil. People got up thinking we had arrived at the station and blocked them. I got off the bus, stopped a car, gave 100 UAH, which at that moment was a hell of a lot of money. It must be said that in Kiev everyone is a taxi, you extend your arm, you give a location, the guy gives you a price (it never exceeds 30 UAH), and you are good to go. At the sight of the 100 UAH the guy didn't even ask me where I wanted to go, I got in, he drove off. I gave a specific address and told him to go as quickly as possible. The guy thought he was F1 driver Hamilton in the city center, astonishing! In 24 hours I organized my disappearance from this country which no longer corresponds at all to my vision of the world nor to that which the European Commission is trying to sell you against the grain of reality... Enjoy the ride!

During the following two days it was a cat and mouse game, guys followed me everywhere I went, I systematically took photos for identification. I even came across a conversation with Finnish mercenaries who had come to fight in Donbass, in the Shato restaurant, right in the center of Khreshchatyk. I had a hard time with this situation, and I started to get scared. On February 20, 6 am, I called a taxi to go to Borispol Airport. I went down to have a last coffee with my bag in a small coffee shop located in an alley at the top of Maïdan to the right of the McDonald's and told myself that I would soon be calmer once in the boarding terminal. A bulldog entered this little cafe, determined, rushing at me, shouting something like that he was watching me on Maïdan and punched me at the C3/C4 vertebra level which cut off my breathing. This earned him a taser barbecue which knocked him to the ground.

I rushed out as best I could, jumped into the taxi that was waiting for me... At the security gate of the Borispol international terminal a group of US soldiers passed by, but what were they doing here? The alarms sounded, they had bags marked "US Army Security," no one said anything to them, I was stunned...Do svidaniya Ukraina.

When I returned I could no longer move two fingers of my left hand, so I was treated with infiltrations through the clavicle between the vertebrae, a pleasure to be being speared with a 15 cm needle in that place... I should have sent the hospital bill directly to the Elysée, just like Dimitry Rogozin, former director of Roscosmos who after being injured in Donetsk, sent back the shrapnel from a Caesar cannon shell that had lodged in his spine during his birthday dinner. Was this the best way to thank him for welcoming astronaut Thomas Pesquet upon his return to earth from Mir Station? These are courtesies that cannot be refused, right Emmanuel Macron?

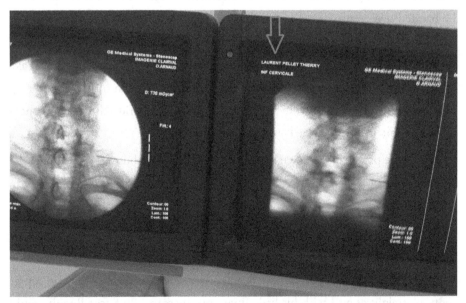

So ten years of hard work and investments vaporized in a coup d'état, without a severance package or a golden parachute. A "Goodbye" à la President Giscard d'Estaing, get out, there is really nothing more to see! So, I came up with an even more brilliant idea: publishing a report explaining this phenomenal attack on

LinkedIn. In the hour that followed I was harassed by a certain Charles Leven, who in his profile didn't hide that he was part of the CIA based in Kiev. I received an avalanche of insults and death threats from some of his henchmen (Sheikh Fall, close to Senator McCain, organizer of Mïidan, James Berger, close to Senator Merkley). Being harassed on the phone dozens of times a day, I managed to escape to my mountains for several months while this matter calmed down... and I managed to get them kicked off the platform for harassment.

This was worth pointing out to me by the president of the economic forum of the Danube region, the general director of the Russian International Affairs council (who works with two former ministers of Russian affairs), and so one thing led to another, the CF2R, then the advisor of the Prime Minister of Malaysia whom I welcomed to my home in France. An absolutely incredible scandal ensued when he handed over a number of my findings on the MH17 affair to Prime Minister Mohamad Mahathir. He gave a press conference and announced that he did not believe for a minute that it was the Russian side which shot down this plane. Take it in your mouth Hollande, it was a bit like confessing, each in turn, we shouldn't believe that it's always the same people who take it all in stride all the same, there must be some memorable backlash!

This little personal revenge may have flattered my ego, but it didn't punish the guilty. One day justice will have to be done for the families of the victims.

THE WESTERN MEDIA, PINOCCHIO'S JUNKIES

Since the start of the conflict, February 2022, the media have been in full psychotic delirium over the model of the line decided by the globalists that Macron represents as straight as an I with his little finger on the seam. Professor Raoult would say "In psychiatry we call it having delusional flashes." A whole range of experts of all kinds have been spreading their venom in the media: a so-called former KGB spy Andrey Zhirnov vomits everything he can about his country (he who was never more than a simple administrative attaché.) If he had been someone seriously posing a risk to the national security of the Russian Federation, it would have crackled in the night like its soup). Zhirnov is just a media rattle. Then it's the turn of a high school teacher from 93 on CNEWS, who is hysterically agitated with a lot of "Me teacher, me this and me that," not speaking a word of Russian but explaining the murders of Boutcha like a public prosecutor. Let's not forget about those retired French generals (the "TV studio Gamelin" the geopolitical analyst Xavier Moreau would say, who adopted the Colonel McGregor tone) who have never seen a battlefield but come to supplement their pitiful income by recounting stupidity after stupidity about the military strategies adopted by the Russian army. This doesn't mean that the Russians did not make mistakes, but they were corrected gradually...

"And Russia is losing, and they are lousy, and they only have frying pans, and they are out of ammo, and they are bombing with washing machine drums, and they are all dead..." 24/7 for 11 months... But, if these people were a little serious, they would know that the Russian military arsenal is absolutely gigantic (13,800 tanks, 4,800 fighter planes, 9,500 artillery pieces, more than 100 million shells in reserve, 1.5 million men...) and that Russia has switched their economy to war mode at the end of 2022, and is starting to manufacture the most recent weapons in (large) series...

They are so bad, that with a strength of ⅓ compared to the Ukrainian army, they took 20% of the territory of a country bigger than France, so bad that the Ukrainian ambassador to England in a private conversation at the beginning of January 2023 declares: "We have hidden the real losses, the figures are enormous and indigestible." We know that more than 33,000 bodies were left on the battlefields and our estimates for having a team assessing the flags flying in the wind in Ukrainian cemeteries gives more than 200,000 graves (as of December 31, 2022), with a number of injured which is impossible to estimate but is still much higher. The information from our working group is solid. They are correlated with those that come to me from US generals with whom I am in contact and my own sources coming from residents in Ukraine.

In this regard, the losers that these "high-ranking" soldiers are talking about have just kicked the Ukrainian army (AFU) out of Soledar, which will allow them to finish off the reserves in Artemovsk (Bakhmut). This logistical node is strategic for their supplies, and they will have to flee across the steppe towards Kramatorsk because the M03 (a sort of highway) is cut, and during these 45 km they will experience the hell of artillery and Russian aviation. They will get whipped.

In the chimerical world of Western media, Ukrainians are the most beautiful, the strongest, the most virtuous, and only the "progressive leftist journalists" know the truth without leaving their sofa. In the real world where we live, us average people, who never understand anything, the facts are still a little different. But if by a terrible misfortune you move away from the decided narrative, then you are the worst of the "collaborator-Putinist", after having been a "Cov-idiot." They want to force you to live in a cognitive distortion leading to a brutal shock when confronted with the very real world. We should remember that:

- The world press is sponsored by Bill Gates ($312M).

- The French press is every year on a drip from the Elysée and 35% is controlled by the German group Bertelsmann owned by Liz Mohn, (a very close friend of Merkel whose husband divorced a first marriage after being discovered in the marital bed in the presence of a man).

With these details known, it becomes very complicated to sell this sauce of lies that they serve you every day... To support this point, we will deal with some thorny topics.

THE BUCHA MASSACRE

Let us remember that Maidan was a small "democratic" celebration where the constitution was respected, and the Ukrainian legal system was respectful and exemplary. The white dove sent to AFP the images of victims murdered by the Russian army and all the media took up the matter, the opportunity of the century to denigrate Operation Z and Vladimir Putin the child-eating butcher (awaiting proof of other wrongdoing). Sometime before, in the various legal cases of murder or sexual assault and other crimes covered on CNEWS, I rightly heard, dear attorney Gilles-William Goldnadel, warning his heated colleagues during prime-time news, that a talk show was not a court of justice, that they were not prosecutors, and without in-depth knowledge, with all facts in hand, judging a case publicly can constitute defamation. That said, it's very fashionable nowadays to proceed with "Gobble style." We condemn during TV shows, we create sweeping judgments in such a way that public opinion is moved and takes sides. Remember this Syrian child who died, Alyan Kurdi, on September 2, 2015. A photo and a shocking sentence on BFM TV.

"If this extraordinarily strong image of a Syrian child washed up on a beach doesn't change Europe's attitude towards refugees, what would?"

They make you feel guilty, and they make you accept a million migrants. This resulted in thousands of women being raped all over Europe. Where are the feminists stunned by sexism, Motus and tight-lipped? And of course, we forgot to tell you that the smuggler is none other than the father of the kid, that it is the French consul in Turkey, Francoise Olcay, who sells the zodiacs to smugglers, making a fortune in the process and it is Georges Soros who finances the entire migration operation through an HSBC hub. The globalism of Open Society and WEF are in action. It's for a good cause, applaud! Faced with the consul's scandal, Hollande had no choice but to dismiss her...

For the alleged massacre of Boutcha, we are witnessing the same emotional process, we take a photo relayed in all the media, and we run it in a loop to play on the sensational side of this horror. But when we know the Kiev birds of ill omen and their methods, the string is a little too thick, and so we have to dig a little into the details without accusing people unnecessarily.

Nothing surprises or shocks you in the photo below? The victim's hands have been exposed to muddy water for a very long time, this is the reason why the fingers are blistered and dirty apart from the necrosis (very clear at the level of the right thumb), stay in your bathtub for two hours and look at your hands. It's surprising to see an immaculate white headband, as well as a clean coat as if it came from a dry cleaner, with a body placed on its stomach. The international political weight of such butchery becomes obvious, and as with MH17, in 30 minutes, the loud-speakers of the global MSM proclaim the name of the culprit without serious investigation or prosecutor: Russia.

Let's take the Luxembourg press: https://tinyurl.com/LU-BUTCHA

(the photos used in France are the same)

Conclusion: the victim was killed, fell on his back in a puddle and remained in this position for a long time, subsequently dressed and tied his hands behind his back and with a hood placed over his head (masking an execution at point blank, as the SBU practiced for eight years on the political opposition?), then moved in order to clearly expose the crime. Of course, the chronic prosecutor Kévin Bossuet, during the CNEWS talk show, did not fail to gesticulate in a hysterical pleading, because between 5 o'clock in the afternoon when he left his college in Seine Saint Denis and 8 o'clock in the evening, he had already gone to the SBU morgues in

Kiev to investigate and conclude that the Russians were guilty. Later, we learned that some victims had combat rations from the Russian army. We can sense a little atmosphere of denunciation in Ukraine. TV courts still have a bright future ahead of them.

This was without counting on the testimony of the former French soldier, Adrien Bocquet, part of a French humanitarian aid NGO, who confirmed that it was indeed the Ukrainians who had done the deed. He escaped a murder attempt in Turkey (perpetrated by the SBU?). He received Russian citizenship from Vladimir Putin as a political prisoner.

You Fail Mr. School Teacher Prosecutor, You Fail!

I am keeping in reserve the case of the mini nuclear research reactor at a university in Kharkov on March 8, 2022. The day before, one of my sources warned me. I sent a notification to a member of CF2R (French Intelligence Research Center) that the SBU was going to bomb this laboratory at the risk of nuclear contamination, copying senators, lawyers, and journalists from CNEWS. The next day, CNEWS announced that the Russians had bombed it.

One of these famous journalists replied to me that I had to stop bothering him. I thought I was helping him do his job, am I stupid?

The collateral victim of all these war crimes is indeed the integrity and ethics of the Western media which turns out to be an arrogant, misleading, lying, accomplice of criminal governments and neo-Nazis rising from its ashes. If a tenth of what happened in this country in eight years had happened in France, the press would be screaming "FASCISM" 24/7, shame on you, you make me vomit.

VI. Biological weapons in Ukraine

Since 2016, I knew from different sources that ten biological weapons laboratories had been installed in Ukraine, without really knowing what was going on there. We had a vague idea of the cities, but it remained a rumor. In winter 2016-17 around February, an event caught my attention. "In a village near Kherson more than 860 people died in one week from virulent pneumonia," my former neighbor, a doctor in Odessa, told me. Travel in this part of Ukraine at that time was very complicated because of the snow and the quality of the roads which is absolutely terrible. (Even during the summer).

At the end of December of the following year in 2017, I was invited to the economic forum in Chisinau in Moldova, which Sergey Glaziev, economic advisor to Vladimir Putin and Russian transport minister, was to attend. Alexandre Dugin, one of the Russian advisors very active in the design of the Eurasian Union and his daughter Daria, a brilliant journalist, were also present. The President of Moldova Dodon welcomed us warmly. Glaziev did not come - he was afraid of being murdered. A week earlier the Russian ambassador to South Ossetia was assassinated and a few months later it was the president of Moldova who escaped death after a truck hit his vehicle for no explainable reason. Dugin and his daughter Dasha traveled separately. Valérie Burgault, a French researcher, gave a presentation on the hegemony of Western currencies, and, during the forum, she was threatened by a member of the DGSE. Well after the forum I learned that a member of the French delegation (senior official close to Marine Le Pen) died of devastating cancer. Coincidence? I don't want to think about it. It feels like a bad dream.

I returned to France, tired and sick, a sort of bad bronchitis which I could not get rid of and which lasted despite heavy treatment (No, it was not polonium, and the Skripals were not present). A few days of respite and mid-January it started again even stronger. I was devastated, fever over 40 degrees for five days. I was hospitalized after a sudden drop in respiratory capacity to 85%; in the emergency room I lost consciousness, my temperature rose to 41.2. I was placed in a negative pressure room and visitors were prohibited. The medical staff were dressed as cosmonauts to enter my unit. My blood was oxygenated by an external mechanism, perfused, nasal tube, my urine was black... A serious condition indeed. It took ten days to stabilize me, I lost 11kg, I couldn't even walk anymore. The doctor told me: "We don't know what the virus you contracted is, we've never seen it and you had a narrow escape." I received high-dose corticosteroid inhalation treatment twice for 45 minutes per day for another month. I only started walking properly again at the beginning of May... I was skeletal, a shadow of myself. Professor Raoult said during the pandemic period, in one of his weekly conferences, that Covid-19 began to circulate well before the pandemic, he did not think he was saying that well and we are going to see how it was already linked to these dear Ukrainians... Did I catch it? I can't confirm it, but based on what we know today in terms of symptoms, it looks a lot like it. Would you believe it, PCR tests were not yet ready for a pathogen still known only to those in the know.

One year later... We met our invisible but very present friend Mr. Covid-19. I was in Paris at the beginning of January 2020, and received a phone call from the advisor to the Malaysian government who is also the advisor to the governments of the Guangdong and Guangzhou regions in China. He texted me: "Don't take the metro anymore or put on an FFP2 mask, there are a lot of Chinese coming to Paris for the New Year and there is a lot of filth that is spreading and killing at a terrible speed." At the moment I thought it was a bad joke but knowing this person, and his knowledge in various fields, particularly in biology and agriculture, I told myself that following this advice was and easy task. Moreover, I had experienced something not very funny two years before, I was not very motivated to experience a similar adventure. I still felt like I was going crazy when I took the TGV to go home in mid-January with a mask on my face. I called ARS Marseille (equivalent to the CDC in the US), who sent me to graze with the cows in the pre-Alps. I went to see my family doctor, and she said, "You're too anxious." They may be right, why should I really worry... At the beginning of March, 11 p.m. I received an SMS from my doctor who apologized and asked me if I could find him some masks because the ARS did not provide any while I told her I had stocked up... The hell of the C19 was beginning.

HOW THE INVESTIGATION BEGINS...

January 2022, I received a message from one of my Bulgarian contacts who gave me information about Dilyana Gaytandzhieva, an investigative journalist who had been investigating biological weapons laboratories in Europe established by the USA for a year. She got her hands on a large number of documents that compromised the governments of Georgia, Romania, Bulgaria, and Ukraine. She told me where I could download them and what I read left me speechless. This is how we started to dig deeper. **Early February 2022**, I called General Paul Vallely, retired US Army, Pacific unit, who at that moment was in Florida playing golf at Mar-a-Lago with the big boss. I told him I wanted to organize a conference call with some of his associates, generals, and colonels for an extremely serious matter. Paul organized the conference on Zoom and I showed them that a certain branch of the Pentagon financed the installation of illegal biological weapons laboratories in Europe, the largest of which was located in Georgia, Tbilisi (Lugar center benefiting from a fund of $180M), 11 laboratories in Ukraine and one being created in Bulgaria (a scientist involved had warned Dilyana) for the development of viruses such as:

Bacillus anthracis (anthrax), Brucella, CCHF virus, Coxiella burnetii, Francisella tularensis, Hantavirus, Rickettsia species, TBE virus, Bartonella species, Borrelia species, Ehrlichia species, Leptospira species, Salmonella typhi, bubonic plague, **and certainly Covid-19.** We discovered much later that during the first three months of Russian Operation Z, forty laboratories were uncovered, most of them dismantled, the samples isolated and secured. And that indeed **Covid-19 has been "studied" in Ukraine**, all financed thanks to Biden's son, Hunter. We found evidence of this in the US government spending database which we outline below.

Surprised, my interlocutors tell me that they will set up an internal investigation to verify my statements and the documents provided. Dilyana managed to obtain a large number of official documents through the emails of ministers in Georgia as well as in Ukraine, and she also followed members of the US embassy in Tbilisi, even in the laboratory they were visiting frequently. Sometime later, a member of the team sent an email to our group (which is substantial and very high-ranking) with mind-boggling details straight from Hunter Biden's laptop, which had been picked up by the former mayor of New York, Rudolph Giuliani, who is part of our network. So we began to unroll the ball of wool. The result was a 180-page document, which was given to my general US contacts and to Igor Lopatonok, production director of the film *Ukraine On Fire*, a long-time friend and Sean Stone (son of Oliver).

Today Dilyana is the subject of an elimination contract issued by Zelensky on Myrotvorets, the truth is always dangerous: https://tinyurl.com/DILYTHREAT

THE BIDENS AND D.O.D INVOLVED TO THE NECK

When Joe Biden was vice-president under Obama, he took advantage of the Maïdan coup to place his son Hunter at the head of the Ukrainian gas consortium Burisma, so that he could "represent" the family there. He was therefore comfortably installed in a board seat. He was so well established that he attracted the wrath of NABU, the national anti-corruption office, a sort of FBI with Ukrainian flavor. On June 22, 2020, a joint press conference took place with the Ukrainian news agency Interfax, during which a member of the Ukrainian Parliament, Andrii Derkach, and the head of a group of Ukrainian prosecutors at the Prosecutor General's Office of Ukraine (GPO) Konstantin Kulyk detailed the evidence of bribery and corruption against Joe Biden and his son, Hunter, his proxy. They discovered bribes from Burisma amounting to $3.4 million in the Morgan Stanley account of Rosemon Seneca Bohai LLC, a company controlled by Hunter. This was only part of the payments made to Hunter, who acted as a front for his father.

Ukrainian investigators caught representatives of the Burisma Oil Company paying a $6 million bribe to the Ukrainian Anti-Corruption Bureau (NABU) in order to obtain… the closure of the investigation into previous bribes and government corruption for the benefit of Burisma. This payment to NABU was only part of the $50 million total diverted.

Suffice to say that corruption still has good years ahead of it in Ukraine, having such institutions. The anti-corruption office, even more ruthless than what they are fighting against, is hardly believable. When we think that the Maïdan pretext was the fight against corruption, there is really something to smile about. We now understand that, on the contrary, it was a way for oligarchs, having lost their previous power, to return to the main stage and accelerate the growth of their bank accounts' assets.

Illegal fund flows (General Prosecutor's Office of Ukraine)

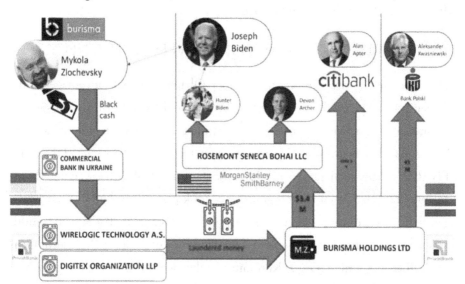

Link: https://www.bitchute.com/video/lcEw4wNEhaJ6/

Shortcut: https://tinyurl.com/HUNTERUABRIBE

Morgan Stanley
PRIVATE WEALTH MANAGEMENT

CLIENT STATEMENT | For the Period March 1-31, 2014

STATEMENT FOR:
ROSEMONT SENECA BOHAI, LLC
C/O DEVON ARCHER

TOTAL VALUE OF YOUR ACCOUNT (as of 3/31/14) $2,436,115.00
Includes Accrued Interest

Morgan Stanley Private Wealth Management, a division of Morgan Stanley Smith Barney LLC.
Member SIPC.

Your Private Wealth Advisor Team
SCHATZ/MOYE/MARKEY/FINNEG
212-296-6000

Your Branch
522 FIFTH AVENUE
NEW YORK, NY 10036
Telephone: 212-296-6000; Alt. Phone: 800-419-2861; Fax: 212-296-6320

#8WNJGWM

ROSEMONT SENECA BOHAI, LLC
C/O DEVON ARCHER
152 W 57TH ST
47TH FL
NEW YORK NY 10019

GOVERNMENT
EXHIBIT
301
16 Cr. 371 (RA)

Client Service Center (24 Hours a Day; 7 Days a Week) : 800-668-8158
+1 201-830-4796 (Int'l Collect)

Access Your Account Online: www.morganstanley.com/PWM

876 · 018483 · 380 · 1 · 0

MS-USAO-0017705

Morgan Stanley
PRIVATE WEALTH MANAGEMENT

CLIENT STATEMENT | For the Period March 1-31, 2014

Page 2 of 8

Active Assets Account   ROSEMONT SENECA BOHAI, LLC
876-018483-380   C/O DEVON ARCHER

Account Summary

CHANGE IN VALUE OF YOUR ACCOUNTS (includes accru...)

This P...
(3/1/14-3/...)

	2,446,561.00
TOTAL BEGINNING VALUE	2,44...
Credits	
Debits	
Security Transfers	
Net Credits/Debits/Transfers	$2,4...
	(10,450.00)
	—
Change in Value	
TOTAL ENDING VALUE	$2,43...
	$2,436,111.00
	4.00
	$2,436,115.00

ALLOCATION OF HOLDINGS

	Market Value	Percentage %
..., BDP, MMFs*	$2,436,115.00	100.0
TOTAL VALUE	$2,436,115.00	100.0%

Map of laboratories identified in Ukraine

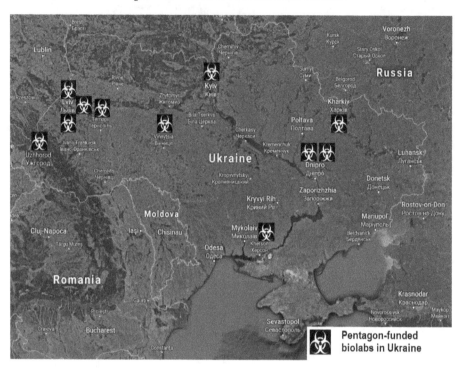

Pentagon-funded biolabs in Ukraine

Since the case was causing a lot of noise, the new Kiev prosecutor (the previous one had been thrown out of the window from his apartment for wanting to investigate the Maïdan murders) summoned Hunter Biden to be indicted. But the father, Joe, offended, went to Kiev, blackmailed Poroshenko then president, by telling him that the indictment of his son would result in a refusal of the USA to write them the next contribution check to the Kiev administration, a check which amounted to $2 Billion. Poroshenko fired the prosecutor and saved Private Hunter which cost American taxpayers dearly. As for the fight against corruption in Ukraine, that will have to wait a few more centuries...

This is how part of the embezzled funds were used directly by Hunter Biden to invest in a company called Metabiota, which uses a front company, Labyrinth Global Health (**LGH**) in order to finance the various laboratories in Ukraine. We note the cynicism of these people, calling a front company "Global Health Labyrinth" is really delicious.

The main company receiving the funds to be distributed and financed by the Pentagon is called Black & Veatch. (**B&V**). **Why adopt such a complex structure**: The Pentagon has a legal obligation for public transparency, so finding funding information by front company entry point into their vendor system is not simple. But by searching carefully from the identified recipient company, the ball of wool unravels much more easily. This is how we learned that B&V received $1.4 billion, the distribution details of which are absolutely **incredible,** as shown below.

Link: https://www.usaspending.gov/recipient/3c7ceda1-5fa1-77a3-fd7a-125db 5426436-C/all

Shortcut: https://tinyurl.com/BNVTotal

BLACK & VEATCH SPECIAL PROJECTS CORP.

Also known by 5 other names ▸

This recipient is associated with multiple parents in the dataset: ⊕
BVH, INC.
BLACK & VEATCH HOLDING COMPANY(788948115)
Hide ⌄

CHILD RECIPIENT

Total Awarded Amount	Details	
$1.4 Billion	Recipient Identifier	C8L3CMNXPAA1 (UEI) 803168931 (Legacy DUNS)
from 5,316 transactions	Address	8800 W 115TH STREET SUITE 2200 OVERLAND PARK, KS UNITED STATES 2420 CONGRESSIONAL DISTRICT: KS-03

Link: : https://www.usaspending.gov/award/CONT_AWD_0004_9700_HD TRA108D0007_9700

Shortcut: https://tinyurl.com/BVFunding

In March 2015, $4.2M were allocated for "**biological cooperation commitment**" in Ukraine. No details were described. It was by digging on the site of the US embassy that we discovered the pot aux roses (see appendix)

Modification Number	Action Date	Amount	Action Type	Transaction Description
5	04/01/2015	$0	M: OTHER ADMINISTRATIVE ACTION	IGF::OT::IGF ADMIN MOD TO ADD COUNTERINTELLIGENCE AWARENESS AND REPORTI
8	03/09/2015	$4,246,919	C: FUNDING ONLY ACTION	IGF::OT::IGF COOPERATIVE BIOLOGICAL ENGAGEMENT PROGRAM IN UKRAINE
7	09/08/2014	-$13,308,000	C: FUNDING ONLY ACTION	PHD (LEVEL OF EFFORT:
6	08/27/2014	$0	C: FUNDING ONLY ACTION	ADMIN ACTION TO REALIGN FUNDS:

However, on November 12, 2019, a fund of $420k was allocated to the LGH Company to study COVID-19 in UKRAINE and this, well BEFORE the pandemic was declared or this virus was revealed to the public (End of December 2019). LGH operates in Kiev and Odessa (Mechnikov Institute). More than $107M is committed to research into biological weapons of all kinds in this country by the Pentagon. On the link provided above, go down to the bottom of the page, select the tab "Sub-Awards" and identify the record #19-6192. This document was given to an attorney general in Dallas, Texas.

Number of Sub-Award Transactions	Sub-Award Obligations	Percent of Prime Award Obligations
115	$107.15 Million	137.8%

Sub-Award ID	Recipient Name	Action Date	Amount	Sub-Award Description
19-6205	CAMFIL USA, INC.	12/11/2019	$63,251	HEPA FILTERS
19-6200	BIOSAFE ENGINEERING LLC	11/26/2019	$735,995	TISSUE DIGESTERS FOR KYIV AND ODESSA ILD
19-6198	CAMFIL USA, INC.	12/11/2019	$63,549	HEPA FILTERS
19-6194	ARKHITEKTURNO-BUDIVELNA GRUPA PALATIUM, TOV	10/22/2019	$75,235	OFFICE FURNITURE FOR KYIV AND ODESA ILDS
19-6192	LABYRINTH GLOBAL HEALTH INC	11/12/2019	$369,511	SME MANUSCRIPT DOCUMENTATION AND COVID 19 RESEARCH
19-6192	LABYRINTH GLOBAL HEALTH INC	11/12/2019	$50,000	TASK ORDER 1
19-6191	GLOBAL SCIENTIFIC SOLUTIONS FOR HEALTH LLC	11/05/2019	$100,000	TRAINING
19-6187	RIVA-STAL, TOV	10/21/2019	$248,953	LABORATORY FURNITURE FOR KYIV AND ODESA ILDS

At the beginning of November 2019, who knew what Covid-19 was? Nobody. If the Pentagon allocated this amount of money to Ukraine to study a virus that was not supposed to exist, who provided it to them and where did it come from? Study what, with whom, and for what? So many questions the D.O.D. will have to answer, preferably before an international court of justice. But above all it means that upstream, **the virus was known well before this date**, authorizations had been put in place, the virus had been collected or its production had been controlled. How its transport was carried out, by whom, who decided, why, etc.

Company Labyrinth Global Health (LGH)

546, 15TH Avenue North East, Saint-Petersburg, FL 33704, it should be noted that after several visits to their website, the address was removed from the site…

Social reason: a small so-called international company founded by Karen Saylors (considered a minority) for biological research around the world, claiming to have operations in six countries (Eastern Europe including Ukraine, Africa, USA), signing millions of dollars contracts with the D.O.D. (US Department of Defense), whose headquarters is a wooden shack in a residential area in a small town of Florida - this is surrealist. Can we imagine the D.O.D allocating such budgets to a registered company (January 2019) just nine months in advance without a trackrecord? This is not a biological weapons laboratory, so it is a mailbox for a shell company. It is impossible to find the registered EIN, but this company is certified by the **GSA** (United States General Services Administration) to be able to apply for the D.O.D RFQ, incredible!

Link: https://opengovus.com/sam-entity/LTG3S98L7A19

Shortcut: https://tinyurl.com/GovLGH

LABYRINTH GLOBAL HEALTH INC is an entity registered with the U.S. General Services Administration (GSA), System for Award Management (SAM). The corporation number is #LTG3S98L7A19. The business address is 546 15th Ave Ne, Saint Petersburg. FL 33704-4707, USA. The point of contact name is *Murat Tartan*.

Entity Information

SAM ID	LTG3S98L7A19
	Unique Entity ID by SAM
CAGE Code	88TL7
	Commercial and Government Entity (CAGE) Code by NATO Codification System
Legal Name	LABYRINTH GLOBAL HEALTH INC
DBA Name	LABYRINTH
Physical Address	546 15th Ave Ne
	Saint Petersburg
	FL 33704-4707
	USA
Mailing Address	546 15th Ave Ne
	Saint Petersburg
	FL 33704-4707
	USA
Congressional District	13
Entity Structure	2L - Corporate Entity (Not Tax Exempt)
Incorporation State	DE
Business Type	2X - For Profit Organization
	8W - Woman Owned Small Business
	A2 - Woman Owned Business
Primary NAICS	541990 - All Other Professional, Scientific, and Technical Services
NAICS Code	541714 - Research and Development in Biotechnology (except Nanobiotechnology)
	541715 - Research and Development in the Physical, Engineering, and Life Sciences (except Nanotechnology and Biotechnology)
	541990 - All Other Professional, Scientific, and Technical Services
	North American Industry Classification System (NAICS)
NAICS Exception	541715 - Research and Development in the Physical, Engineering, and Life Sciences (except Nanotechnology and Biotechnology)
	North American Industry Classification System (NAICS)

The company **LGH** declares Murat Taran to be the resident contact point executive 458 Karra CT, Chula Vista, CA 91910, while his LinkedIn profile indicates that he lives in Washington State, while working in Florida. A company declared as a "Woman-Owned Small Business" whose declared representative is a man (transgender?) ... An activation date **SGA** in November 2021 having the capacity to receive government funds in November 2019, an SME operating in six different countries... We still sense an air of fraud...

None of the **LGH** board members live in Florida (LinkedIn source) and a single employee registered in the USA, a certain Joe Sharp, chief scientist, who previously specialized in the study of video systems, is the founder of the company Prism Video Technology, 2015. What relationship does he have with biology? A mystery! What is the link? **One thing employees have in common: almost all of them have worked for Metabiota.**

Leadership Team

KAREN SAYLORS, PHD
CHIEF EXECUTIVE OFFICER

MARY GUTTIERI, PHD
CHIEF SCIENCE OFFICER

MURAT TARTAN
CHIEF FINANCIAL OFFICER

Karen Saylors · 3rd
CEO at Labyrinth Global Health
San Francisco, California, United States · Contact info
500+ connections
🔒 Message   More

Mary Guttieri · 3rd
Chief Science Officer at Labyrinth Global Health, Inc.
Frederick, Maryland, United States · Contact info
500+ connections

Murat Tartan · 3rd
Chief Financial Officer
Washington, District of Columbia, United States
1,754 followers · 500+ connections

Team Management	LGH	Meta biota	previously
Karen Saylors (USA) https://tinyurl.com/KTLnkin	x	x	Johns Hopkins, Doctors Without Borders
Murat Taran (USA) https://tinyurl.com/TMLnkin	x	x	Prism, BoA, Harris, St James
Mary Guttieri (USA), https://tinyurl.com/GMLnkin	x	x	D.O.D Bio defense
Inna Yevsieienko (Ukr) https://tinyurl.com/InnYLnkin	x	x	Black & Veatch

Kateryna Palyshniu (Ukr) https://tinyurl.com/KPLnkin	x	x	Fellow researcher veterinary medicine
Bethany Edison (Canada) https://tinyurl.com/BELnkin	x	x	Government
Serah Sidique (Sierra Leone) https://tinyurl.com/SSLnkin	x		ICAP at Columbia University

The PDG (CEO) of LGH, Karen Saylors, Ph.D has worked in international public health for over a decade and spent many years living in Africa establishing global surveillance networks, "working with partners to improve global health policy on detection, response, and control of infectious diseases."

At the house of **LGH**, Dr. Saylors specializes in studies that aim to understand and mitigate the biological and behavioral risk of disease transmission. Dr. Saylors has worked with the University of Oxford Vietnam Clinical Trials Network on zoonotic disease surveillance research and continues to coordinate with regional partners on emerging outbreaks in animal and human populations. But with whom did Dr. Saylors and **LGH** choose to work? None other than **Ecohealth Alliance,**[*] and **Metabiota** (a company linked to the financing of Hunter Biden).

Dr. Saylors, Ecohealth Alliance and Metabiota worked together on the **PREDICT** program from the United States Agency for International Development (**USAID**) from 2009, while **Labyrinth Global Health** worked alongside **EHA** and **Metabiota** on the program **PREDICT** from 2020.

(https://tinyurl.com/PredictProject).

---

[*] Controlled by Doctor Fauci having granted access to viral gain-of-function technologies to a Chinese researcher from the P4 laboratory in Wuhan, contrary to US security policy. This famous laboratory built and financed under the supervision of Minister Buzin's husband gave rise to a challenge from a French scientist regarding the true level of security and the activities carried out there.

Launched in 2009 and partially funded by USAID, **PREDICT** was an early warning system for new and emerging diseases in 21 countries. It was led by the University of California (UC) Davis One Health Institute, and key partners which included **EcoHealth Alliance** (FOUR), **Metabiota**, Wildlife Conservation Society, and the Smithsonian Institute, and as we have just revealed, **LGH**. PREDICT was a precursor to the more ambitious Global Virome project.

USAID describes **PREDICT** as having made "significant contributions to strengthening global laboratory surveillance and diagnostic capabilities for known and newly discovered viruses within several important virus groups, such as filoviruses (including Ebola viruses), influenza, paramyxoviruses and **coronavirus**." This is one of the many studies published by **Ecohealth Alliance, Metabiota and LGH** proved by the link. https://tinyurl.com/SRSC19

Example of a funded project: "Predicting zoonotic transmission potential and host associations for novel viruses." The grant **NIAID** is defined by the code: U01-AI151814/AI/NIAID-NIH-HHS/United States

https://pubmed.ncbi.nlm.nih.gov/35986178/

Here is the team that participated, we found the three companies.

Juliana Triastuti, Indonesia

Ehab Abu-Basha, Jordan

Kwallah Allan, Kenya

Kamau Joseph, Kenya

Mutura Samson, Kenya

Bouaphanh Khamphaphonphane, Lao PDR

Watthana Theppanga, Lao PDR

Jim Desmond, Liberia

Sandra Samules, Liberia

Mei Ho Lee, Malaysia

Jimmy Lee, Malaysia

Batchuluun Damdinjav, Mongolia

Enkhtuvshin Shiilegdamba, Mongolia

Ohnmar Aung, Myanmar

Manisha Bista, Nepal

Dibesh Karmacharya, Nepal

Rima Shrestha, Nepal

Julius Nziza, Rwanda

Jean-Claude Tumushime, Rwanda

Subash Morzaria, external advisor

Wantanee Kalpravidh, FAO

Yilma Makonnen, FAO

Sophie Von Dubscheutz, FAO

Filip Claes, FAO/Bangkok

Katie Pelican, OHW-Minnesota

Casie Barton Behravesh, U.S. CDC

Elizabeth Mumford, WHO

John Pauli Clark, World Bank

Trong Duoc Vu, NIHE/Ministry of Health

Karen Saylors, Labyrinth Global Health

Bethany Edison, Metabiota

Jason Euren, Metabiota

Amethyst Gillis, Metabiota

Christian Lange, Metabiota

Mat LeBreton, Metabiota

David McIver, Metabiota

Chris Walzer, WCS

Amanda Fine, WCS

USAID

Cara Chrisman

Andrew Clements

Ricardo Ecalar

Lisa Kramer

Timothy Meinke

Amalhin Shek

IN-COUNTRY

Arif Islam, Bangladesh
Shainful Islam, Bangladesh
Zia Raman, Bangladesh
Vibol Hul, Cambodia
Veasna Duong, Cambodia
Moctar Mouiche, Cameroon
Julius Nwobegahay, Cameroon
Kalpy Coulibaly, Côte d'Ivoire
Charles Kumakamba, DRC
Eddy Kambale Syaluha, eDRC
Jean-Paul Lukusa, eDRC
Desalegn Belay, Ethiopia
Negatu Kebede, Ethiopia
William Ampofo, Ghana
Sammuel Bel-Nono, Ghana
Richard Suu-Ire, Ghana
Kalivogui Douokoro, Guinea
Huda Dursman, Indonesia
Imung Pamungkas, Indonesia
Novie Rachmitasari, Indonesia
Suryo Saputro, Indonesia
Wirda Damanik, Indonesia
Tina Kusumaningrum, Indonesia
Maya Rambitan, Indonesia
Beounly Rey, Indonesia
Dodi Safari, Indonesia
Amin Soebandrio, Indonesia

Modou Moustapha Lo, Senegal
Amadou Ndiaye, Senegal
Mame Cheikh Seck, Senegal
James Bangura, Sierra Leone
Edwin Lavalie, Sierra Leone
Grace Mwangoka, Tanzania
Zikankuba Sijali, Tanzania
Ricky Okwir Okello, Uganda
Benard Ssebide, Uganda
Supaporn Wacharpluesadee, Thailand
Nga Nguyen, Viet Nam

GLOBAL

Simon Anthony, EcoHealth Alliance
Jon Epstein, EcoHealth Alliance
Emily Hagan, EcoHealth Alliance
William Karesh, EcoHealth Alliance
Alice Latinne, EcoHealth Alliance
Anne Laudisoit, EcoHealth Alliance
Hongying Li, EcoHealth Alliance
Catherine Machalaba, EcoHealth Alliance
Stephanie Martinez, EcoHealth Alliance
Kevin Olival, EcoHealth Alliance
Noam Ross, EcoHealth Alliance
Ava Sullivan, EcoHealth Alliance
Carlos Zambrana Torrelio, EcoHealth Alliance
Peter Daszak, EcoHealth Alliance
John Mackenzie, external advisor

Daniel O'Rourke, Metabiota
Tammie O'Rourke, Metabiota
Suzan Murray, Smithsonian Institution
Marc Valitutto, Smithsonian Institution
Dawn Zimmerman, Smithsonian Institution
Jaber Belkhiria, UC Davis OHI
Brian Bird, UC Davis OHI
Hannah Chale, UC Davis OHI
Eunah Preston, UC Davis OHI
Nicole Gardner, UC Davis OHI
Brooke Genovese, UC Davis OHI
Tracey Goldstein, UC Davis OHI
Kevin Gonzalez, UC Davis OHI
Zoe Grange, UC Davis OHI
Christine Kreuder Johnson, UC Davis OHI
Lucy Keatts, UC Davis OHI
Terra Kelly, UC Davis OHI
Elizabeth Leasure, UC Davis OHI
Jonna Mazet, UC Davis OHI
Corina Monagin, UC Davis OHI
Pranav Pandit, UC Davis OHI
Nistara Randhawa, UC Davis OHI
Brett Smith, UC Davis OHI
Woutrina Smith, UC Davis OHI
Eri Togami, UC Davis OHI
Alex Tremeau-Bravard, UC Davis OHI
David Wolking, UC Davis OHI
Carolina Churchill, WCS

Subsequently we will discover that Karen was directly involved in the sequencing of the Covid-19 genome whereas previously she was involved in the monitoring and/or collection of viruses such as coronaviruses on bats in Asia…

https://pubmed.ncbi.nlm.nih.gov/36346652/

Targeted genomic sequencing with probe capture for discovery and surveillance of coronaviruses in bats

Kevin S Kuchinski [1] [2], Kara D Loos [3] [4], Danae M Suchan [3] [4], Jennifer N Russell [3] [4], Ashton N Sies [3] [4], Charles Kumakamba [5], Francisca Muyembe [5], Placide Mbala Kingebeni [5] [6], Ipos Ngay Lukusa [5], Frida N'Kawa [5], Joseph Atibu Losoma [5], Maria Makuwa [5] [7], Amethyst Gillis [8] [9], Matthew LeBreton [10], James A Ayukekbong [11] [12], Nicole A Lerminiaux [3] [4], Corina Monagin [8] [13], Damien O Joly [11] [14] Karen Saylors [7] [8], Nathan D Wolfe [8], Edward M Rubin [8], Jean J Muyembe Tamfum [6], Natalie A Prystajecky [1] [2], David J McIver [11] [15], Christian E Lange [7] [11], Andrew D S Cameron [3] [4]

Affiliations

[1] Department of Pathology and Laboratory Medicine, University of British Columbia, Vancouver, Canada.

[2] Public Health Laboratory, British Columbia Centre for Disease Control, Vancouver, Canada.

[3] Department of Biology, Faculty of Science, University of Regina, Regina, Canada.

[4] Institute for Microbial Systems and Society, Faculty of Science, University of Regina, Regina, Canada.

[5] Metabiota Inc, Kinshasa, Democratic Republic of the Congo.

[6] Institut National de Recherche Biomédicale, Kinshasa, Democratic Republic of the Congo.

[7] Labyrinth Global Health Inc, St. Petersburg, United States.

[8] Metabiota Inc, San Francisco, United States.

[9] Development Alternatives, Washington, United States.

Despite the disappearance of the **LGH** address on their website, a large number of publications attest to their location in Florida.

Abstract

Public health emergencies like SARS, MERS, and COVID-19 have prioritized surveillance of zoonotic coronaviruses, resulting in extensive genomic characterization of coronavirus diversity in bats. Sequencing viral genomes directly from animal specimens remains a laboratory challenge, however, and most bat coronaviruses have been characterized solely by PCR amplification of small regions from the best-conserved gene. This has resulted in limited phylogenetic resolution and left viral genetic factors relevant to threat assessment undescribed. In this study, we evaluated whether a technique called hybridization probe capture can achieve more extensive genome recovery from surveillance specimens. Using a custom panel of 20,000 probes, we captured and sequenced coronavirus genomic material in 21 swab specimens collected from bats in the Democratic Republic of the Congo. For 15 of these specimens, probe capture recovered more genome sequence than had been previously generated with standard amplicon sequencing protocols, providing a median 6.1-fold improvement (ranging up to 69.1-fold). Probe capture data also identified five novel *alpha*- and *betacoronaviruses* in these specimens, and their full genomes were recovered with additional deep sequencing. Based on these experiences, we discuss how probe capture could be effectively operationalized alongside other sequencing technologies for high-throughput, genomics-based discovery and surveillance of bat coronaviruses.

Keywords: DNA sequencing; bat; coronavirus; genome; infectious disease; microbiology; probe capture; viruses.

Conflict of interest statement

KK, KL, DS, JR, AS, ML, NL, JM, NP, AC No competing interests declared, CK, FM, PM, IN, FN, JA, JA, CM, ER, DM were employed by Metabiota Inc, MM, KS, CL are employees of Labyrinth Global Health Inc and were employed by Metabiota Inc AG is an employee of Development Alternatives Inc and was employed by Metabiota Inc, DJ is an employee of Nyati Health Consulting and was employed by Metabiota Inc, NW is an employee of Metabiota Inc

This is how part of the Covid-19 octopus is defined

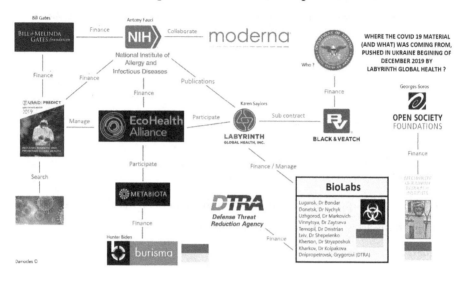

What were the goals of the laboratories in Ukraine?

The few official documents that we were able to recover tell us that they transformed the Ukrainian population into laboratory rats. The Defense Threat Reduction Agency (**DTRA**) financed a project, codenamed UP8, similar to those developed in Georgia (which caused 320 deaths in two years while testing vaccines coming from the Gilead laboratory) using soldiers in Ukraine, to supposedly control a possible spread of the virus. **Crimean-Congo hemorrhagic fever virus** (CNRS Classification, Category 4) and hantaviruses in Ukraine, and the potential need for differential diagnosis in patients suspected of leptospirosis.

The project began In 2017 and was extended several times until 2020, according to internal documents. Blood samples were taken from 4,400 healthy soldiers in Lviv, Kharkov, Odessa, and Kiev. 4,000 of these samples were tested for antibodies against hantaviruses, and 400 of them for the presence of antibodies against the Crimean-Congo hemorrhagic fever (CCHF) virus.

Blood test results were not provided to study participants. There is no information on what other procedures were put in place, except that "serious incidents, including deaths, were reported within 24 hours." **All deaths of study subjects suspected or known to be related to research procedures were required to be** brought to the attention of bioethics committees in the United States and Ukraine.

In Donbass, Lisichansk Cemetery is 15 km from the FarmBioTest laboratory installed in Rybezhnoye. A large number of graves of very young people as well as blood samples were found as well as documents linking the US Food & Drug administration (FDA), USAID, the Gilead, Beger, Pfizer laboratories... by the Russian army, put in place evidence by Colonel Konachenkov and Colonel Vasili Prozorov former SBU...

DTRA activities in Georgia and Ukraine fall under the protection of special bilateral agreements. Pursuant to these agreements, Georgia and Ukraine would absolve themselves of any liability, take no legal action, and indemnify the United States (and engaged personnel), subcontractors (and subcontractors' personnel), for property damage, death or injury to any person resulting from activities under this Agreement. **If DTRA-sponsored scientists cause death or injury to local people, they cannot be held responsible.**

All the details are listed on the website of the US Embassy in Kiev, they don't even have the decency to delete the information that follows. This is behavior of unspeakable criminal arrogance. Ukraine rejected the proposal for public control over Pentagon-funded laboratories while Pentagon contractors were given full access. Independent experts were refused access under the pretext that they harbored particularly dangerous pathogens... Were category P2 laboratories not authorized for this? According to a letter from Ukrainian Deputy Minister for European Integration Oksana Sivak, dated **October 21, 2016,** disclosed the Ministry of Health of Ukraine refused access to experts of the scientific journal *Problems of Innovation and Investment Development.* The Ministry of Health of Ukraine considered it inappropriate to create a working group for public control and it was not possible to allow members of the group to enter the premises of infection laboratories under pretext of security.

In the program **DTRA**, according to a letter dated **July 2, 2019** by Ukrainian Health Minister Ylana Suprun, full access was given to **Black & Veatch Special Projects Corp** (already mentioned) to all Ukrainian laboratories involved in the US military biological research program. Ylana Suprun is an American citizen who received Ukrainian citizenship from former President Petro Poroshenko in 2015.

Thus the USA transformed Ukraine into a veritable opaque biological weapons factory without real security, control, or safeguards, opening the door to bioterrorism.

The European Union has also benefited from Ukrainian corruption in this area. German and Ukrainian scientists conducted biological research on particularly dangerous pathogens in birds (2019-2020). The project was implemented by the Institute of Experimental and Clinical Veterinary Medicine (Kharkov) and the Friedrich Loeffler Institute (Greifswald, Germany). According to the project description, the main objective was to carry out the sequencing of the genomes of orthomyxoviruses (agents responsible for avian influenza), as well as to discover new viruses in birds (See appendix).

A NEW TURN OF EVENTS APRIL 2022

A member of our team, who was an instructor on weapons of mass destruction for the American army, was able to obtain an internal Moderna document that was disturbing to say the least. If the US government was funding research into Covid-19 before its existence was publicly known, that suggests at a minimum that they either knew Covid-19 existed naturally, and perhaps they were involved in the development of this virus in a laboratory.

But if the formal evidence isn't enough for you to reach that conclusion, then perhaps pair it with the evidence linking the US National Institute of Allergy and Infectious Diseases (**NIAID**) and **Moderna** as indicated in all documents below. Subsequently in April 2023, Stéphane Bancel, in a senatorial hearing before Senator Rand Paul, will admit what we discovered: **NIAID** was responsible for the development of vaccines and Moderna for their industrial implementation and marketing under their brand.

If you still doubt the findings associated with the documents below then the testimony of Dr David Martin to the European Parliament at the end of May 2023 will dispel your doubts definitively. You will hear him say explicitly that COVID-19 was indeed a subject of bioengineering and patented by **NIAID**/Chapel Hill in 2002; and **PFIZER** knew since 1990 that **any mRNA vaccine did not work** on a coronavirus, whose mutation cycle is very short. In 2005, this virus was described as a biological weapon designed to eliminate humanity. Who was at the head of **NIAID**? Anthony Fauci, White House health advisor.

Conclusion: "Vaccination cannot be imposed, it is a crime," says Dr. Martin, a crime which was the subject of a colossal financial operation, during which Gates and Soros became rich. You were the turkeys of a horrible and cynical farce masterfully orchestrated.

Link: https://odysee.com/@ExcaliburTraduction:4/International-Covid-Summit-Iii-Dr-Martin-Wlt--1:3

Shortcut: https://tinyurl.com/EUDRMARTIN

Confidential Disclosure Agreement

In order to protect confidential information relating to research, development, business plans, and other technology, which may be disclosed between them, the Vaccine Research Center, National Institute of Allergy and Infectious Diseases, National Institutes of Health ("NIAID"), and the "Collaborator" identified below (individually, a "Party"; collectively the "Parties"), intending to be legally bound as of the date of the last signature hereto ("Effective Date"), agree that:

1. A Party ("Disclosing Party") may disclose information to the other ("Receiving Party") for the purpose of assessing their interest in research collaboration (the "Purpose"). The Disclosing Parties are: **NIAID; Moderna Therapeutics, Inc. and its affiliates,** Proprietary Info   (the "Collaborator").

2. The Parties' representatives for disclosing or receiving information (if known):

For NIAID: Barney Graham and other employees and contractors of NIAID as needed to fulfill the Purpose.

For Collaborator: Giuseppe Ciaramella,
                       Stephane Bancel,
                       Lee Cooper, and other employees of the Collaborator as needed to fulfill the Purpose

3. The information disclosed under this Agreement ("Confidential Information") includes any and all technical, business and financial information, including third party information, relating to the Disclosing Party, including but not limited to: (a) non-public patent applications; Proprietary Info   and (c) other proprietary information, ideas, gene sequences, samples, chemical compounds, biological materials, techniques, works of authorship, non-public inventions, know-how and processes related to the current, future, and proposed products and/or services of the Disclosing Party or its partners, and including without limitation, information concerning research, experimental work, development, design details and specifications, engineering, financial information, procurement requirements, purchasing, manufacturing, customer lists, investors, employees, business and contractual relationships, business forecasts, analyst reports, marketing plans and any additional non-public information that the Disclosing Party provides.

The Confidential Information disclosed under this Agreement is described as:

> For NIAID: NIAID's proprietary information and data relating to the development of vaccines for HIV, influenza, Ebola and MERS and development of broadly neutralizing monoclonal antibodies for preventative and therapeutic use.
>
> For Collaborator: Moderna's proprietary and confidential information related to design and manufacture of a messenger RNA platform and messenger RNA constructs for treatment and prevention of disease.

4. The Receiving Party will not disclose the Confidential Information of the Disclosing Party to any person except its employees, consultants, contractors, directors, or professional advisors or authorized representatives to whom it is necessary to disclose the Confidential Information for the Purpose described above, and any such disclosures shall be under terms at least as restrictive as those specified herein. Any of the persons mentioned above who are given access to the Confidential Information shall be informed of this Agreement. The Receiving Party shall protect the Confidential Information by using the same degree

Moderna Therapeutics, Inc.
320 Bent Street
Cambridge, MA 02141

Vaccine Research Center, NIAID, NIH
c/o Technology Transfer & Intellectual Property Office
Suite 6D, MSC 9804
5601 Fishers Lane
Rockville, MD 20852

Authorized Signature:

Authorized Signature:

Carol A. Salata -S

Name: ____Benjamin Enerson____
              Corporate Counsel

Carol Salata, Ph.D.
Senior Technology Transfer Advisor
Technology Transfer & Intellectual Property Office, NIAID

Title: _____

Date: ____11/6/2015____

Date: _____
Acknowledged by VRC Representative(s)
Disclosing/Receiving Confidential Information:

Date: 9 Nov 2015

Barney Graham, M.D., Ph.D.

Enerson did work for Moderna in 2015/16, when the document below was signed.

https://www.linkedin.com/in/ben-enerson-47580a7/

Ben Enerson
VP, Legal Affairs

Corporate Counsel
Moderna Therapeutics
2015 - Mar 2017 · 2 yrs 3 mos
Cambridge, Massachusetts

Drafted and negotiated a wide range of agreements, including patent license, supply, sponsored research, clinical trial, consulting and services agreements.

So this is the **NIAID** who develops vaccines and **Moderna** which is implementing them using an mRNA platform, starting in 2015. Considering the collaboration established over so many years, there is no doubt that they must have operated on the same principle with COVID-19.

To put an end to these dark vaccine stories, a research hospital was in partnership to test the effectiveness of the result on human guinea pigs: The University of Chapel Hill in North Carolina. The agreement was also signed by two representatives of **NIAID**, including Amy F. Petrik PhD, technology transfer specialist who signed the agreement on December 12, 2019 at 8:05 a.m. The other signatory was Barney Graham MD PhD, researcher for the **NIAID**, but this signature was not dated.

MATERIAL TRANSFER AGREEMENT
SIGNATURE PAGE

FOR RECIPIENT:

Recipient's Investigator

Ralph Baric, PhD
Professor

Date: 12/12/2019

Mailing Address for Materials:

Attention: Dr. Rachel Graham, Department of
Epidemiology, University of North Carolina at
Chapel Hill, 135 Dauer Drive, 2101 McGavran-
Greenberg Hall, CB #7435, Chapel Hill, NC 27599-
7435

Duly Authorized

Jacqueline Quay
Director, Licensing & Innovation Support, OTC

Date: 12\16\11

Mailing Address for Notices:

The University of North Carolina at Chapel Hill
Office of Technology Commercialization
109 Church Street, Chapel Hill, NC 27516

Tel: 919-966-3929 Fax: 919-962-0646

Recipient signatories found on page 107

Tel:919-966-3895_____Fax: _____

FOR PROVIDERS:
NIAID's Investigator

Barney Graham, MD, PhD

Date: _____

Duly Authorized

Amy F.   Digitally signed by Amy
              F. Petrik -S
Petrik-S   Date: 2019.12.12
              08:05:23 -05'00'
Amy Petrik, PhD
Technology Transfer Specialist, TTIPO, NIAID

Date: _____

Mailing Address for Notices:

Technology Transfer and Intellectual Property Office
National Institute of Allergy and Infectious Diseases
Department of Health and Human Services
Suite 6D, MSC 9804
5601 Fishers Lane
Rockville, MD 20852
Tel: 301/496-2644   Fax: 240-627-3117

NIAID signatories found on page 107

A confidentiality agreement which can be viewed below, stipulates that suppliers **Moderna** alongside the **NIAID** have agreed to transfer the MERS-CoV mRNA coronavirus vaccine candidates jointly developed and owned by the **NIAID** and **Moderna** to the University of North Carolina at Chapel Hill on December 12, 2019.

It should be noted that MERS-CoV was discovered in 2012 and this vaccine would be released just when SAR-CoV2 appeared and when **LGH** received SAR-CoV2 (COVID-19) material. The coincidence is really disturbing knowing that MERS-CoV is extremely rare, why spend so much energy on something that we haven't heard about for seven years? Wouldn't this be a smokescreen for the SAR-CoV2 vaccine?

Attached is the document signed by the different parties:

https://tinyurl.com/C19-Moderna

Chronology of events

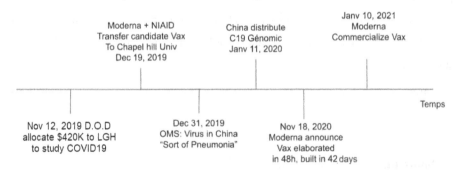

My research and distribution work within the influential group of senior US officers led to my introduction to a number of US Army doctors during private online conferences, for example Lt Colonels Theresa M. Long and Lawrence Sellin.

Remember that it takes between 17 and 23 years for the Food & Drugs Administration (FDA) to grant marketing authorization for a vaccine. **This pseudo-experimental vaccine was authorized for mass use in a few months on a lie.**

In May 2020, during a private conversation I told General P. Vallely: "I think that Covid is a military psy-ops type which was prepared for a long time and piloted for several reasons, the first being that since Trump destroyed the globalists' plan, they want to eject him. What could be simpler than to be blamed for hundreds of thousands of deaths, the second being the destruction of the European economy to restore the dollar as a single currency reserve and the destruction of the Belt & Road Initiative." He asked me to write a letter to the president to my surprise, which he would hand-deliver to him in Washington. I was far from suspecting that I could be approached in this way.

Later on, I received an invitation to attend the September 17, 2021 FDA online conference from Lt. Colonel Lawrence Sellin through General P. Vallely. It was a public conference due to legal obligations. It concerned the use of the booster (3rd dose). It lasted eight hours, and I got help from a doctor to understand what was a bit technical but overall the speakers spoke very well and it was easily understandable.

Link: https://www.fda.gov/advisory-committees/advisory-committee-calendar/vaccines-and-related-biological-products-advisory-committee-september-17-2021-meeting-announcement

Shortcut: https://tinyurl.com/FC19V3D

We heard several professors begging to stop the Pfizer carnage, due to a number of out-of-control side effects leading to death and hospitalization from cardiac arrest and stroke (as well as many other serious symptoms such as paralysis, blindness…). We also heard certain Israeli doctors underline the explosion in the appearance of extremely virulent cancers unknown until then which they will subsequently name "Turbo Cancer," or many others saying that at this stage of propagation (250 Million officially infected), it is not with a QR code or a pseudo vaccine which is at best useless (*) and at worst even dangerous for the populations that this scourge will be contained, but rather with treatments (prophylactic or in the 1st phase infection). In short, let the doctors do their job, which was deliberately hindered. Besides, any serious doctor would tell you that we NEVER vaccinate during an epidemic, because if a patient is injected while he is incubating the disease, you can aggravate infectious shock and kill him (4th year medical course). All the rules have been broken during the pandemic.

Shortcut: https://tinyurl.com/FDAVOTEC19

Conclusion of the conference WITHOUT CALL ; The FDA's Vaccines and Related Biological Products Advisory Committee, or VRBPAC, **voted 16 to 2** Friday afternoon to not recommend a booster dose of Pfizer-BioNTech's COVID-19 messenger RNA vaccine to Americans aged 16 and older. However, the committee voted unanimously to recommend booster doses for people aged 65 and older, as well as those at risk for severe COVID-19.

(*) Coronaviruses are known for their very short mutation cycle, it's a losing race.

The Biden/Fauci administration ignored the recommendations for the third dose from the chairman of the FDA board, and resignations are pouring in. The American military is rebelling, and this is how General Burger, in charge of the US Marine Corps, called Secretary of State for Defense Austin Lloyd, threatening to march on Washington in arms, if unfortunately they made vaccination compulsory after noting a worrying number of deaths among young recruits in great shape. (Testimony of Lt. Colonel Theresa M. Long, MD at the Dallas Capitol).

During my correspondence with senators, journalists and other politicians regarding the Ukraine/Biological weapons/Covid-19 chapter, **NONE** of my interlocutors wanted to raise the enormous problem. Although I called Senator P. Bas's attaché, Jérémi de Maisonville, copied the journalists from CNEWS, and many other political leaders including Gérard Larcher, they didn't care. "How? Being bothered by a simple person coming off the street, how dare he?" Isn't that right Mr Bock-Côté? Would the French be much more interested in LGBTQXYZ-Wokist analytical sociology than in their health and safety?

The only ones who listened and integrated what I told them are the two MEPs, Juvin and Mariani. And I once again see the label "Facho-Komploto-Putinist" stuck to my forehead. I am proud of it in advance, we kill the messenger when the message is disturbing and cannot be attacked for its own sake, a very well-known process. No matter how much we cite the facts, there is nothing to be done, no one is banging their fist on the table...

Bill Gates controls the W.H.O

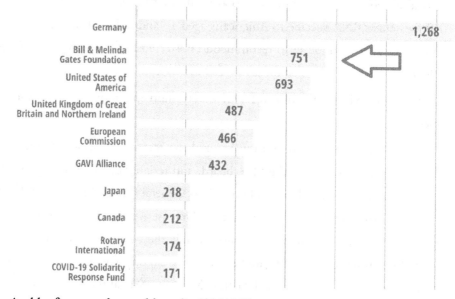

And he finances the world media ($319M between 2020 and 2021):

https://tinyurl.com/BGFMedia (Alan McLeod· Nov 21, 2021)

The Gates Foundation has also contributed heavily to academic sources, with at least $13.6 million going toward content creation for the prestigious medical journal *The Lancet*. And more broadly, even money paid to universities for pure research projects ends up in academic journals and, ultimately, in the mass media. Neither these grants nor grants funding the printing of books, or the creation of websites count toward the total, although they are also forms of media. He announced the financing of vaccine factories in February 2020 with his great friend

George Soros. The world press is quick to say that we cannot treat covid with AZT + HCQ to be able to justify the use of a vaccine because if a treatment works, the law says that it is out of the question to inoculate someone. This is how the machine ran wild with passive and active corruption.

Who talked about a COVID pandemic preparedness at a meeting in New York in October 2019? Philippe de Villiers. This one is being shot at with red bullets all over the media, notably in the newspaper *Le Monde*, which is very virulent…**This same newspaper receives more than $4M from the Bill & Melinda Gates foundation.** Sacred Bill Gates, deeply altruistic, whose wife is divorcing him for his involvement in the Epstein affair (more than thirty visits to rape island), a dark story of sex scandal and prostitution of minors.

During an interview to exonerate him, when the journalist asked him the question about these visits to the famous Epstein Island, it was obvious that Bill was not really convinced of his own answer. We can clearly see the contraction of his face expressing unease.

Thus, Bill was cleared by "the decoders" transforming the "real news" into fake which will be denounced later by Idriss Aberkane on Sud Radio: the main newspapers and media paid these crook-checkers, to deny the real news and torpedo their authors in Wikipedia.

Le Monde

ACTUALITÉS ⌄   ÉCONOMIE ⌄   VIDÉOS ⌄   DÉBATS ⌄   CULTURE ⌄   LE GOÛT DU MONDE ⌄

LES DÉCODEURS · VÉRIFICATION

Philippe de Villiers recycle l'infox de la simulation de l'épidémie de Covid en 2019

L'ex-député relaie dans son livre, ainsi que dans les médias, une vieille théorie du complot qui dénonce le rôle des élites dans la survenue de la pandémie.

Par Les Décodeurs

Publié le 20 avril 2021 à 17h55, mis à jour le 20 avril 2021 à 18h09   ⏱ Lecture 2 min.

THE WORLD OF LIARS IS COLLAPSING!

There is a third reason which is today very clear, but which was difficult to predict although already perceptible. When you want to make an individual accept anything and submit, immerse him in fear long enough.

Let's take a simple example, **the Bataclan carnage**. The group of attackers is made up of three French people who no longer "like" France: Fouad Mohamed-Aggad, 23 years old, originally from Wissembourg in Bas-Rhin, Ismaël Omar Mostefaï, 29 years old, originally from Courcouronnes and living in Chartres, and Samy Amimour, 28 years old, from Drancy. The room was crowded and could hold 1700 people. 130 dead, more than 400 injured, 99 of them very serious. Three individuals were able to paralyze 600 times more people with fear. The law of numbers prevailed, if twenty strong guys had jumped on them, certainly, some would have died, but the attackers would have been smashed. This shows to what extent French society has become incredibly cowardly, preferring sheep-like slaughter to fighting for its survival (which also applies to the ban on police officers carrying their service weapons off duty, a ban which has cost lives in particular to the police officers present).

Now let's take an invisible enemy, COVID-19, with the media telling you over and over again that everyone is going to die (by the way, you note that no one wore a mask during a TV show at that time)... You paralyze the global population because it doesn't know when it can be hit and so you will make it accept all kinds of technocratic madness coming from the head of who-knows-what furious scribbler like being forced to sit down to have a coffee. And yes everyone knows that if you sit down, the virus will pass over your head... Two years kept in fear of dying from pseudo-vaccines that don't work (Many of my relatives have been vaccinated and have caught covid between three and four times. A real success!) and you create a population of sheep who will swallow anything like, let's quote at random (drum roll):

THE WAR IN UKRAINE

The Azov group, neo-Nazi paramilitary militiahaving guaranteed the success of Maïdan,adopts the butcher's hook, symbol of **division SS Das Reich** and also, to remove any chance of doubt,the black sun so dear to **Heinrich Himmler**.

VII. Was the Conflict Inevitable?

During the presidency of Donald J. Trump (**DJT**), the Ukrainian conflict was frozen, and **DJT** had several reasons not to not talk to Poroshenko.

The first is the involvement of Hunter Biden in some very repugnant corruption rings in Ukraine, and the desire of DJT to use these abuses to rightly neutralize the Democrats.

But the main one comes from the transfer of ICBM technology from the Izhmash and Yzhnoy companies to North Korea through the intermediary of the sulphureous Ukrainian oligarch Igor Kolomoisky who reigns supreme in the Dnepropetrovsk region where these companies are located. I did not fail to pass the information on to my general US contact, which made him angry.

How could these companies have survived after Maïdan? They worked mainly for the Russian army, which after this American-democratic masquerade could no longer trust them. They had to find markets that would allow them to survive.

North Korea, whose long-range delivery programs had stalled for years, was an easy commercial target. Eight months after the implementation of the technology transfer and its integration, Little Rocketman, the name that **DJT** gave to Kim Jong Un, is able to send a big "firecracker" into the Pacific Ocean passing over Japan to the surprise of everyone. Money definitely has neither smell nor color in Ukraine.

A little over a week before Operation Z, my US general contact asked me the following question: "Is Vladimir Putin going to attack Ukraine?" (His question referred to rumors of Russian troop movements on the Donbass/Russia border.) First of all, I was a little surprised because I knew from my various contacts on site that 100 tons of military equipment were coming from the USA every day for the last three months on the Donbass border to attack these dissident regions. Since the start of the conflict in 2015, Russian military bases in the Krasnodar region were already well stocked and had no need for equipment. Therefore, if one of the parties had war-like intentions it was the Ukrainians.

Two weeks beforehand, the Russian Communist Party and far-right had tabled a bill aimed at recognizing the republic of Donbass, the Minsk II agreements having in fact lapsed since December 2015. It was obvious that Kiev would never respect them even though that was the solution and the most elegant way to resolve this conflict. The USA and Russia are federations, why not Ukraine?

Russian legislative practice gives the president thirty days to decide on the text. From an internal political point of view, he had no choice but continue to think because he knew full well that signing them would immediately trigger a major conflict. Despite a certain degree of military preparation for two years, nothing was really planned to venture there. The economic consequences of a conflict - more sanctions - were hazardous, and he was not really motivated. In addition, four days before Operation Z, Russia had purchased several billion US bonds. If there had been an intention to attack, this transaction would never have taken place. Here is the response given to my interlocutors: "If the Ukrainians start bombing again, and they will, Vladimir Putin will sign the agreements recognizing the LNR and DNR but be careful of the consequences because these will include several areas: Economic, cultural and security (i.e. NATO style). If the Ukrainians do not want to understand its meaning, it will cost them dearly and they will be hit with a hail of shells like they have never seen. **Russia will no longer have a choice and will prevent the continuation of a genocide that has lasted too long.**"

And I add: The West has pushed the patience of the Russians to its limit, the proposal for Ukraine to join NATO is the red line of red lines. The first spark will ignite a full blow. There is a proverb in Russia which says: "We take a long time to jump on a horse, but once we do, we ride very quickly." In fact, for ten years, Vladimir Putin offered Merkel the Eurasian economic union, and it was she who refused, blocked by the USA which knew her little Stasi secret. Through frenzied obscurantism, Western elected officials did not want to see the European interest (which is to guarantee sustainable access to Russian natural resources in advantageous conditions), which brought us to an extremely dangerous clash.

In his last speeches well before February 24, Vladimir Putin's tone changed radically. I felt his exasperation toward the attitude of his opponents. The vocabulary chosen by V. Putin was hardened, his face was closed, his tone was dry. There is no longer any doubt: at the first misstep he will order strikes.

BEHIND THE SCENES OF A "MASCARONADE"

The administrator Macron, as usual, decided to perform one of his favorite media stunts to show off, he went to Moscow in order, he says, to persuade Vladimir Putin not to respond to Kiev's provocations on February 8, 2022. Did he know anything at that time? He was not greeted in a formal manner at the airport and returned to the Kremlin through a back door. Vladimir Putin made him wait, because he would have denied a PCR test (Why?), and they found themselves at the ends of a six-meter table while the week after the Israeli Prime Minister, Naftali Bennett was welcomed face to face. The attitude of the master of the Kremlin is unequivocal: "Keep talking, I have no interest in your bullshit." Trust was broken, the West should have respected its commitments, and it was too late. Long after, Merkel's declaration of January 2023 was a thunderclap in diplomatic space, which confirmed the bad faith of the Western guarantors of the Minsk agreements… Vladimir Putin was therefore right!

The Putin-Macron meeting, symbolized in 2 images

Later, during the staging of the Macron-Putin telephone exchange, we realized that Macron understood absolutely nothing about this issue, or he pretended not to understand. He dared to tell Vladimir Putin that it was out of the question to take into consideration the requests of the republics of Donetsk and Lugansk when this was the precise object of the Minsk II agreements. This was the straw that broke the camel's back, the break was complete, Vladimir Putin would no longer take him on the phone; he only speaks to serious leaders, not to diplomatic puppet showmen whom he considers unprofessional... It was not an old KGB vet that a young WEF leader would teach to make faces.

So, this is how the facts unfolded, which unfortunately proved me right to the total surprise of my contacts. In fact it is very simple to understand this character to anticipate what he is going to do, he says it explicitly so it's no rocket science:

- On February 19 and 20, there was heavy bombing of Donbass by Kiev (note that it is the anniversary of the Maïdan massacre).

- On February 21, an exasperated Vladimir Putin signed the recognition of the Donbass republics and a NATO-type protection agreement (article 5).

- On the 22nd and 23rd Kiev ordered a massive bombardment of Donetsk

- On February 24, the ruler of St. Petersburg, when the fight could be avoided, struck first... Russia, **at the request of the LNR & DNR republics,** fell on the accumulated Ukrainian forces in the Donbass because their intentions were to massacre the entire population, to the amazement of the international community. This, at the request of Kiev oligarchs including Rinat Akhmetov, owner of the Azovstal factory in Mariupol and Igor Kolomoisky whose interests in the port of Odessa and its traffic are essential. This small detail helps clarify the real reasons for the current conflict; territorial integrity is of no interest to the real gravediggers of Ukraine. Preserving their respective interests is what really matters.

18 months later, General P. Vallely, forwarded me a flattering email in which I could read from the moderator of our group: "Regarding this conflict, only two men got it right: Colonel McGregor and Mr. Laurent Pellet." Being included with a man who was an advisor to the White House was quite a compliment.

Russia is gambling with its existence, because it knows the final goal of **US hawks** is to dismantle it to recover its resources, and of course to justify themselves as an enemy in order to be able to pass colossal arms budgets, allowing the military-industrial complex to survive. The **useful idiots** (another species of very corrupt bird), are at attention in Brussels and on TV shows, in ideological battles aligned to respond to the Biden administration's demands. They do not see that the ground is slipping away from under their feet because the grass that grows there is so lush, watered with Monsanto and Dupont de Nemour... The well-oiled narrative comes out of the box:

"Yzhas kakoy ya ne mogu, Russia invades Ukraine."

Could this conflict have been avoided? Yes if...

- The Obama/Biden administration did not shy away from Russian natural resources, because it is the main cause of the conflict to the great displeasure of human rights in search of freedom and other democratic concepts. An administration who imposed its choices on its vassals - the European ruling classes.

- The Ukrainians, in their desire for independence, had respected their own population and avoided massacring the majority Russian speakers in Ukraine and had accepted federalization without neo-Nazi nationalist murderous madness...

- The European Union had pushed Kiev to execute the Minsk II agreements, which was very simple: "If you do not implement the signed agreements then no more funding!" We would have seen Poroshenko or Zelensky crawling on the ground with their hands outstretched, begging for their respective real estate assets to continue to increase indecently.

- Diplomacy was taken seriously by taking into account Russia's security, financial and social interests, and not playing last-minute excitement in panic mode to better use this agitation for internal political communication purposes and support the warlike mood of the taxpayers.

Suffice to say that none of these criteria have been met, European diplomacy is braindead. Instead of trying to set up a preventive negotiation, the Western side poured fuel on the fire with both feet in the blaze by underestimating Russia's capacity to resist economic sanctions. The European Union thought that this country was still formatted on the model of the 90s.

I met Sergey Glazyev, Vladimir Putin's economic advisor, during the 2019 Yalta economic forum, and could easily understand the fatal error in the assessments of the brainless Brussels technocrats, without forgetting of course the strategic genius of the French ego elites, centered on alleged "French exception" I named (drumroll) the great Bruno Le Maire, minister of the economy.

These financial geniuses caused the ruble to plunge in 15 days with an incredible set of sanctions, believing that it would kill the Russian economy. They did not know what awaited them... After some disturbances, the ruble appreciated much better than before the crisis... What a slap in the face for the aficionados of useless boomerang sanctions!

Euro to Russian Ruble

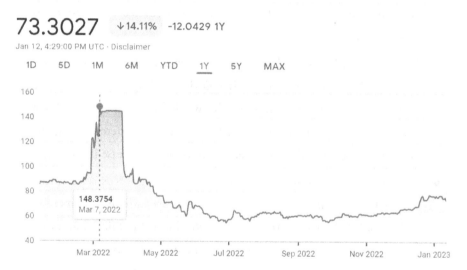

73.3027   ↓14.11%   -12.0429 1Y

Jan 12, 4:29:00 PM UTC · Disclaimer

The immediate indexation of the ruble to gold and the obligation to purchase oil and gas in rubles lead to a spectacular rise in its price, but not only that... A new payment procedure was put in place to which the geniuses of the sanctions did not expect! While much of the media has focused on the currency conversion element, what the Russian government was asking for, was not exactly being paid for gas in rubles. The substance of the request must be paid in foreign currency in an account with the government bank Gazprombank in Russia, rather than in a Gazprom account in any Western bank.

From Russia's perspective, this achieves two key results. First, it prevents the Europeans from enacting sanctions that would freeze gas payments to European bank escrow accounts - which would only be accessible to Russia after its troops withdraw from Ukraine. This option was discussed, but the Russian decree makes it very clear that Europeans cannot have their cake and eat it: as long as they want Russian gas delivered, they will have to pay for it into a Russian Gazprombank account which cannot be frozen. If payment is not made according to the procedure described in the decree, the gas supply may be interrupted. This was putting European governments in a bind: if they wanted to prevent Russia from accessing energy-related funds, they would have to make the politically much more difficult decision to stop importing Russian energy rather than just keep buying and holding the money. This has already proven to be a divisive issue in the EU and the Russian move risks increasing political fragmentation at the worst possible time.

Second, gas payments under the scheme could significantly undermine sanctions already imposed. So far, Gazprombank has been allowed to maintain SWIFT access due to its role in energy transactions. But this creates a risk that the bank will become a conduit for sanctioned companies to and from Russia. Experiences in other sanctioned jurisdictions (Iran and Venezuela) suggest that banks can become adept at creating shell companies and layering opaque transactions so that it is almost impossible to tell who the ultimate beneficiaries of transfers are. The new gas payment system presents a similar opportunity: once funds reach Gazprombank, it becomes impossible to trace them through the system.

Another important change introduced by the presidential decree concerned the stage and conditions at which payment for natural gas would be deemed to have been made. Under the "normal" payment procedure, the buyer has full ownership of the payment process, and the obligation is considered fulfilled once the currency transfer from the buyer's account reaches the seller's account. Under the new regime, on the other hand, the obligation of the foreign buyer to pay for the supply of gas is considered fulfilled only from the moment the funds received from the sale of foreign currencies are credited - that is, when Gazprombank converts the euros it received into rubles.

The execution of the buyer's payment obligation is de facto transferred to an agent (Gazprombank) and is entirely beyond the buyer's control. If payment is not made in accordance with the procedure provided for in the decree, the supply of gas under existing contracts may be interrupted at the discretion of the customs authority. It follows that the continuous and stable flow of gas to Europe in this new framework would depend not on the payment of the invoice by the buyers, but on Gazprombank which will carry out the EUR-RUB conversion in accordance with the letter of the decree and within the deadlines stipulated in the contract. Thus, Russia has put the troublemakers out of the game and, as icing on the cake, benefited from its own payment system implemented (MIR and ISPs) since 2017 in order to allow Crimea to integrate into the Russian economic system.

This crisis is the worst known in Europe since the Second World War because it involves nuclear powers and the risk of escalation is very high, yet a much more serious event is taking place under the noses of the European populations. without anyone reacting: **The coup d'état of the European Commission by Von Der Leyen. It decides on sanctions, and the allocation of funds to arm and support Ukraine without a mandate** and is almost certainly supported by the CIA or its accomplices, whose ultimate goal is to destroy the Euro by annihilating the German economy, which would be the worst crime. Conspiracy?

THE REAL REASON FOR THE CONFLICT

The Rand Institute claims that the following document is a fake, it also claims that the laboratories in Ukraine are only a Russian hoax while the documents of the financing of all biological weapons laboratories in Ukraine are accessible online from the US Embassy in Kiev and in all the documents described above. Hidden URL links (see appendix) that I did not fail to forward to a group of Lt Colonel doctors in the US army as well as their associated generals. When you lie once, you lie all the time!

https://tinyurl.com/RANDBIOWEAPON

Two Swedish journalists, Isaac Bonan and Markus Andersson, whom I contacted directly, confirmed to me that their source was in contact with the German

BND (intelligence service). They were given a confidential document developed by the think-tank "Rand Corp" and addressed to:

(Top right) US Secretary of State Antony Blinken, White House Chief of Staff Ron Klain, CIA Director William Burns, National Security Advisor Jake Sullivan, and NSA Director Paul Nakasone are listed as recipients of the document, along with the Democratic National Committee. In the background, the RAND Corporation headquarters in California.

https://tinyurl.com/UKREEUC https://tinyurl.com/UKREEUC

They put in place a formidable plan:

1. Trigger a major conflict between Russia and Ukraine which will lead to sanctions whose content was in ready-to-go mode from the sending of the above document on January 25, 2022. It allows the decoupling of the Russo-German energy partnership by using useful idiots that are easy to manipulate: the green "decarbonizers" of the economy. The German economy would be killed, and its losses are guesstimated at between 200 and 300 billion Euros.

However, even when the SPD and the FDP are ready to go against the Greens, the possibility for the next government to return relations with Russia to normal soon enough will be noticeably limited. Germany's involvement in large supplies of weapons and military equipment to the Ukrainian army will inevitably generate a strong mistrust in Russia, which will make the negotiation process quite lengthy.

If war crimes and Russian aggression against Ukraine are confirmed, the German political leadership will not be able to overcome its EU partners' veto on assistance to Ukraine and reinforced sanctions packages. This will ensure a sufficiently long gap in cooperation between Germany and Russia, which will make large German economic operators uncompetitive.

A reduction in Russian energy supplies - ideally, a complete halt of such supplies - would lead to disastrous outcomes for German industry. The need to divert significant amounts of Russian gas for winter heating of residential and public facilities will further exacerbate the shortages. Lockdowns in industrial enterprises will cause shortages of components and spare parts for manufacturing, a breakdown of logistic chains, and, eventually, a domino effect. A complete standstill at the largest in the chemical, metallurgical, and machine-building, plants is likely,

2. By band effect, being able to replace the source of Russian gas supply with US GLN at an exorbitant price in order to make European companies uncompetitive and therefore migrate towards areas where energy is cheaper to produce: the USA.

The cumulative losses of the German economy can be estimated only approximately. Even if the restriction of Russian supplies is limited to 2022, its consequences will last for several years, and the total losses could reach 200-300 billion euros. Not only will it deliver a devastating blow

3. Trigger the economic collapse of the Eurozone, and eliminate its currency in order to reestablish the hegemony of the dollar.

to the German economy, but the entire EU economy will inevitably collapse. We are talking not about a decline in economy growth pace, but about a sustained recession and a decline in GDP only in material production by 3-4% per year for the next 5-6 years. Such a fall will inevitably cause panic in the financial markets and may bring them to a collapse.

The euro will inevitably, and most likely irreversibly, fall below the dollar. A sharp fall of euro will consequently cause its global sale. It will become a toxic currency, and all countries in the world will rapidly reduce its share in their forex reserves. This gap will be primarily filled with dollar and yuan.

4. By creating a huge depression, well-educated young people (between 300K and 400K) would rush to market opportunities offered on the American continent, and therefore this would induce a growth of 6 to 7 trillion dollars because the capital would shift from Europe to the American stock market.

Another inevitable consequence of a prolonged economic recession will be a sharp drop in living standards and rising unemployment (up to 200,000-400,000 in Germany alone), which will entail the exodus of skilled labour and well-educated young people. There are literally no other destinations for such migration other than the United States today. A somewhat smaller, but also quite significant flow of migrants can be expected from other EU countries.

The scenario under consideration will thus serve to strengthen the national financial condition both indirectly and most directly. In the short term, it will reverse the trend of the looming economic recession and, in addition, consolidate American society by distracting it from immediate economic concerns. This, in turn, will reduce electoral risks.

In the medium term (4-5 years), the cumulative benefits of capital flight, re-oriented logistical flows and reduced competition in major industries may amount to USD 7-9 trillion.

Unfortunately, China is also expected to benefit over the medium term from this emerging scenario. At the same time, Europe's deep political dependence on the U.S. allows us to effectively neutralise possible attempts by individual European states to draw closer to China.

Economic situation of the European Union today:

- On October 29, the North Stream gas pipelines were destroyed. Who benefits from the crime? American Secretary of State Victoria Nuland boasted to the Senate in Washington: "As you say, I like to say that we are at the Department of Foreign Affairs, very satisfied that the pipelines in the North Sea are a pack of scrap metal at the bottom of the sea…" See also the text message intercepted from Liz Truss's phone: "It's done," which no media cares to talk about. Today, the EU buys US GLN at four times the price… Huge questions remain unanswered: **Why doesn't Scholtz raise his voice against the United States when his country's economy is being completely destroyed?** https://tinyurl.com/NSPIPEBLOW

- Capital invested in Europe is fleeing abroad, the monetary volume is estimated at €152 billion.

- France cannot supply as much electricity as necessary because a large part of its nuclear reactors are under maintenance. It sets up a deal with Germany where it supplies gas in exchange for electricity to compensate for the loss of power from the Ukrainian Zaporozhye power plant (closed by the Russians due to daily Ukrainian bombings). The necessary capacities are not balancing the level of demand, the producer price index in Germany increased during the month of August by 45.8%. Under the impact of persistent increases in energy prices in the country, energy-intensive factories are laying off workers and closing or moving (Siemens, BASF, etc.)

- **German chemical production**

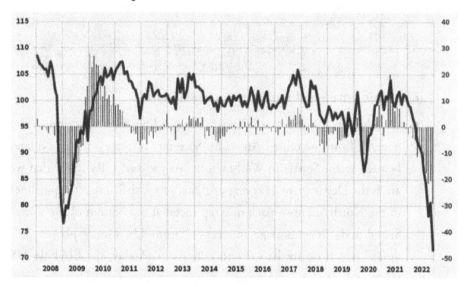

- Macron went to beg for cheaper LNG in the USA, he discovered life with a bitter end of rejection. Uncle Sam didn't care about our economic difficulties, business is business. Europe's gas supplies are becoming exorbitant.

- Europe is experiencing extremely violent inflation, bringing households to their knees, particularly in the food sector (between 17 and 25% depending on the product range). Overall consumption has collapsed by 40%, there are an incredible number of bankruptcies, particularly in the textile and distribution sector and this impacts all supply chains.

- The D.E.A and the Mexican army are waging a merciless war against drug cartels in the regions bordering the USA in order to allow the establishment of free zones to accommodate European companies whose needs in energy and cheap labor would be a necessity.

- The ECB is increasing key rates by wanting to apply the magic formula of overconsumption while inflation is due to the energy cost of production and transport, corporate debt is becoming more and more expensive, especially after financing the Covid crisis. Borrowing dries up because people are afraid, the economy collapses, because without consumption, mass unemployment looms. How can you be so stupid, Christine Lagarde?

- Employees across industries are demanding salary increases, thus contributing to accelerating inflation in a vicious spiral while the financial markets remain in good shape, a scenario looming in the subprime crisis, a remake of 2008.

- If we refer to the gas supplies established after cutting off the Russian source, we realize that Ukraine, France, Romania, and Lithuania will go into critical mode because the critical threshold of 20% stock will be reached. During the month of April 2023. Germany's stocks were in disarray as most of its energy-intensive industries have been shut down.

Member States are counting on a collapse of Russia to negotiate to their advantage (source close to Macron); it is a terrible mistake and the fall will be hard. The countries that are doing best are those that have maintained good relations with Russia, such as Hungary, Bulgaria, and Austria. However, despite sanctions, the Ukrainian government is delighted by Russian gas, due to its climate, Ukraine (UA) has colossal gas needs.

We also note a collapse in gas reserves in rolling months for all countries in the Eurozone, which reflects the fact that supplies are not functioning properly and that filling is collapsing.

If the winter of 2022-23 went almost well, the fall of 2023 will be a different matter. Sanctions diehards should realize that their effects are likely to be devastating for themselves. We noticed a significant drop in supply from November 2022 to continue this trend in a pronounced manner from January 2023.

Gas stock in European countries in Million m3 (Feb-Apr 2023)

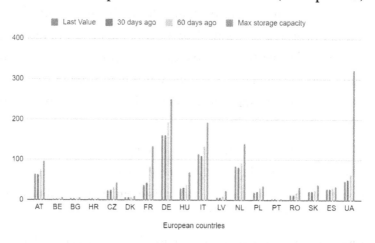

Gas supply in Europe (in Million m3), the orange zone representing the lack of supply 2022/2023.

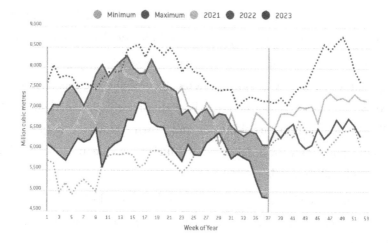

Source: bruegel.org, official partner of the EU.

The lack of imports for the first 25 weeks of 2023 was -23%, substantial. The fall of 2023 promises to be all the more complicated as France risks experiencing harsh social movements in the face of Macron's stubbornness in pushing through unpopular reforms by triggering harsh strikes.

The European populations will not be able to absorb an exorbitant cost of production due to energy costs in the long run being squeezed by inflation which continues to climb. As purchasing power diminishes, we are heading inexorably towards cascading bankruptcies.

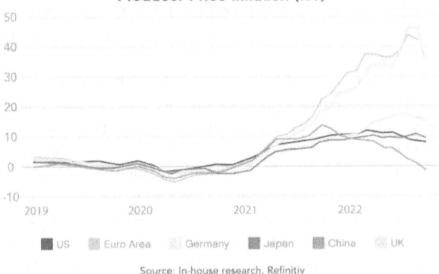

Producer Price Inflation (%Y)

Source: In-house research, Refinitiv

The US plan may have worked wonderfully and from the discussions I have with various auditors, I hear that in France 40% of SMEs/SMIs could disappear within 18 months.

During this time the European deputies are "pampered" (internal source in the parliament). These virtual living room warriors have not yet understood that when the populations realize that they have been the farce of this neo-Nazi prank, all the "Marie Antoinettes" in heels have an interest in negotiating with their backers for a warm spot in Florida because the next generation of yellow jackets may not be as conciliatory as the previous one.

WAR AND CORRUPTION

The graph below expressing the evolution of Ukrainian GDP is self-explanatory, the previous government in Maïdan had done a very good job to redress the post-crash economic situation of 2008 triggered by the subprime crisis in the USA. In 2012-2013 the Hi-Tech industry contributed to strengthening the economy while Yanukovich was completely denigrated by Europe, not corresponding to the geo-political orientations of the USA and the European Union. The consequences of Maïdan caused the Ukrainian economy to collapse and various global institutions took over by injecting already colossal sums of money.

In 2021 the figure of $200 billion was completely artificial (see diagram below) and did not correspond to the economic reality of the country. Donbass no longer contributed to the country's wealth, even though it was its industrial activity that kept Ukraine's economy afloat for thirty years, due to the wealth of its subsoil. Moreover, the population systematically complains about the cost of living and specifically the cost of energy due to policy imposed by IFM. Households are spending on average 30% of their income on heating in winter due to Madame Lagarde's recommendations (when heading the IMF), because she did not care a second about the situation in this country. Despite GDP collapsing in 2022, the fortune of the oligarchs, Zelensky included, is skyrocketing.

Evolution of Ukrainian GDP

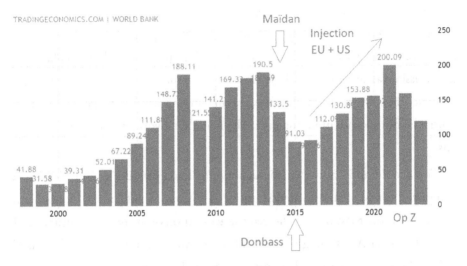

We are therefore entitled to ask for a few explanations on how a TV show actor who had such a personal distinction of playing piano (with his peewee), was able to accumulate $650 million before the crisis, his fortune increasing by $950 millions in ten months of wartime while he spent his time playing hero on TV or in fashion magazines, his nose stuffed with "powdered sugar": villas in Tuscany, Florida, Crimea, several luxury apartments in London and Batumi with a stuffed bank account at Deutsche Bank Costa Rica... A real KGB secret!

A US general explained to me how it has always been so easy in times of war for the crooks to make mountains of easy money; simply by diverting war supplies or funds used to purchase them...

Today the crooks in Ukraine are no exception, this is how two Caesar motorized cannons from the French army were resold by executives of the Ukrainian army to the Russian army for $150K each while the cost "ex-factory" was €11M at the expense of French taxpayers. The dark web is flooded with Stinger and MLRS Javelin US man pads found in Mexico, Colombia, Kosovo, and Africa.

The Ukrainian army even published a catalog of 1000 items which are sold all over the world (source Scott Ritter, US Navy intelligence service). All the personal equipment for soldiers sent by the West is resold in stores in Odessa to soldiers whose families are ruining themselves for their protection. There is even traffic in morgues; to recover the remains, families must pay up to $300 to carry out the funeral service and avoid cremation. When the European media howled like a wolf that Russia was starving the whole world by preventing the transit of grain from Ukraine, they forgot to say that it was transiting by truck through Romania towards the European Union, thanks to the mafia's network, in exchange for weapons.

You should also know that the deputies of Rada passed a law in Ukraine to authorize the sale of lands, whereas until 2015 it was forbidden for a foreigner to own it. Thus the Kievan elites allowed the acquisition of the best agricultural lands by all the major American groups such Cargill, Monsanto, Dupont... That is 17 million hectares out of 40, therefore 42.5% of all Ukrainian arable lands representing 25% of the surface area of the total country!

One can very well imagine that such a decision lined the pockets of the Verkhovna Rada deputies. This is also one of the reasons for the determination of the Biden administration to maintain itself in the Donbass and the adjacent agricultural regions. They want to maintain their interests in these arable lands which, in any case, will revert to Russia. Nazi Germany showed the same interest during WWII. The Nazis sent loads of trains to collect the soil in these regions because of its fertility. This was without understanding the biological mechanisms that made them fertile. The financial vultures have not failed to show their beaks since today all Ukrainian transport infrastructure belongs to the Blackrock company. They blackmailed Zelensky to finance his administration, in a reconstruction deal far from advantageous to the country. So, when the nationalists scream while beating their chests "Slava Ukraina," they are forgetting a small detail... The lands and essential assets no longer belong to them, they want to die for the foreign owners representing the "Woke" ideology at odds with their exacerbated nationalism. Ridiculousness doesn't kill, they say? There are always exceptions to the rule!

We also see all kinds of rackets springing up, from doctors' offices for combat disability certificates (up to $5k), protection of a fighter's widow, embezzlement from the purchase of combat rations, prostitution trafficking at the border, organ trafficking, children (65,000 have disappeared). The latest scandal comes from the province of Lviv where we learned that the administration in place made 60K potential conscripts wanting to flee to Europe pay an average of $5K, some individuals have enriched themselves by $300M. Ukraine was a country walking the red line, it has just jumped into the abyss of chaos and corruption with both feet, far from the Maïdan coup justification.

The biggest beneficiaries of this trafficking of all kinds are indeed in Kiev within the different ministries. It is absolutely impossible to be able to justify such increases in fortune in such a short time, off our consent! This is how Reznikov, Minister of the Ukrainian Armies, was able to offer an €8M villa to his daughter on the French Riviera. Do you remember the episode of the entrepreneurial pigeons in 2012 during which Hollande increased taxes in a dramatic manner for those creating jobs? Well you all joined us! Rhoo! Rhoo!

The United States tried to stop the uncontrolled black-market sale of weapons transferred to Ukraine. A document titled "Strategic Oversight Plan for Aid to Ukraine" was posted on the website of the Office of Inspector General of the United States Agency for International Cooperation. It refers to the creation of a special monitoring group which, in addition to USAID representatives, includes employees of the US Department of Defense and the US State Department.

Clearly, the problem of the theft of weapons and other aid is so big that America is creating an entire agency to try to solve it. In 2022, when Western countries provided the Kiev regime with a record amount of weapons, equipmen, and humanitarian aid, most of what was delivered was stolen.

Link: https://tinyurl.com/USAIDCTRL

HUMANITARIAN AID

In Zaporozhye, in the fall of 2022, the Ukrainian authorities appropriated the contents of 389 railway wagons and 220 trucks. Products intended to be distributed free to the population were put on sale in the city's stores with prices inflated by 300%. The Ukrainian president's entourage was suspected of having stolen this aid intended for refugees and the army. The country's National Anti-Corruption Bureau (NABU), created under Western pressure and effectively serving as an instrument of external control, has opened a criminal investigation.

The representative of the Bureau, Yevgeny Shevchenko, declared (source Vassily Prozorov, former SBU colonel) that almost all humanitarian aid had been stolen in the Zaporozhye region. The suspects are the chief of staff of the Ukrainian President Andriy Yermak, his deputy Kyrylo Tymoshenko, the chairman of the Servant of the People faction in the Verkhovna Rada David Arakhamia, and his friend Vemir Davityan. According to NABU, they developed a criminal scheme and its executors were the head of the military administration of Zaporozhye Oleksandr Starukh with his deputy Zlata Nekrasova, the secretary of the city council Anatoly Kurtev, and the local deputy Viktor Shcherbina.

But then, justifying the virtuous Maïdan becomes very complicated and the howls against Yanukovych who allegedly raided small businesses seem ridiculous compared to the industrialization of fraud which started well with Poroshenko, and which today has passed into "full production" mode with Zelensky. "Money, give me money!" When I listen to him speaking, I have the impression of hearing a Romanian begging at a traffic light!

Summing up the 2022 results, the highest echelon of the Ukrainian state properly corrected its affairs.

February 2022 December 2022

Volodymyr Zelenskyy	$650 млн	$1.5 млрд
Oleksii Reznikov	$780 млн	$1.3 млрд
Dmytro Kuleba	$450 млн	$1.2 млрд
Vitali Klitschko	$150 млн	$800 млн
Mykhailo Podolyak	$620 млн	$1 млрд

Джерело: Forbes, Getty Images   BBC

WEAPONS TRAFFICKING

The weapons that the US and EU transfer to the Ukrainian military subsequently surfaced in:

Africa: Weapons used in the Ukrainian conflict are being smuggled into the Lake Chad region and used by terrorists, Nigerian President Muhammadu Buhari said. "Unfortunately, the situation in the Sahel region and the conflict in Ukraine have been the main sources of weapons and militants, replenishing the ranks of terrorists in the Lake Chad region. A significant portion of the arms and munitions acquired for the war in Libya end up in the Lake Chad region and other parts of the Sahel. Weapons used in the Ukrainian conflict are flowing into the region,"

Buhari told a summit of heads of state organized by the Lake Chad Basin Commission (LCBC) in *the Daily Trust*.

Kosovo: Weapons supplied by the West to Ukraine were noticed in the arsenal of Kosovo radicals. Against the background of a serious escalation on the border between Serbia and Kosovo, sources reported Swedish AT-4s and NLAW disposable anti-tank grenade launchers, as well as man-portable air defense systems. Officially, Kosovo does not have these weapons, however, they have been sent in large quantities to Ukraine in recent months. Information about the appearance of radicals with Western-style weapons in the border zone appeared after Serbia began firing with armored vehicles towards the border zone with Kosovo and moving combat aircraft to this area. However, there are no documented facts about the use of AT-4s and NLAW grenade launchers by the Kosovo army and militias.

We will not be surprised if we very soon find a stock of weapons in the Parisian and Marseille suburbs ready to be used by all the sleeper cells of DAESH and the drug underworld...

VIII. Military Operations According to Sun Tzu

Napoleon I tried in Moscow in 1812, Napoleon III tried in Crimea in 1853, Hitler tried in Stalingrad in 1941… The EU and the Biden US administration wanted to try in Donetsk in 2022. And we all know how that will end! Faced with the media uproar giving a sad emotional spectacle forgetting the systematic analysis of the facts, it was necessary to judge on the basis of what is going on by referring to the most comprehensive book available on the topic: *The Art of War* by Sun Tzu (the quotes of which will be marked in bold to support the different phases observed).

"Anyone who doesn't have goals is unlikely to achieve them."

Demilitarized, denazifying Ukraine, bringing security to the Russian-speaking populations, the objective is clearly defined.

"In war, everything is about speed. We take advantage of what the other is not ready for, we appear unexpectedly."

On February 24, the Russian army attacked without warning and took as much territory as possible with very few men compared to the opposing forces.

"Any war campaign must be based on pretense; feign disorder, never fail to offer a bait to the enemy to lure him, simulate inferiority to encourage his arrogance, know how to arouse his anger to better plunge him into confusion: his lust will throw him at you in order to break it."

A decoy column of Russian tanks advanced on Kiev with old equipment but stopped on the outskirts of the city. The Ukrainian army was fixed on the capital, they attacked massively in the south and take 100,000 km2 with three times fewer men and in a very short time, a first in the annals of war since Rommel's breakthrough in 1940.

"Do not repeat the same victorious tactics but adapt to the particular circumstances each time."

Certainly, errors were made but quickly rectified by radical changes of command, in operational adaptation mode. In addition, we have been able to observe the use of new technologies to be more effective in combat, in particular with the use of the Geranium and Lancet drones, which cannot be intercepted by antimissile batteries because they are too small. The Lancet, which can be controlled remotely, has proven to be formidable due to its flexibility of unprogrammed flight, for the neutralization of mobile units and the destruction of artillery units. It is also used by tank commanders to target the enemy at out-of-sight distances, which is completely new because a tank is made to fire visually over rather short distances and not as an artillery piece.

"Capable, pass for incapable; ready for battle, don't let him see; near, therefore seem far; far, therefore seem close. Lure the adversary with the promise of an advantage; trap him by feigning disorder; if he concentrates, defend yourself; if it is strong, avoid it."

Russian generals know their limitations in human resources and are intelligent enough to understand that they must be preserved. Taking cities like Kharkov is extremely costly in lives because the defense positions are simpler.

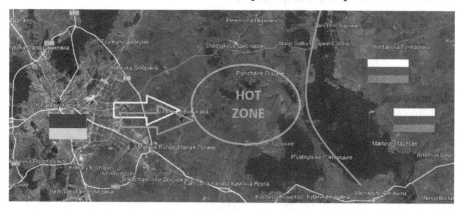

In addition, the city's architecture is drowned in thalwegs and hills. The withdrawal to the outskirts of the city was perceived as a weakness, and the Ukrainian forces pursued them in the steppe zone called in military language "fire bag" (indefensible zone because there are no protective structures) while the Russian army took shelter behind their artillery pieces on the left side of the Donetsk River. This very skillful maneuver cost the lives of 17,000 Ukrainian soldiers and very few Russian casualties because they were in retreat.

The same maneuver was observed in Kherson. The city was crossed by the Dnieper River, 1 km wide in this place with only one main bridge. If this bridge was destroyed, and it was bombed every day, the Russian army would have suffered heavy losses because it was cut off from its supply chain and 30,000 men could have been killed or taken prisoner. Operational strategy: the entire city was evacuated and civilians were accommodated in Mariupol, which is being rebuilt at incredible speed. We note that the position of the bridge being off-center from the city, its protection is all the more difficult and an evacuation in panic mode would have been dramatic. Anticipating an inevitable outcome in a calm and tidy manner was the best option.

Of course, the media around the world will turn these strategic withdrawals into bitter defeats insulting the Russian generals who until today have made very few mistakes. (Dixit Scott Ritter, former US military intelligence executive or Colonel Douglas McGregor, former military advisor in Donald Trump's White House). Remember the Covid affair, journalists are the best medical teachers in the world, they are the ones you consult when you are sick. Same scenario, they became the tearoom "Patton" and "Zhukov" who explained to you that Sun Tzu was an idiot.

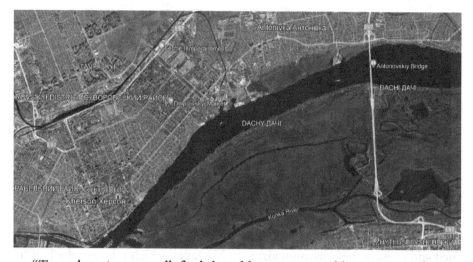

"Treat the prisoners well, feed them like your own soldiers; ensure, if possible, that they are better off with you than they would be in their own camp, or in the very heart of their homeland. Never leave them idle, take advantage of their services with appropriate distrust, and, to put it in a nutshell, behave towards them as if they were troops who had enlisted freely under your standards."

In the various speeches of Vladimir Putin, we hear the same rhetoric "Russians and Ukrainians are the same people" this is one of the reasons why the Russian army behaves well towards prisoners of war (all the videos are attesting to this statement, including the journalists on site from all over the world... Stratpol, Donbass Insider, Patrick Lancaster...) because they do not want to make martyrs of their own brothers. Well, those who do not wear tattoos and other insignia recalling difficult times of the story (Swastika, black sun)...

Reciprocity is far on the Ukrainian side where torture and summary executions are commonplace, especially in neo-Nazi reprisal battalions who behave worse than animals. I collected the testimony of a young man from the Foreign Legion who went to fight on the Ukrainian side in the Donbass and who resigned because he was afraid of being assassinated during the night by these crazy people. Zelensky's government even bombed the Yelenovka camp where the Russians were sheltering prisoners of the Azov group, to prevent them from speaking. (Dixit Xavier

Moreau, French geo-political analyst living in Moscow, who went there to interview the prisoners).

"If you are ten times more numerous than the enemy, surround him on all sides; do not leave him any free passage; make sure he can neither escape to camp elsewhere, nor receive the slightest help."

The Defense Line of the Ukrainian Army (AFU) Seversk-Artemovsk (Bakhmut)-Soledar has been consolidated since 2015, it is made up of support points, salt galleries in which considerable volumes of weapons have been stored. Krasnyi Liman was a very important railway supply point to recover for the Ukrainian army, at the end of September 2022, they recaptured the city in a great strategic move during which the Russian army withdrew so as not to be surrounded and suffer unnecessary losses. This is how Seversk was able to be kept under the Ukrainian yoke when it was on the verge of falling. Seversk is strategic because it is the entry point supporting the consolidated front line from the West.

In mid-January, the Wagner group recaptured the town of Soledar after battles of incredible violence, we learned from fleeing Ukrainian soldiers that fourteen battalions of 1,200 men were literally sacrificed to hold this point before it fell, this which broke the supply line to Artemovsk (Bakhmut). It's tragic because huge troops were fighting in this city. Thus, having no more supply of ammunition, they had to flee in light clothing north towards Kramatorsk and/or Slavyansk across the steppe without protection against Russian aviation and artillery, the M03 road was under control of the Russian army. Thus by interposing between the two points, the front line opened a piercing opportunity and Seversk could be surrounded by the North West, the consolidated front line could collapse... To note: Krasnyi Liman and Seversk are still under Ukrainian control...

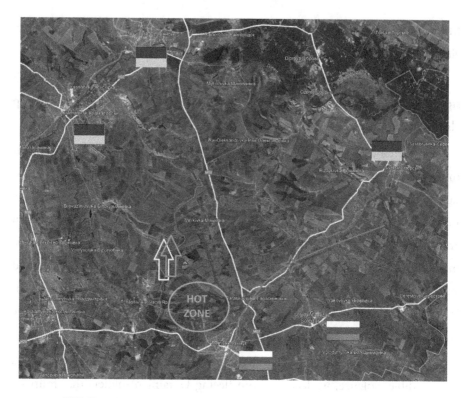

WHY UKRAINE CANNOT WIN THIS CONFLICT

It's not a question of troop numbers, it's a question of inventory and the supply chain, as surprising as that may seem. A high intensity conflict is synonymous with high consumption of large caliber ammunition because it is the artillery which makes all the difference, by erecting an impenetrable wall of explosions it is putting a brake on the adversary's progress. The parameters for success are therefore:

1. Stocks available and their access to stock according to needs

2. The capacity and speed of delivery of equipment and consumables

3. The resistance of the material to the conditions of use: climate, terrain, and intensity

4. The ability to maintain equipment as quickly as possible

5. Renewal of stock (production)/replacement of equipment

6. Turnover of units for rest to avoid exhaustion

In the first phase of the conflict, Ukrainian military infrastructure was destroyed (airfields, warehouses for storing military equipment and fuel of all kinds, telecoms, arms factories, and repair workshops), thus annihilating Kiev's warlike ambitions.

NATO then partially remedied this by providing expensive, fragile, disparate equipment, of different origins, with particular constraints of usage, never tested in current conditions (intensity, environment), without prior training and with terribly complex maintenance logistics (parts and labor). In addition, a conflict of this type requires setting up an economy of war by assigning massive ammunition and equipment production chains, as well as associated logistics. But this also means having to justify the establishment of such mechanisms from a political standpoint, and Ukraine's respective partner governments are careful not to do so because it would not pass muster with public opinion. This is a huge political risk and involves an implicit declaration of war with an already pissed off nuclear bear. These governments want to set up a hybrid war where Ukrainians die stupidly but not a direct and open conflict because the outcome would be the total destruction of the planet. They are crazy enough to play with matches but not to sit on the barrel of TNT.

Let's take an example of logistical complexity: US M777 artillery pieces are very fragile and often break due to an intensity of use never before equaled. The modules are then removed from the front line and are brought to the NATO base in Poland more than 1,400 km away using chaotic roads, where they will be maintained by trained personnel and then returned to the front line, God willing. The time cost is enormous, and this comes at the expense of their troop support operations, and supply columns are always vulnerable.

On the other hand, Russia uses equipment that is much less sophisticated but proven in field conditions and climate, therefore more robust, and which has a rather low maintenance requirement. It has also major stocks of ammunition and parts in opposition to what the TV generals ("Gamelins" - X. Moreau) are claiming. Russia has a stock of more than 2 million 155 mm shells, 1,500 artillery pieces, and around 2,500 tanks on the front line. The front is located less than 200 km from Rostov in Russia, and Crimea is within reach. They have no problem with training or adapting to unfamiliar material. Needless to say, logistical and maintenance problems are a little simpler on the Russian side.

All the TV specialists who have never seen a rifle in their life and who are beating the drums of war should realize that sending a hundred additional tanks to Ukraine will not change the outcome of this conflict and will only increase the number of victims significantly on both sides, but especially on the Ukrainian's. These great Parisian sofa strategists do not know that a tank crew takes at least three months to be trained, the demand for maintenance of this type of equipment (Leclerc, Leopard 2) is enormous, and therefore requires logistics of a rare complexity because the workshops are far from the front line, the transfer times in the event of a need for repair are prohibitive (one week round trip with risk of destruction during transfer).

The US/UK tanks (Abrams/Bradley) are way too heavy for the Ukrainian infrastructures (65-72T vs 50/55 Tmax), they must therefore be transported on special barges on which they become easy targets; moreover they are not adapted to this type of climate and are gas guzzlers (autonomy ~3 hours). Worse, the Abrams tank has a gas turbine engine running on JET-A1 aircraft fuel. Where will they find this type of fuel so far away? A mystery! These disparate types of equipment require substantial maintenance teams (20 people per model). So these little geniuses should understand that when everything will be in place (if possible), the NATO Tank offensive in June 1943 Kursk mode should take place at the time of Rasputitsa (deep spring mud preventing any movement of heavy equipment). Especially because last winter was particularly mild, the ground did not freeze but it rained a lot, the ground is therefore waterlogged and impassable. The soil of Donbass is an ancient alluvial humic soil which acts like a sponge. Heavy vehicles sink deep into it because the ground gives way under their weight and they end up on the chassis. If powerful tractors are available they would get them out of the mud but they should contact Mittal in India (or closer...) to come and collect the cheap burnt metal to make metal T-beams.

Rumors from the Pentagon are circulating that at least a quarter of a million would be the number of Ukrainian soldiers dead at the end of January 2023, as I close this book. The Kiev administration, in the midst of a debacle of corruption and dismissals, launched an eighth mobilization facing a painful and great resistance from the potential conscripts. This will go nowhere and will end with 100,000 new deaths, as well as the final death of European diplomacy and the economy. We are therefore at the mercy of hysterical and worthless politicians without any vision or ability to truly understand the facts, the world, and our true national interests, all of it, dubbed by a corrupt vulture press to state lies.

IX. Crisis Exit Scenario

"He who excels at resolving difficulties does so before they arise."

— *The Art of War*, Sun Tzu.

It would seem that if many of those who caused this crisis had read this book, it would have saved us a lot of disappointments and last-minute knitted sweaters. Before developing negotiation scenarios, it is necessary to take stock of the situation and the interests of each party, taking into account diplomatic and economic precedents.

However, if we understand the financing flows and their economic consequences, we can easily realize that many have no interest in stopping the hellish war machine. US Congress allocates budgets to Ukraine? Which only gets refurbished old army material when the US D.O.D is in huge need of renovation. In fact, the budgets end up in the pockets of the US military-industrial complex, the financial markets rub their hands, and the shareholders, including members of Congress and small investors applaud, the banks make huge profits, and the yellow and blue scoundrels fill their pockets, while poor guys get massacred. We swim in "the best of all worlds." -Aldous Huxley.

ASSESSMENT OF THE OVERALL SITUATION

Ukraine: A totally devastated country from a demographic point of view, with a colossal loss of population through immigration (in Russia and Europe), not to mention the human losses due to the conflict, which will lead to a significant demographic hole in a generation. Ukraine has lost 35% of its population, it is irreparable. An Oligarchy that has pillaged this country for decades, continues to profit from the conflict. A die-hard executive is disconnected from the reality on the ground or deliberately lies to continue to divert the resources sent by the West that are supposed to support the country. And an indisputable social breakdown whose scar will remain engraved for a long time. A painful divorce under a backdrop of neo-Nazi-sounding racism. A destruction of energy infrastructure from which the economy can hardly recover and, of course, a territorial loss with associated economic resources leaving a gaping hole in GDP. A remaining population plunged into inextricable poverty and deprived of religious support by an executive plunging into total obscurantism. The loss of Odessa would be fatal because the remaining Ukraine entity will no longer have any viability and will most certainly be abandoned to its sad fate by the West frightened by the mountain of debts. A total fiasco which will end in the nothingness of history, a nothingness moreover where this geopolitical ersatz coming out of nowhere comes from...

Europe: A worrying situation, with elites totally disconnected from military, economic, and social reality. This syndrome seems global. Disruption or even collapse of energy and consumable supply chains, inflationary explosion in foodstuffs, energy, and transport, with the result being a depression and social movements whose outcome is hazardous against a backdrop of bellicose desire to fight with Russia through NATO. But internal dissensions due to considerations of national interests and a total blindness to the real intentions of the USA which wants to completely subjugate Europe to the detriment of the populations, and risk leading to its dismantling. Having used sanctions that are illegal from an international law point of view, the precedent will be difficult to forget. A collapse awaits at the end of spring or in the fall. A real irresponsible suicide.

USA/NATO: Despite a successful masterstroke by destroying the European economy and cutting off its Russian gas supplies by terrorist methods, the result is half-hearted because the majority of countries on this planet have just understood that the hegemony of the USA was based on the destruction of opponents or simply rivals.

The so-far-successful Russian rebellion to the Machiavellian New World Order plan, with the help of China, has opened the eyes of the rest of the non-Western world, which has become emboldened and is putting itself into battle against the dollar. Saudi Arabia, Egypt, Algeria, Iran, Malaysia, Venezuela, etc... a total of fifty countries have decided to abandon it in favor of their local currency as a support for international trade. This is a major event bringing the share of the dollar in global foreign exchange reserves to 58% from 71% less than fifteen years ago.

Moreover, most countries are abandoning the purchase of US bonds, which is putting the US economy at risk of collapse because its debt will no longer be supported. The BRICS currency, if introduced, will seriously hurt the global dollar reserve and a 30% fall can be expected in the next ten to fifteen years. A military victory for Russia after a terrible debacle in Afghanistan would signify the definitive end of NATO and a bitter humiliation for the USA. The Republicans do not forgive the social and geopolitical excesses of the US Democrat administration "led" by senile old man Biden, who is doing everything possible to avoid his son's corruption and drug scandals, in which he himself was involved. The split between Democrats and Republicans is complete, the latter wants to put an end to the Democrats who have forgotten America and the Americans in favor of a deviant oligarchy. Ukraine is a perfect opportunity to neutralize them in a lasting manner. The USA is experiencing unprecedented debt ($33T), which is causing foreign buyers to flee in fear of insolvency but above all because of a loss of confidence due to the freezing of Russia's assets. The US economy is collapsing (vertiginous drops in car and real estate sales, etc.) with a debt rate that has pushed Secretary of State of the Treasury Janet Yellen to stop issuing debt, while the financial markets completely ignore the situation in the real economy. As for NATO, it is certainly experiencing its last year in Europe because it has proven not to understand the real economic and global issues that are at stake while trying to justify itself in order to survive. It has just shown only one thing: it does not have the means to achieve its ambition and it only serves personal careerist interests and parallel organizations (WEF, Open Society, W.H.O). Biden is trying to save Private Biden before the 2024 election, through the last Ukrainian stand when he no longer has the means.

China: The grand winner of this conflict. It has understood that it is becoming the centerpiece of the world economy and is establishing itself as No. 1. Patiently, it strengthens its links with Russia because the latter is the key to its energy supply. In the last quarter, China-Russia trade broke records in dollar equivalent. China seems to be waiting for NATO to exhaust itself so as not to be able to react when it knocks on the door of its neighbor Taiwan but the potential for conflict is very low. That said, interest in the production of precision semiconductors (nano engraving) that the Taiwanese company TSMC produces for the whole of Silicon Valley has dried up for two major reasons:

- The first is that TSMC relocated its operations to Phoenix, Arizona with the establishment of two factories.
- The second is that China has developed the necessary UV mask technology to etch transistors with nanometer precision.

Taiwan therefore remains just a matter of internal politics for the CCP. China is setting foot in South America and its expansion into the China Sea does not please Uncle Sam. Its diplomacy also seems to be rising and establishing its authority. China accuses, China proposes, and China imposes herself on the international scene and leaves Europe to contemplate its own end. A tour de force was to reconcile Iran with Saudi Arabia, which is a powerful symbol of China's weight in the world.

Russia: It responded to an arrogant and egocentric geopolitical vision of the West in a harsh and firm manner to protect its security, economic, and societal interests after having exhausted its diplomatic means. It is certainly not Pierre de Gaulle who would contradict me. Russia does it without qualms or equivocation. Since the fall of the Berlin Wall it has suffered constant aggression, where the West is implementing Brzezinski's plan, and we are witnessing a cold war which has turned hot and is ending definitively in Ukraine with a proxy conflict bringing mercenary companies of all sides financed by NATO to a nameless slaughter.

The exposure of serious diplomatic intentional lies, the confiscation of individuals' property owned abroad, the destruction of strategic transnational assets lead it to take increasingly harsh economic counter sanctions and military actions. The West's stubbornness in adding fuel to the fire by escalating the type of weaponry sent to Ukraine is pushing it towards all-out war with NATO. From an economic point of view, it is doing very well, generating more profits than it ever did thanks to the essential raw materials exported to Western economies, via Chinese and Indian trade hubs (which cost us astronomical commissions for nothing), and the implementation over the past fifteen years, accelerated over the past ten years of an import substitution policy.

Russian merchandise exports in 2022 set a historic record of $591.5 billion, and the merchandise trade surplus also turned out to be a record $332.4 billion, according to Federal Service data of Customs (FTS) on foreign trade. Thus, Russia entered the Top 10 world economies in 5th place from 15. After Vladimir Putin's statements commenting on Merkel's interview: "Negotiate? What and with whom?"

We understand that Russia wants to end things in its own way because no other choice is available and suitable. Russia takes its time, manages the military situation masterfully with minimal losses; it advances its diplomatic and economic pawns until the moment of the final blow. Its greatest success is none other than its diplomacy, rallying all the countries that have been pressured by the USA to put an end to the hegemony of the dollar. These countries wind up as one man and are joining the BRICS one after the other. It means the end of the role of the US dollar in the exchange of raw materials, so beneficial for the American economy: a future monetary tsunami and the symbol of the worst miscalculation made by the USA.

Who owns the resources? Russia. Who produces goods using them? China. Who needs them to exist and today to survive? The West. **There are ideological battles that can kill you without a single shot being fired.**

Mineral and Energy Resources of Russia

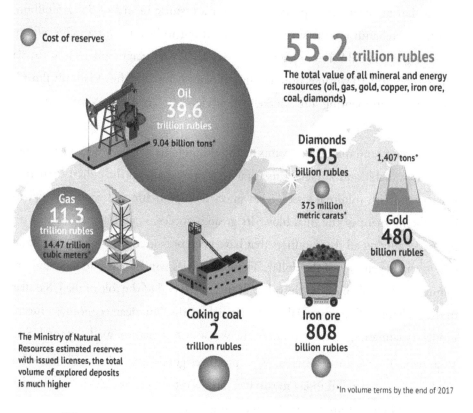

Cost of reserves

55.2 trillion rubles

The total value of all mineral and energy resources (oil, gas, gold, copper, iron ore, coal, diamonds)

Oil
39.6
trillion rubles
9.04 billion tons*

Gas
11.3
trillion rubles
14.47 trillion cubic meters*

Diamonds
505
billion rubles
375 million metric carats*

Gold
480
billion rubles
1,407 tons*

Coking coal
2
trillion rubles

Iron ore
808
billion rubles

The Ministry of Natural Resources estimated reserves with issued licenses, the total volume of explored deposits is much higher

*In volume terms by the end of 2017

"Know your enemy and know yourself; if you had a hundred wars to fight, a hundred times you will be victorious."

— *The Art of War*, Sun Tzu

The media and the politicians, instead of crying wolf about the collapse of Russia should have consulted the real and tangible data issued by serious organizations to get out of their denial of reality. The United Kingdom and France are the most indebted countries in the world, so Bruno Le Maire, Cocorico? There is an Anglo-Saxon proverb that says: "You can fool someone all the time, you can fool everyone for a short while, but you cannot fool everyone all the time."

Summary of the debt of the main players in the Ukrainian crisis

Country	Nat Debts ($)	GDP ($)	Debts/GDP	Debts (ext)/GDP
USA	31.5T	25.9T	94.9%	94.2%
Chine	14.1T	17.5T	80.8%	17.2%
Japon	13.2T	4.5T	296%	114.5%
Allemagne	3.3T	4.2T	78.6%	181%
UK	3.7T	3.4T	107.6%	297%
Inde	3.2T	3.4T	95.1%	21.5%
France	3.6T	2.9T	126.5%	286.2%
Italie	3.5T	2.1T	170.5%	142%
Russie	0.4T	2.2T	19.2%	26.3%

One day the truth will emerge, spread, and depending on the damage caused you will pay. The failure of Ukraine will be no exception, but it is the populations who will pay, moreover they are already paying, without really understanding or knowing why because the expression of the contradiction is well muzzled and the few channels which allow forming an opinion are not very easy to access and are accused of dissidence or conspiracy.

MEPs are careful not to take the path of opposition to the Biden dictatorship because their pockets are filled by supporting this geopolitical line against the interests they are supposed to represent. In this regard, I suggested to an EU MP whose name I will not mention, to motivate the creation of a European FBI in order to control the already very comfortable lifestyle of the people at the head of these opaque institutions, to say the least. When Von Der Leyen was asked to make available to the justice system the various emails and text messages exchanged with the CEO of Pfizer Albert Burla, as well as a copy of the contracts signed to obtain vaccine doses (€35 billion) and a commission of €750 million that has been paid, (but to whom?), we faced a dead end of silence. The European Commission refuses to give details, thus positioning itself above the law, in an anti-democratic manner. In such operating conditions, it would be interesting to explore the arms shipment contracts to Ukraine by observing the financial movements from Ukraine to tax havens like the Cayman Islands, wouldn't it? The European Union claims to be transparent and democratic when in fact it is an autocratic regime which enacts laws to be self-sufficient for the benefit of its administrators. In other words, it is called an unelected mafia.

DIFFERENT AREAS OF EXIT FROM THE CRISIS

The difficulty in establishing a common basis for negotiation will be extremely difficult because a gap has just widened between two worlds, and the Western protagonists have not yet integrated or understood this violent rupture which will lead to their destruction.

During the Davos 2023 summit, where neither Russia nor China participated, we heard the voices of the USA, France, Germany, the IMF, and the ECB, in a concert of bustles. They are trying to define their dominance and their orientation of the future world without yet seeing that the cards are no longer in their hands. Furthermore, they refuse to recognize that the system represented is out of breath and that it will not be saved thanks to the decarbonization of our economies: China would therefore be the only one responsible for the slowdown in global growth and then for the galloping inflation the next minute. We thus heard Kristalina Georgieva (President of the IMF), announcing that global growth would be 0.5% this year 2023, fantastic news because the world economy has stopped its decline but seriously worrying about the fragmentation of the world by inviting participants to do everything in their power to maintain global cohesion…

Sorry Kristalina but this schizophrenic burst does not prevent the divorce from not only being completed for more than six months but motivated by the same arsonist firefighters. Then it was Christine Lagarde's turn saying that headwinds will blow against the effectiveness of increasing key rates to calm inflation because China's economy will pick up again.

China is pre-empting Russian gas and oil which you have deprived us of due to megalomaniac considerations by wanting to monopolize Ukraine. This same China resells us the same product, only much more expensive. Incredible to see such stupidity and such bad faith, not only incapable of recognizing their own errors of judgment and incompetence, they have the nerve to accuse their neighbor. To top it off, Bruno Le Maire, in astonishingly youthful candor in terrible English verbiage, explains that we must reindustrialize Europe while "decarbonizing" it, in the context of competition with the USA, without sinking into a trade war with the US. This, under the sly eye of former Treasury Secretary Larry Summers who openly makes fun of him. He knows very well that the war in Ukraine was started to kill European competitors. So we can clearly see that all the protagonists have a very different agenda with a seemingly common but totally biased desire under a background of dissension hidden in a deafening denial of reality.

At the end of January 2023, the last 48 hours gave rise to events which completely confirmed some of the predictions I made to a group of US generals. They realized the considerable error made by the Biden administration, namely the dedollarization of the global commodity trading system and the risk of escalation of nuclear conflict. For the sake of transparency I am obliged to clarify the following facts:

- Towards my interlocutors, being clearly opposed to the Kiev regime, I have never hidden my position and justified it with complete intellectual honesty. I established that I admired soldiers like General Patton, Admirals Nimitz, Leyton, Colonel Doolittle but also like General Zhukov. And because of my family's history it was out of the question that I could accept a regime whose neo-Nazi Banderist support in Ukraine is absolutely beyond doubt.

- During my various discussions I asked them if they would agree to see Russian missile batteries in Terlingua or Tijuana, the respective borders between Texas & Mexico, California & Mexico. Not out of provocative desire but out of concern for contextual clarification. I don't even need to describe the response, some of them had experienced the Cuban Missile Crisis of 1962 during their active-duty positions.

We are at a pivotal moment in this conflict which in any case will not be won by Ukraine to the great dismay of all the "Bojo" (Boris Johnson), tank and squadron commanders who have perhaps watched too much of *Top Gun, Maverick*. Having followed military operations very closely, having professional contacts in the field and debating them objectively on a daily basis, I can easily say that "it seriously smells like pine tree (wood used for coffin) for Kiev" at a time when Artemovsk is about to fall. Therefore, here is what we could reasonably consider. The negotiations would be oriented along three axes:

– Territorial resolution, social consequences

– Overall security

– Economic balance

TERRITORIAL RESOLUTION, SOCIAL CONSEQUENCES

The partition of Ukraine. Russia will impose its conditions for ending the conflict on Kiev. The cost will be exorbitant and proportional to the time taken to postpone its resolution in terms of humans, infrastructure, and territories losses. Zelensky's cocaine-fueled obstinacy only leads to more losses of all kinds except for his bank account. From the discussions that I have had in particular with Alexandr Dugin in the past and in view of my understanding of the various events I can say that Novorossia (Donbass, up to Odessa especially due to the massacre of May 2, 2014) will live under the Russian flag. Until the Minsk II agreements there was no question of it but Merkel-Hollande coming out was the straw that broke the camel's back. Russia is taking off its gloves to make the West understand that playtime is over and that tolerance has moved to the red zone. Putting the rest of Ukraine into "landlocked" mode will bring its economy to its knees because the loss of access to the Black Sea will force Kiev into customs agreements for the passage of goods and considerable additional costs and dependencies, not to mention the loss of agricultural capacity and mining resources. The Ukrainian immigrant population will only return in part, especially after having tasted the comfort of Western life or having settled in Russia where the economy is way more solid and structured, the people calmer, what is more, allowing an easier cultural integration for Russian speakers. The depopulation of Ukraine has caused their fiscal capacity to collapse and Kiev today only lives on massive injections of Western capital. The sweet music of hard cash will stop because the financial backers' situation will no longer be able to support their own functioning.

We are on the eve of a major financial crash. The intended destruction of the European economy by the USA will plunge the remaining Ukrainian population into terrible poverty for the next thirty years.

This chapter ignores the now obvious views that Poland, Hungary, and Romania have allowed to emerge, but with the Ukrainian army destroyed, it will be very difficult to prevent this tacit partition of Western Ukraine. A limitless waste when we know that a non-alignment could have propelled the economy of this country into the stars by becoming a free trade zone between two blocs, a real Switzerland of Eastern countries. A once-in-a-lifetime opportunity was turned into the greatest disaster of the 21st century by a minority. This shows how exaggerated nationalism, forced by the greed of a few, is only the paved path to destruction and chaos. The Ukrainian leaders are absolutely worthless, not to mention their limitless greed and selfishness.

Neo-Nazi groups. It will remain to resolve the thorny problem of neo-Nazi nationalists who will never accept a capitulation, and any negotiation will be perceived as a betrayal. This is certainly what scares Zelensky the most. Russia represents humiliation, but the extremists, a guaranteed death.

Moreover, the bombing of the Azov prison camp in Yelenovka will be a price to be paid, and those who made this decision will have to protect themselves so as not to be confronted by the survivors, who are dangerous and determined individuals. During the last few months, my sources on the Ukrainian side have reported to me a number of abuses against civilians that are impossible to describe; these individuals have no complexes or restraint. We can clearly see that the coming years post-conflict in Ukraine will be turbulent: sabotage, attacks, crimes, and score-settling of all kinds...

Stability is not there yet and a large number of psycho people will end up either in Siberia or at the bottom of a hole in a forest. Generally speaking, and this is what is most shocking, the population is totally lobotomized and refuses to consider the crimes committed by their successive post-Maïdan regimes as unacceptable. Torture, public executions, what could be more normal! This denial can only be resolved by the explicit exposure of these crimes and the recognition by a large part of the population of their overall mental drift.

When the Charlie Hebdo journalists were murdered, the world population took to the streets; when the journalists and MPs were murdered in the streets of Kiev, the nationalists threw them in trash cans while the French watched sitcoms and their associated morons. Have the Ukrainians really understood the concept of human rights so declaimed by the European Union? I doubt it! Do they really have their place in Europe? This is the question Arno Klarsfeld asks himself, a lawyer, whose parents had the Nazi criminal Klaus Barbie arrested. He said:

"**Ukraine is not innocent. If in Ukraine, with the approval of the European Union, we worship Banderists who massacred hundreds of thousands of Jewish families during WWII, sooner or later we will achieve Hitler's rehabilitation.**"

There is no doubt that Russia will establish courts to try the various civilian crimes that have been committed over the past eight years, and that these procedures will continue over time.

Embezzlement and corruption. As for the Kievan elites, apart from Zelensky in his warm bunker, they are already in Europe, on the French Riviera, in Monaco, in Vienna or in Dubai, driving around in luxury cars, buying back properties confiscated from Russians on the Riviera or in the south of France, thanks to our funds while waiting for the monsoon of shells to stop before returning to turn the easy money pump. In the meantime, they can still wave their flag above a tray of bottles of Cristal champagne for 12,000 euros on the terrace of the Bagatelle restaurant in Courchevel or the penthouse of the Odéon tower in Monaco (Two Ukrainian families live there and pay an annual rent of €6M)... Europeans, don't forget to save money on heating and wear a turtleneck.

Behind this auspicious ironic pamphlet, we will therefore have to look at the seizure of the ill-gotten goods of Kievan's golden youth in order to redistribute them to the population that has been despoiled for decades. Not to mention that it will also be necessary to analyze in depth the mechanisms of tax evasion and zero-interest financial loans allocated to anyone close to the Kiev administration during the conflict. Loans of millions of euros without guarantee which evaporate in nature or in tax havens. It's good to be the son of an administrative person or a banker in Ukraine. Senior administration executives and other oligarchs will also have to justify the growth of their bank accounts by several tens or even hundreds of millions of dollars (Zelensky is better paid than the CEO of BlackRock). This chapter highlights that Ukraine will have to be placed under administrative supervision in order to control financial flows for reconstruction because it is incapable of managing itself in an honest and reasonable manner without plunging both hands into the banks' coffers.

Rehabilitation of seriously injured soldiers, post-traumatic stress treatment, military pension. This chapter deserves attention because the costs will be colossal. The average cost of rehabilitating a soldier in the USA is $100K, generally these are serious pathologies requiring complex and often multiple prostheses for the same war veteran patient, rehabilitation, psychological assistance, etc. Assuming that the care is 50% lower in Ukraine, estimating a figure of 300 thousand cases to be processed, the sum very quickly exceeds $14 billion. This does not include disability pensions, death compensation ($50 billion), the specialized centers that will have to be built... Over twenty years we can easily imagine a sum of $100 billion, or more than the annual GDP of Ukraine, a total failed state, which will have to be faced. That said, Kiev does everything to make the bodies disappear by abandoning them or burning them so as not to pay. Knowing the Ukrainian leaders, this will become a considerable source of revenue to be diverted to the detriment of those who really need it. Recently, I sent a request concerning this "small problem" to Viktoria Tigipko, wife of the former deputy prime minister, who presented a pharaonic project for the construction of a Hollywood center in Odessa on Facebook… I still have no answer, but I am convinced that this delusional and irrelevant project in this context of destruction, will never see the light of day!

Financial compensation. A complex topic due to Russia's care of its own populations and territories but also Ukraine's inability to take care of its own. It may be necessary to consider an energy supply at very low prices over a period of time to be determined depending on the infrastructure loss suffered, and commercial agreements allowing Ukraine to restructure under the best conditions to become a commercial hub between both blocks. That said, it will also be necessary to consider the colossal investments that were made by Russia in Ukraine during thirty years of its existence as well as the settlement of the share of the Ukrainian debt to which the USSR had subscribed and which Russia graciously repaid. The USA and Europe will have to take charge of a large part of the reconstruction of the rest of Ukraine for having provoked and fueled this conflict. The newly acquired Russian territories having been damaged will undoubtedly be rebuilt thanks to the funds allocated by Russia, which is already the case in Mariupol since thousands of brand-new housing units including all the necessary infrastructure (school, hospitals, leisure centers, and commercial) have already been rebuilt. This phenomenon is accelerating considerably, in the style that I observed in Crimea. Crimea under Kiev authority was Tijuana, under Russia it became San Diego. That said, with regard to information revealed to me, the company AEGIS AVIA was mandated by the French embassy in Kiev to evaluate the cost of rebuilding the country and the report turned out to be minimal due to the fact that Russia only targets military infrastructure and not civilian interests.

THE SECURITY ASPECT IN EUROPE

The Ukrainian crisis results from a US hegemonic desire to expand NATO in order to corner Russia aided by a vassalized Europe, thus establishing a problem of insecurity to be addressed with the greatest seriousness. For this to be possible, trust must be reestablished and this requires a state of recognition of the mistakes made. Unfortunately, we never ask those who generated a problem to resolve it because if it was created it is because their initiators were not able to avoid it or worse still, they deliberately provoked and organized it. Which means in other words that European management must be ignored or even neutralized, and the solution to be implemented imposed by a third party. The solution can only come through a team made up of civil society engaging realistic military personnel or even politicians who are capable of understanding the true global collaborative interests to be put in place. When we listen to the narrative on Rossia 1, Russia's most popular channel, we hear a presenter proposing a pre-emptive strike on France.

Macron has brought us from a position of support to a position of co-belligerence, he no longer has any credibility. In his habit of "at the same time," he dares to speak of dialogue and negotiation, his trademark does not work with leaders who know how to decide very clearly.

Let's consider the following situation that unfolded… The president of Azerbaijan, Ilham Aliyev, made it clear to Macron, Tartuffe the first, that it was out of the question for him to participate in negotiations with Armenia. The response to his arrival was as sharp as a Japanese katana: "We will not meet Armenian Prime Minister Nicol Pashinian if he (Macron) is present."

Our proposal is all the more legitimate since those who started this madness are doing everything to aggravate the situation even though it is desperate and it is so important to stop this human carnage. The losses in men compared to what we observe in Ukrainian cemeteries are appalling. They say they want to negotiate and are sending more and more weapons while the Ukrainian troops are exhausted.

We are therefore experiencing a shortage of fuel, energy, and medicines, our bakeries are ruined, hotels are closing, and businesses are moving abroad or collapsing, which results in the impoverishment of European populations. We cannot be the judge and jury or continue in this direction.

Deployment of nuclear weapons among NATO constituent countries throughout Europe creates a permanent Cuban Missile Crisis putting a nuclear threat on Moscow's doorstep, which significantly increases tensions. The withdrawal of NATO's nuclear vectors becomes an absolute necessity as well as establishing a comprehensive Pan-Eurasian security concept which would avoid potential future overflows. This is essentially linked to economic agreements of strategic interest that the political classes cannot understand due to their intellectual corruption or worse. Terrorism, Islamism, trafficking in weapons, drugs, organs, and human beings are more civilizational threats than Russia is. The media have a huge responsibility in the perception of the biased security paradigm that has been established, and their motivations will have to be examined. Is it Russia that distributes crack in Paris? Who murdered hundreds of passers-by in Nice? The real security issues are not addressed or left drifting because keeping populations in a form of insecurity allows the same authorities to justify their positioning as saviors, without any action or real taking of responsibility. A multi-party agreement must be concluded to ensure the security of Ukraine, and particularly the dismantling of armed gangs trafficking in all kinds (weapons, drugs, humans). We will not forget the terrorist threat that Ukraine will pose in Europe from ISIS fighters who have flowed in via UK-based mercenary companies, recruiting them to support neo-Nazi factions. The Baltic belt of states and Poland will be a considerable obstacle to this type of approach because they have not yet digested their history and Russophobic soup is still served for breakfast.

ECONOMIC BALANCE

Russia is an essential continent in terms of economic strategy linked to supply chain dynamics and access to natural resources. It offers three supply routes from China to Europe which are allowing our companies to have much more efficient cash flow, thanks to a frequency minimizing stocks, a speed of transfer and a diversity of routing allowing a turnover of goods. Less bulky therefore less expensive, not to mention a limited "**carbon dioxide**" footprint. These routes are the Northern Corridor passing through Moscow to Poland, the Central European Corridor passing through Kiev towards Vienna (Austria), the Southern Corridor, passing through Crimea Sevastopol towards Constanta (Romania) or Burgas (Bulgaria). The last being a considerable shortcut to southern Europe. These routes allow a time saving of more than a month compared to maritime routes and with very high security (no piracy in the Gulf of Aden, nor sinking trains). This can give rise to export optimization platforms for specific, characteristic products to Asia for our SMEs/SMIs whose need for market expansion becomes vital in such a tense context. There are around 1000 multi-billionaires and the number of multi-millionaires in China stands at 6.2 million and is expected to double in 2026, to 12.4 million (20% of the French population). They represent a colossal market to address. When I wrote to Martine Vassal and Christian Estrosi (all in charge of PACA region, south of France) in 2018, returning from the economic forum of the Danube region, explaining that French ports and railways must set up BRI partnerships, I received a total rejection... No response. The elites are supposed to help entrepreneurs, but they understand absolutely nothing about the world in which they live. They take care of their privacy and comfort while ignoring the reasons for their positions. Furthermore, as one of the advisors to the PM of Malaysia indicated during the Danube region forum in 2017, Asian populations are in full demographic expansion, to feed them, Africa will become an essential production player, which positions Europe as the pivotal hub of this necessary chain. I would like to quote Paul-Antoine Martin. In his book, *The Clan of Lords*, he explains that the mafia of the major schools does everything to keep its meadows and prevents any type of development of our economy: "The country's railway infrastructures have contracted, due to freight transport lack of activity, penalizing industry and the so-called ecological transition." He adds that after a visit to a ministry to one of these zealous civil servants who had never done anything in his life, he was told in a smug and contemptuous tone, "I have a little music in my head and my song will not change its tone."

Wasn't it Alexis Kohler, on the board of the Italian maritime freight company MSC? Would he have protected his own interests by refusing the development of rail freight? Can we also deprive ourselves of a market of 150M people? Can we continue to buy GLN at four times the price? It's high time to be rational!

Commercial recovery. Can the world afford to do without Russian-produced natural resources or Chinese manufacturing? In a world of remarkable complexity where humanity has progressed exponentially over the last fifty years, claiming to have the capacity to produce everything necessary to function is completely illusory.

The resources on earth are limited and considering that the economy can grow infinitely is an enormity. **As a result, common intelligence would allow balanced functioning and rational and more economical use of resources. This can only happen through technological research collaboration and not through constant geopolitical confrontation leading to the terrible fragmentation of the world that we are facing today.**

The survival of humanity is at stake. The Ukrainian conflict has highlighted the fragility of world economies and their energy and functional interdependencies. We must therefore come to a stable compromise so that this does not happen again. This crisis was perhaps necessary for us to become aware of it. Above all, we are witnessing the brutal awakening of a bloc of the world emerging from its torpor to understand that it has been spoiled all this time, especially in Africa.

We are witnessing not an ideological clash, but a split motivated by access to natural resources. The West has very limited resources and has used force or corruption to access them for too long and finds itself faced with the consequences of its shortcomings, lies, and contradictions. Having heard of a meeting of some central bank officials from oil-producing states, it seems that the tone has changed radically, even extremely. It is time for the Davos community to realize that arrogance is no longer appropriate and that continuing down this path will end in a dead end, on a bicycle, perhaps electric!

The oil & gas "price capping" established by the G7 is the blatant proof of this arrogance, have you ever seen a customer enter a store and say "I do not agree with the price you charge, I limit your price to xxx..." Good luck! Trade negotiations are fair game, but this type of behavior ends with a door closing. Perhaps we should impose control on market speculation with regard to raw materials in order to avoid excesses and abusive behavior by those who organize the shortages. We can imagine a blockchain system of certified exchange between producers and institutional buyers using an appropriate electronic currency (indexed on gold appreciated by a variant reflecting the exchanges it supports?).

A relaxation of the sanctions which have totally destroyed our economic production capacity and trust between blocs would already be a first step towards a renormalization of international relations and everyone would benefit in an intelligent way.

Private influence networks. Some individuals have boasted of having participated, financed, and organized the 2014 overthrow of Ukraine's government, notably George Soros saying he spent a modest amount of $1 billion (which Jean Claude Juncker reimbursed him to organize African migration to Europe). We also heard from Philippe De Villiers that 200 Euro MEPs were eating out of his hand. It is therefore time to clean out the Augean stables and neutralize the harmful capacity of this type of individuals and ensure that these corruptive behaviors can no longer operate. It is the same with the hundreds of lobbying agencies that revolve around Brussels institutions. The deviations of global corruption systems must be stopped because the result goes against the common interests.

How can we explain the psychotic autocratic excesses of certain oligarchs like Bill Gates announcing pandemics and the ways in which they must be contained. Does Gates have a medical degree? His latest statement to the Australian Department of Health is beyond disturbing. Announcing that the next pandemic will be more violent and triggered by a virus emerging from a laboratory (Ukrainian?) is most surprising. Could he be a medical Nostradamus or did he have information that we didn't have? You now know where Covid comes from…

Financial power decides on global governance to ensure its survival and expansion, it finances the organizations it controls to represent this governance and uses financial and media bias to impose it globally. If you do not comply with their demands then you will be ostracized by society or brought to your knees by your own government: "No vaccine? No restaurant!"

A part of the Davos Forum Nebula

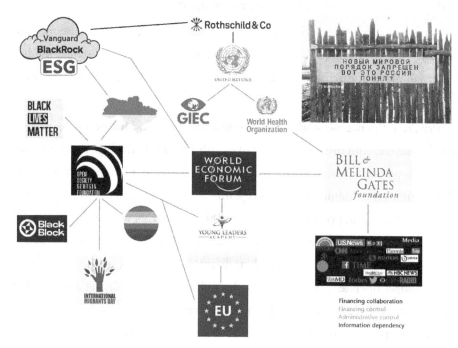

(*) No New World Order, this is Russia… Understood?

X. Epitaph of the Ancient World

The French historian Georges Bensoussan, editorial manager at the Shoah Memorial in Paris, said: "From the summer of 1942 the information concerning the massacres of Jews in the territories conquered by the German army was total, the political elites also knew both among the Allies and in neutral countries." From Treblinka to Auschwitz via Sobibor, millions of Jews were exterminated while political leaders turned their heads.

At the start of the Russian military operation in April 2022, the Israeli NGOs Abad and Ley Leyev exfiltrated Jewish populations from the Zhytomyr region of Ukraine to Israel through Romania because the nationalists began to behave as they had done under Bandera during WWII, with total media indifference. The same indifference and omerta with which they treated the assassination of the French rabbi Mendel Deutsch in this same city in October 2016 by the same individuals. "We must sell the war, no scandal please!"

When the dissidents of the one-track thinking dare to declaim the problem posed by the Ukrainian neo-Nazi totalitarian drift, the entire French political class turns its head in the name of the sacrosanct democratic concept. What would have happened if that neo-Nazi coup in 2014 had occurred at the Place de la Concorde in Paris? That double standard is unsustainable.

History repeats itself tirelessly, we find the same cowardly behavior of the elites which is matched only by their mediocrity. According to these people, Russia should have turned a blind eye to all the massacres perpetrated throughout Ukraine for eight years without saying anything, it should have applauded the genocide in Donbass which was in preparation. And one day in 2025, as in 1945, we will discover with horror Dachau, Timisoara, and other carnage in mass graves. One or two useful idiots will be presented to the court in The Hague, imprisoned for thirty years like Milosevic, and we will turn the page... It was a poor understanding of Vladimir Putin, whose patience has been flouted and insulted on numerous occasions despite the efforts of his diplomatic corps, whose desire for appeasement in the person of Sergey Lavrov is beyond doubt.

Western governance, an arsonist firefighter, in a disorderly and hysterical agitation armed with a truly sickening hypocrisy has swept away our ways of life with the wave of the hand and is trying to keep us under the yoke of the metal manipulative media of fear. So, like sheep they will go and get vaccinated without complaining because Bill Gates, the Grand Ayatollah of the W.H.O, decided so. How long will this mass lobotomy last? When are the populations going to stand up as one man to fire all these self-congratulatory "Fat Cats," like the little marquises living off the hook of a 17th century royalist court? I feel a great anger that is boiling, a dull anger that is just waiting to be expressed, like a pot on the fire from which the safety valve has been removed.

I fear that when the limit is exceeded, the consequences will be terrible for those who plunged us into this forced and illegitimate chaos. The world has just fractured in a lasting way and this will cost us, Westerners, very dearly. The BRICS, aided by emerging oil & gas producing countries and many others, are rising like a chain of young mountains and imposing themselves on the global economic scene. In this world of interdependence, the globalism so desired by Klaus Schwab in his megalomaniacal vision of total control is dying. A grain of sand is blocking the cogs of the infernal machine of the new world order, his name is Vladimir Putin. This new order invented without a civilizational basis, in its last breath, will want to take us down so as not to die alone, it is up to us to defend ourselves.

Multi-polarity has just been born, certainly in order to rebalance the forces present and for the sake of humanity.

XI. Predictions for 2023

The latest (end of February 23) events are significant, the start of corruption purges within the Kiev government are the signal which will allow the populations to accept the next financial package, it is just a smoke screen because the big names of embezzlement remain in place: Zelensky, Kuleba, Podolyak, Reznikov.

Secretary of State Blinken, in panic mode after the note from the Californian think-tank Rand in January 2023, explaining that a long conflict would be detrimental to the US economy, makes the following proposal:

- Territorial concessions must be made including Crimea, Donbass, Zaporozhye and Kherson, the land bridge that connects Crimea and Russia.

- West of the Dnieper River, to the north around Kharkov and to the south around Odessa and Nikolaev, the United States' acceptance of a "demilitarized status" for Ukraine.

- Additionally, the United States' agreement to limit the deployment of HIMARS, U.S., and NATO infantry fighting vehicles, to one point in western Ukraine from which they can "maneuver" as a deterrent against future attacks.

Will Vladimir Putin accept a proposal authorizing what has already been achieved? I doubt it... The positioning of a NATO land armed force in western Ukraine results in the installation of a NATO base on the rest of Ukraine, which is much of the initial problem. A ridiculous proposal at a time when Artemovsk is falling. We see here an attempt to want to take a break to better recover. Indeed, US General Wesley Clark, in an interview at the beginning of February, is explicit: If Artemovsk (Bakhmut), central point of the Ukrainian resistance line falls, the entire line falls with a reopening towards Kherson then Nikolaev and finally Odessa. With such momentum and potential, will Russia miss this opportunity?

Closing the access line to the Black Sea means the total economic death of Kiev. Odessa is the symbol of the atrocities of the neo-Nazis in May 2014, this symbol should fall because it would represent a scathing political victory, the end of the lies of the West but more than all it would wash away the shame that has hung over this city for too long, not to mention trafficking of all kinds (drugs, prostitution, weapons, etc.).

The sweeping declarations of all the fragile and hysterical people in the European Parliament in Brussels will be lost in the noise of the night, and it is not the four fire-breathing pieces of scrap metal that NATO wants to send that will make a difference, nor planes which can only be piloted by highly qualified military personnel, therefore non-Ukrainian. Will the different foreign air units accept such involvement? I doubt it. Can the European economies put themselves in battle order as requested by NATO Admiral Rob Bauer. France can no longer produce bread; the German BASF factories have been closed... The European Union is at the dawn of the worst recession since 2008. The conflict may still last for months because Zelensky, living in the snowy Metaverse of his muddled mind and too attracted by easy and massive gains, does not want to face the harsh reality: the total loss of his army. The Russian steamroller will be in place in a few weeks to take back Kramatorsk and Slavyansk...

The capitulation of Ukraine is obvious except to the the small armchair politicians, besides they don't care if thousands of Ukrainians are still chopped up, that would perhaps represent more choice in European and Middle Eastern brothels.

Poland's views on its former empire attract attention, the fact that one mobilization of 200K men was put in place says a lot about the warlike intentions of Duda, their president. The Polish government buys land in the Lviv region of Ukraine, and distributes passports, for identical historical reasons linking Russia and the formerly Ukrainian Russian-speaking regions. I see from here the sending of troops to better withdraw them at the appropriate time but running out of fuel in Galicia (Lviv region) and Volhynia (Rivne region). Orban may have the same idea without sending troops because the purchase of lands and the distribution of passports in Transcarpathia are going well. Same technique that Albania had put in place to acquire Kosovo from Serbia.

It would not be surprising if, emboldened by its neighbors, Romania had the good idea to seize the Chernivtsi region. By absorbing Moldova it would constitute a sort of pan-European NATO security belt to contain Russia. Which would leave Ukraine looking like a few plots of lands around a dying Kiev, like a whore on the side of the road after the Napoleonic army had passed through. To avoid it, Kiev is forcing mobilization in these regions to eliminate the ethnic threat by sending these conscripts to the hottest parts of the front. In any case, the partition of Ukraine is inexorable... That said, Poland has already announced its desire to maintain the security of the western part of Ukraine by positioning troops there. I doubt that this will be to Vladimir Putin's taste, who would see it as a maneuver to install a NATO military base right under his nose by being hundreds of kilometers closer.

What will happen to the Zelensky & Co. regime? A great waltz of exfiltration helicopters will take shape in the sky like dragonflies or a rain of corpses of thugs will fall on the streets of Kiev... Will the Russo-Ukrainian populations be able to forgive themselves? This social trauma will be difficult to absorb, only time and the exposition of the facts will help them, provided that the Ukrainians come out of their denial of genocide and recognize that massacring the Russian-speaking population in their own country led to their downfall.

Manipulated by authorities who have enjoyed themselves well with other tax-payer funds, they will see financial support dry up as quickly as it appeared. When a people insists on making its own culture disappear by eradicating a language that has always been its own, when it brings down statues as if to erase the evidence of its history, when it burns the supports of its literature, ignores its songwriters... It is condemned to disappear and to be absorbed into a subcultural mixture. The immigration of Ukrainians is proof of this, the demographics will decline and they will be diluted. This is the process of disappearance of the West in an accelerated mode that we are witnessing like an open-air laboratory. It's an immeasurable waste and a lesson like no other. When we forget ourselves by accepting anything and everything at the call of financial or Wokist mermaids, who have no other face than this hideous, depraved old man Soros, the price to pay is terrible.

The big winner in the fight for values is undoubtedly Russia, which that crazy Soros wanted to destroy. It emerges strengthened in its transcendental existence. Today we see a well welded and united people around their president who has clearly understood the message that has been sent for years. Of course you will hear the Durak (idiots) and other journalists imploring the god "Revolution" for the dismissal of the master of the Kremlin but that will not happen. And as I pointed out to my fellow US generals, those who call for this wish could regret the arrival of the replacement, he could be much less complacent and patient. Let them not be surprised, because the contenders to succeed Vladimir Putin are not altar boys. Its close rapprochement with China, its gigantic natural resources, and its agile adaptation to the new sanction situation are all motivating factors which have allowed its economy to consolidate and solidify itself. This conflict sounded like the wakeup call of Russian society pampered in its winter torpor. It will count as a major economic and geopolitical power in the future. Moreover, France is the one that will suffer the most because it is being kicked out like dirt from Africa which, under the leadership of Russia and China, now refuses its subjugation to Françafrique. Macron takes a colossal slap in the face, and yes, you don't entrust a great lady to a puppet. We went from Francophonie to Frankaput in a few years.

Faced with the NATO deception, the Western world will put away its little yellow and blue flags, still dazed from the psycho-economic shock it will have inflicted on itself. A number of actors in this crisis will have to be held accountable before an international court of justice set up for this purpose by the BRICS for having done nothing or having encouraged this major crisis through lies.

The chasm that has just widened between the BRICS+ blocks and the West, the scars that this conflict inflicts, will mark future decades indelibly and as a result natural resources will become more and more expensive. This crisis will have highlighted the fragilities of the so-called European leaders and their inability to approach the world in a rational and intelligent manner. They sawed off the branch they have been sitting on for too long. Like a pack of cubs, they projected their anxieties and psychoses: "Russian tanks will soon be in Paris if we don't stop them in Ukraine," but what bullshit! Vladimir Putin has nothing to do with Europe, he has many other fish to fry because Europe's worst enemy is its leaders. This artificial European entity is set to die due to internal dissensions antithetical to national interests and the incapacity for a true long-term global vision. We cannot lead such a juggernaut with a few little pugs worse than those of the decadent USSR, worrying more about whether a man is a woman and whether a transsexual can participate in a women's athletics competition because 99.9% of the people will think these people are just crazy.

For almost two years, populations were restricted and plunged into fear of a virus. Today, like an anesthetized woman waking up, they are recovering from this shock. The politicians do not want to realize that they are losing their power, they are trying to channel the information as much as possible and do not want to understand that they have lost the control and confidence of their voters and citizens. When the real reasons for this conflict are understood and the populations realize that they have been duped from A to Z, presenting them with the bill will end in a volcanic explosion of unprecedented magnitude. So dear politicians, park your helicopters on the roof of your administrations because the tornado is on the horizon, governments will inexorably fall, and Brussels will be swept away in the bathwater along with the €uro.

The great unknown will come from the USA, an unnamed battle is taking place between Democrats and Republicans, or rather between globalists and patriots. Due to the latest discoveries made within Twitter by Elon Musk by opening the sordid cupboards, tensions are only growing and we can feel a fierce mutual hatred. More and more evidence is being exposed, showing that the Democrats, through the positioning of FBI executives (former director James Comey was placed at the head of Twitter's legal department) were able to control the results of the last elections and censor anything. The FBI also hid the Biden laptop affair, the full contents of which have just been given to me. A true horror, drugs, corruption, prostitution, influence peddling, incest... We are entitled to all the chapters of human darkness (https://tinyurl.com/HBLAPTOP2023). America has split into two blocs who cannot and do not want to discuss with each other, the Wokists living in a new world, and the traditionalists inclined to preserve their culture and sense of reality.

Namely, what twisted move awaits the "again" candidate Donald Trump to eliminate him from the political scene? At the same time, Congress will have to legislate in June on the increase in the US debt ceiling, the emissions of which have been frozen and the initial attraction collapsing for reasons already mentioned. A US debt default would lead to an unlimited global financial cataclysm.

This negotiation will become a pre-election political weapon of mass destruction, as evidenced by the same thing circulating at the moment – "The Democrats are blackmailing Americans – either you elect us and give us a mandate to destroy America, or…we destroy America."

Within the Republicans, a large number of voices are raised against the financing of Ukraine to the detriment of the US population and the support of their economy in a context of bank collapse which will make the subprime crisis seem like a little joke. At the beginning of March when the book was finished I sent to my general American contacts a summary of the losses of a sample of fourteen regional banks (small/medium cap) which amounted to $112 billion in less than a week, I dare to imagine the total loss of US financial institutions over this period while we are just at the start of hostilities.

I stressed to my contacts that the Biden administration, by attacking Russia, had shot the USA in the head at the end of March 2022 with the implementation of the steamroller of de-dollarization. The Eurasian geopolitical tectonic movement will awaken an African volcano which will put an end to Western hegemony and trigger the predicted crisis of financial crises bringing America to its knees and Europe to its stomach.

Evolution of world monetary reserves (the sharp decline of the dollar)

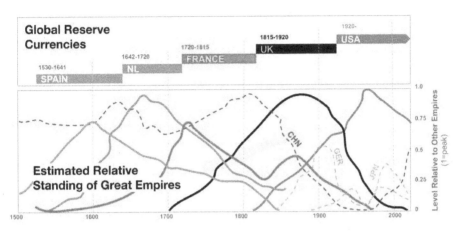

A question therefore arises…

Will Biden, cornered politically by the successive defeats of Ukraine, push to commit the unthinkable, that is to say push NATO to intervene directly on the front or continue to maintain chaos at the expense of the European Union? Despite the fact that the Pentagon is controlled thanks to safeguards, will Zelensky, in a moment of despair or madness, after having abused this white powder that he loves so much, cross the red line leading to a nuclear or other disaster? The latter boasted to a select committee during his visit to the headquarters of the European Union that he was in possession of an isotope weapon ("dirty bomb") and that he was considering its use, while his behavior significantly worried the deputies who witnessed his erratic gesticulation. This leads us to believe that Ukraine has become a dangerous and out of control country, with the potential for nuclear, bacteriological, and terrorist risks.

In Russian we say, "A dog that barks doesn't bite."

Let the West be wary of Vladimir Putin's silence

in front of this hysterical agitation.

XII. Annexes

A. BIOLOGICAL WEAPONS

B. SAGA OF EMAILS TO FRENCH OFFICIALS

C. SOROS

D. FUTURE OF UKRAINE. PROPOSAL
   FOR AN END OF CONFLICT

A. Biological Weapons

In the press we could read in February 2022 that the web admin of the US embassy in Kiev had removed part of the information relating to the development of biological weapons laboratories in Ukraine. But the cache from Google allowed us to make the connection between some of the file names which were provided to us on the financing of these laboratories and the US embassy in Kiev. This is how we were able to realize that these documents are very real and they still appear on the website, but are not easily accessible hence the reason for the link below so as not to lose sight of them. (See "Fact Sheets" column).

apar.tv/societe/lambassade-americaine-vient-de-retirer-de-son-site-web-tous-les-documents-relatifs-aux-laboratoires-darmes-biologiques-en-ukraine/

ACCUEIL   ART ⌄   MODE ⌄   SOCIÉTÉ ⌄

L'ambassade américaine vient de retirer de son site web tous les documents relatifs aux laboratoires d'armes biologiques en Ukraine

Les laboratoires biologiques américains en Ukraine sont-ils l'une des raisons de l'invasion russe ?

by **Mary Josephson** — 26 février 2022   Reading Time 22 mins read   ᴀA

Some of the viruses studied in these laboratories of the Ukrainian type P2 (low security level) are considered category 4 by the CNRS in France and would require a very high level of security (accessibility to the building protected by exterior fencing and guarding; in Odessa the Mechnikov Institute is in the center city and anyone can access it). Just go to the website of the US Embassy to realize the risk humanity is running. In 2016, the armed militia of Praviy Sektor attempted to access the Zaporizhya power plant to steal nuclear waste to make a dirty bomb.

What would happen if, in a fit of desperation, a group of this type seized vials of extremely dangerous viruses?

Link: https://ua.usembassy.gov/wp-content/uploads/sites/151/Pathogen-Asset-Control-System-Eng-ver3.pdf

Shortcut: https://tinyurl.com/US-UA-DTRO

D.T.R.O: (Defense Threat Reduction Office)

Biological Threat Reduction Pro... x +

← → C 🔒 ua.usembassy.gov/embassy/kyiv/sections-offices/defense-threat-reduction-office/biological-threat-reduction-program/

Visas   U.S. Citizen Services   Our Relationship   Education & Culture   **Embassy**   News & Events

Laboratory Construction

BTRP has upgraded many laboratories for the Ministry of Health and the State Food Safety and Consumer Protection Service of Ukraine, reaching Biosafety Level 2. In 2019, BTRP constructed two laboratories for the latter, one in Kyiv and one in Odesa.

Science Writing Mentorship Program (www.SWMProgramUA.com)

The Science Writing Mentorship Program (SWMP) was initiated focus of SWMP is to advance One Health initiatives and disease effective dissemination of scientific findings at BTRP-supported improve the science writing skills of participants to afford them obtaining grants for projects.

In addition, there is an annual Ukraine Regional One Health Rese participants of SWMP and many others. In 2019, the Symposium presentations.

Active Research Projects

BTRP supports many collaborative research projects through which Ukrainian and American scientists work together. A few recent examples are:

- "Risk Assessment of Selected Avian EDPs Potentially Carried by Migratory Birds over Ukraine"
- "Prevalence of Crimean Congo hemorrhagic fever virus and hantaviruses in Ukraine and the potential requirement for differential diagnosis of suspect leptospirosis patients"
- "The Spread of African Swine Fever Virus (ASFV) in Domestic Pigs and Wild Boars in Ukraine –

CNRS Classification

AGENT BIOLOGIQUE	Groupe	Note
Hantavirus		
Hantaan (fièvre hémorragique avec syndrome rénal)	3	
Virus Séoul	3	
Virus Puumala	2	
Virus Prospect Hill	2	
Autres Hantavirus	2	
Nairovirus		
Virus de la fièvre hémorragique de Crimée/Congo	4	
Virus Hazara	2	

Lviv Research Institute of Epidemiology and Hygiene (LRIEH) (PDF 101 KB)

Fact Sheets

Lviv Diagnostic Laboratory (PDF 101 KB)

Lviv Regional Diagnostic Veterinary Laboratory (PDF 101 KB)

Kharkiv Diagnostic Laboratory (PDF 98 KB)

Luhansk Regional Diagnostic Veterinary Laboratory (Luhansk RDVL) (PDF 91 KB)

Dnipropetrovsk Diagnostic Laboratory (PDF 102 KB)

Vinnytsia Diagnostic Laboratory (Vinnytsia DL) (PDF 99 KB)

PATHOGEN Asset Control System The Pathogen Asset Control System (PACS) is an electronic system for accounting, management, and control of biological agents. The application is designed to monitor the receipt, transfer, movement, and destruction of agents, as well as other actions performed with biological material. The system allows you to track materials of all kinds. Each item in the repository is marked with a unique barcode label. Barcode technology using a barcode reader allows for fast, error-free data entry, and provides an additional level of pathogen tracking security. With the help of barcode technology, the repository process is quick, convenient and secure.

PACS offers configurable access rights and a user management system. It also allows users to produce a variety of custom reports. PACS is a highly customizable tool that can be configured to meet local needs and regulations, simplify the data entry process, and organize data optimally. Extensive search and reporting capabilities allow users to produce the necessary data sets in the appropriate formats. PACS was first installed in Ukraine in test mode in November 2009 at the Interim Central Reference Laboratory of **Particularly Dangerous Pathogens (ICRL), located at the Ukrainian Anti-Plague Research Institute in Odessa (URAPI). All program interfaces and database information have been translated and localized for Ukraine. PACS is a turnkey solution.**

Implementation includes deployment, staff training, and support. The training program includes basic computer training for users with limited computer skills and in-depth PACS training. PACS is supported by a multi-layered technical support team including a hotline and support specialists based in Kiev.

The beneficiary of the technical assistance project is the Ministry of Health of Ukraine. The main objective of the program is inventory support for the consolidation of particularly dangerous pathogens within the ICRL.

The integrated electronic disease surveillance system (**AIDS**) is a software system designed to strengthen the surveillance and prevention of human and animal diseases under the One Health concept and facilitate compliance with the International Health Regulations (IHR) 2005. Key modules of the system include the human cases module, module vector surveillance module, laboratory module, epidemic module, administrative module and analysis, visualization and reporting (AVR) module with geographic information system (GIS) capabilities.

AIDS manages case data, case- and disease-specific investigations, aggregated data with corresponding samples, and case-related laboratory data. The system collects and distributes data, notifies events in near real time, provides access from desktop, web, and mobile devices, allowing it to link different levels and ministries of a national disease surveillance network in a secure manner. **AIDS** is customizable for each participating country to contain relevant content: list of diseases, specific reports, disease-specific investigation forms, among others. In 2011, EIDSS was introduced in Ukraine with installations at the following locations:

- Epidemiological sanitary center in Kiev (**CSES**)

- Mechnikov Anti-Plague Research Institute in Odessa (**BELOW**)

- Vinnytsia Oblast Sanitary- Epidemiological Station

- Vinnitsa City Sanitary- Epidemiological station

- Kalinowska Rayon Sanitary- Epidemiological station in Vinnytsia Oblast

- Zhitomir Oblast Sanitary- Epidemiological Station

- Khmel'nyts'ka Oblast- Epidemiological station regional site

-

The Mechnikov Institute sponsored by Soros, Open Society Foundation.... What was Soros' interest in sponsoring laboratories where extremely dangerous viruses are handled without the necessary level of security? It would be interesting to be able to access the recordings of the **AIDS** in order to see what was tested after the transfer of Covid-19 materials in November 2019 within this laboratory. Have they stored the provenance information of the transmitted strain?

I. I. MECHNIKOV
UKRAINIAN
ANTI-PLAGUE
RESEARCH INSTITUTE

ADDRESS

I. I. Mechnikov Ukrainian
Anti-Plague Research
Institute
of the Ministry
of Public Health
of Ukraine
2/4 Tserkovna St.
Odesa 65003, Ukraine
Tel./fax: +380 482 238-172

Yuriy Boshchenko,
Director
sn.u@te.net.ua,
vitatest@ua.fm
usas@tm.odessa.ua

trol over new foci formation;

• Biological properties of EDI, in order to estimate their epidemic potential;

• New chemical preparations against EDI;

• Reduction of EDI resistance to antibiotics by joint application of proteolysis inhibitors and antibiotics;

• Methodology for forecasting epidemics and principles of organization of preventive and counter epidemic measures;

• Improved diagnostics for EDI;

• Immuno-biological preparations and vaccines against emerging diseases;

• Evaluation of new antiviral and antimicrobial preparations by computer-assisted technologies; and

• Improvement of the system of sanitary protection of the territory of Ukraine from penetration and distribution of EDI.

The Institute has strong collaborative research connections with organizations from around the world, and it receives financial support from a variety of international organizations, including the STCU, SOROS Foundation, Civilian Research and Development Foundation, NEDA and the University of London. The I. I. Mechnikov Anti-plague Institute is included in the list of possible International Cooperative Centers in creating the Global Network for Monitoring and Control over biological pathogenic agents.

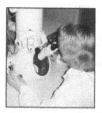

Electron microscopy

Working in the biosecurity unit

Below is a copy of all documents received and verified on the website of the US Embassy in Ukraine. More than $20M spent on laboratory installation, B&V cited in terms of systematic subcontracting, which corroborates the information found in the government database in the chapter concerning laboratories.

Source: https://ua.usembassy.gov/wp-content/uploads/sites/151/Kyiv-IVM-Fact-Sheet-Eng-1.pdf

Institute of Veterinary Medicine of the National Academy of Agrarian Sciences

Fact Sheet

Technical Assistance Project – Memorandum on technical assistance for project recipients of the State Committee of Veterinary Medicine of Ukraine and National Academy of Agrarian Sciences of Ukraine. Registration card #2225-04, dated 05.21.2012

Donor – The Department of Defense of the United States of America (DoD)

Beneficiary/Executive Agent - The State Committee of Veterinary Medicine of Ukraine (now the State Veterinary and Phytosanitary Service of Ukraine)

Recipient – Institute of Veterinary Medicine of the National Academy of Agrarian Science
Address: 30, Donetska street, Kiev, Ukraine
POC: Dr. Serhiy Nychyk, Director

Contractor Team - Integrating Contractor: Black & Veatch. Ukrainian Subcontractors: Project Technichniy Center (Designer) & Mediamax (Construction & Equipment supply).

Design Oversight (Avtornadzor) – Mutilin Sergey Volodimirovich

Construction Oversight (Technadzor) - Ziryanov Dmitro Vicktorovich

Expert Examination of Design Approval – The Conceptual Design was approved by the MoH Central Regime Commission on July 11, 2012. The Working Design was approved by Dr. Nychyk, Director of IVM on August 29, 2012.

Construction permit – The Declaration for the beginning of construction was signed by Dr. Nychyk, Director of IVM and registered by GASK (State Architectural Construction Inspection in Kiev oblast) on September 07, 2012.

State Acceptance - "Construction Ready for Operation Declaration" was signed by Dr. Nychyk, Director of IVM on April 08, 2013 and applied for registration by GASK (State Architectural Construction Inspection in Kiev oblast) on April 15, 2013.

Transfer of Custody and Sustainment Memorandum of Understanding - Transfer of Custody is in process.

EDPs Permit - Permit for working with Pathogens is in process.

USG Investment - Total cost of laboratory: **$2,109,375.23 USD** ($1,217,164 for design and construction and $762,134 for equipment and furniture)

Source: https://ua.usembassy.gov/wp-content/uploads/sites/151/Zakarpatska-DL-Fact-Sheet-Eng.pdf

Zakarpartska Diagnostic Laboratory
Zakarpartska Oblast Laboratory Center
96, Sobranetska Street., Uzhgorod

Fact Sheet

Technical Assistance Project - Technical Assistance Plan for designated recipients of the Ministry of Health of Ukraine. Registration card #2225-04 dated 21.05.2012.

Donor – the Department of Defense of the United States of America

Beneficiary/Executive Agent - the Ministry of Health of Ukraine

Recipient – Zakarpatska Oblast Laboratory Center (former Zakarpatska Oblast SES)
Address: 96, Sobranetska Str., Uzhgorod
POC: Dr.,Vladimir Mikhailovich Markovich, Director if the Oblast Laboratory Center

Contractor Team - Integrating Contractor: Black & Veatch. Ukrainian Subcontractors: - Ekzotika LTD-Uzhgorod (Designer) & RK-Center (Construction) & Mediamax (Equipment supply).

Design Oversight (Avtonadzor) - Ivan Andriyovych Mygalko

Construction Oversight (Technadzor) - Sergey Yurievich Petrovsiy

Expert Examination of Design Approval - Conceptual Design was approved by the MoH Central Regime Commission on August 11, 2010. The Working Design was approved by Zakarpatska Oblast "Ukrbudderzhexpertise" on December 07, 2010.

Construction permit - The Construction Permit was signed by GASK (State Architectural Construction Inspection in Zakarpatska oblast) on December 29, 2010

State Acceptance - "Construction Acceptance Act" was signed by the Chief Doctor (Dr. Vladimir Mikhailovich Markovych) on July 15, 2011. Building Certificate Compliance was signed by GASK (State Architectural Construction Inspection in Zakarpatska oblast) on July 23, 2011.

Transfer of Custody and Sustainment Memorandum of Understanding - The TOC and S&T MoU were signed by the Chief Doctor (Dr. Vladimir Mikhailovich Markovych) on February 16, 2012.

EDPs Permit - The permit for working with Pathogens was issued by Regime Commission of MoH on March 02, 2012.

USG Investment - Total cost of laboratory: **USD$1,920,432** (USD$1,516,354 for Design & Construction; USD$404,078 for lab equipment and furniture)

Source: https://ua.usembassy.gov/wp-content/uploads/sites/151/130202-Vinnitsa-DL-Fact-Sheet.pdf

Vinnytsia Diagnostic Laboratory (Vinnytsia DL)
Vinnytsia Oblast Laboratory Center
11, Malinovskogo str., Vinnytsia

Fact Sheet

Technical Assistance Project – Technical Assistance Plan for designated recipients of the Ministry of Health of Ukraine. Registration card #2225-04 dated 21.05.2012.

Donor – the Department of Defense of the United States of America

Beneficiary/Executive Agent – the Ministry of Health of Ukraine

Recipient – Vinnytsia Oblast Laboratory Center (former - Vinnytsia Oblast SES)
Address: 11, Malinovskogo str., Vinnytsia
POC: Dr. Valentina Grigoryevna Zaytseva, Head of the Laboratory Center

Contractor Team - Integrating Contractor: Black & Veatch. Ukrainian Subcontractors: Vinnytsia Design Institute of MoH-Lviv (Designer) & RK-Center (Construction) & Biolabtech (Equipment supply).

Design Oversight (Avtonadzor) – Architectural Construction Engineering Company Vinnytsia

Construction Oversight (Technadzor) – O.I.Kuprienko

Expert Examination of Design Approval - The Conceptual Design was approved by MoH Central Regime Commission on November 06, 2009. The Working Design was approved by Vinnytsia "Ukrbudderzhexpertise" on November 13, 2009.

Construction permit - The Construction Permit was signed by GASK (State Architectural Construction Inspection in Vinnytsia oblast) on May 05, 2010.

State Acceptance – "Construction Acceptance Act" was signed by the Chief Doctor (Valentina Grigoryevna Zaytseva) on August 30, 2010. Building Certificate Compliance was signed by GASK (State Architectural Construction Inspection in Vinnytsia oblast) on August 31, 2010.

Transfer of Custody and Sustainment Memorandum of Understanding - The TOC and S&T MoU were signed by the Chief State Doctor Valentina Grigoryevna Zaytseva on December 01, 2010.

EDPs Permit – The permit for working with Pathogens was issued by Regime Commission of MoH on December 22, 2010.

USG Investment - Total cost of laboratory: **USD$1,504,840** (USD$1,106,610 for Design & Construction; USD$398,230 for lab equipment and furniture)

Source: https://ua.usembassy.gov/wp-content/uploads/sites/151/1301231-
Ternopil-DL-Fact-Sheet.pdf

Ternopil Diagnostic Laboratory
Ternopil Oblast Laboratory Center
13 Fedkovycha str., Ternopil

Fact Sheet

Technical Assistance Project - Technical Assistance Plan for designated recipients of the Ministry of Health of Ukraine. Registration card #2225-04 dated 21.05.2012.

Donor – the Department of Defense of the United States of America

Beneficiary/Executive Agent - the Ministry of Health of Ukraine

Recipient – Ternopil Oblast Laboratory Center (former Ternopil Oblast SES)
Address: 13 Fedkovycha str., Ternopil
POC: Stepan Semenovych Dnistrian, Director of Oblast Laboratory Center

Contractor Team - Integrating Contractor: Black & Veatch. Ukrainian Subcontractors: Techno Project (Designer) & Macrochem (Construction & Equipment supply).

Design Oversight (Avtornadzor) - Vasyl Petrovich Lysenko

Construction Oversight (Technadzor) - Yaroslav Nikolaevich Malichenko

Expert Examination of Design Approval - Conceptual Design was approved by the MoH Regime Commission on November 24, 2011. The Working Design was approved by Ternopil "Ukrbudderzhexpertise" on April 11, 2012.

Construction permit - The Declaration for start of construction was signed by the Chief Doctor of Ternopil Oblast SES (Dr. Stepan Semenovych Dnistrian) and registered at GASK (State Architectural Construction Inspection in Ternopil oblast) on April 20, 2012.

State Acceptance - "Construction Ready for Operation Declaration" was signed by the Chief Doctor (Dr. Stepan Semenovych Dnistrian) and registered at GASK (State Architectural Construction Inspection in Ternopil oblast) on December 25, 2012.

Transfer of Custody and Sustainment Memorandum of Understanding - Transfer of Custody is in process.

EDPs Permit - Permit for working with Pathogens will be obtained after signing TOC and MoU.

USG Investment - Total cost of laboratory: **USD$1,755,786** (USD$1,312,810 for Design & Construction; USD$442,976 for lab equipment and furniture)

Source: https://ua.usembassy.gov/wp-content/uploads/sites/151/130121-Lviv-DL-Fact-Sheet_final-ENG.pdf

Lviv Diagnostic Laboratory
Lviv Oblast Laboratory Center
27, Krupyarskaya Str. Lviv

Fact Sheet

Technical Assistance Project - Technical Assistance Plan for Designated Recipients of the Ministry of Health of Ukraine. Registration card #2225-04 dated 21.05.2012.

Donor – the Department of Defense of the United States of America

Beneficiary/Executive Agent – the Ministry of Health of Ukraine

Recipient – Lviv Oblast Laboratory Center (former Oblast SES)
        Address: 27, Krupyarskaya Str. Lviv
        POC: Dr. Lubamira Evgenivna Shepelenko, Acting Director of Laboratory Center

Contractor Team - Integrating Contractor: Black & Veatch. Ukrainian Subcontractors: Central Design Institute - Lviv (Designer) & RK-Center (Construction) & Mediamax (equipment supply).

Design Oversight (Avtonadzor) – Central Design Institute, Lviv - Evgeni Vasiliovich Svetlichniy

Construction Oversight (Technadzor) - Bogdan Ivanovich Ostrovskiy

Expert Examination of Design Approval - The Conceptual Design was approved by MoH Central Regime Commission on August 11, 2011. The Working Design was approved by Lviv "Ukrbudderzhexpertise" on August 12, 2011.

Construction permit - The Declaration for start to construction was signed by the Chief Doctor of Lviv Oblast SES (Dr. Roman Mikhailovich Pavliv) and registered at GASK (State Architectural Construction Inspection in Lviv oblast) on July 13, 2010

State Acceptance - "Construction Ready for Operation Declaration" was signed by the Acting Chief Doctor, Dr. Mikola Vasilievich Urbanvoich, and registered at GASK (State Architectural Construction Inspection in Lviv oblast) on December 25, 2012

Transfer of Custody and Sustainment Memorandum of Understanding - The TOC and S&T MoU were signed by the Chief Doctor of Lviv Oblast SES, Dr. Roman Mikhailovich Pavliv, on July 24, 2012.

EDPs Permit - The permit for working with Pathogens was issued by Regime Commission of MoH on July 2, 2012.

USG Investment - Total cost of laboratory: **USD$1,927,158** (USD$1,523,080 for Design & Construction; USD$404,078 for lab equipment, furniture, and installation)

State Regional Laboratory of Veterinary Medicine
Luhansk Regional Diagnostic Veterinary Laboratory (Luhansk RDVL)
9a, Krasnodonnaya Str. Luhansk

Fact Sheet

Technical Assistance Project - Memorandum on technical assistance for project recipients of the State Committee of Veterinary Medicine of Ukraine and National Academy of Agrarian Sciences of Ukraine

Donor – the Department of Defense of the United States of America (DoD)

Beneficiary/Executive Agent - the State Committee of Veterinary Medicine of Ukraine (nowadays – the State Veterinary and Phytosanitary Service of Ukraine)

Recipient – State Regional Laboratory of Veterinary Medicine
          Address: 9a Krasnodonnaya Str. Luhansk.
          POC: Dr. Valeriy Nikolayevich Bondar, Director

Contractor Team - Integrating Contractor: Black & Veatch. Ukrainian Subcontractors: Project Development Center (designer) & Mediamax (Construction & Equipment supply).

Design Oversight (Avtornadzor) – Sergiy Vladymyrovych Mutili

Construction Oversight (Technadzor) - Dmytro Vyctorovych Zyvianov

Expert Examination of Design Approval - The Conceptual Design was approved by MoH Central Regime Commission on March 13, 2012. The Working Design was approved by Luhansk Director of the Laboratory, Dr. Valeriy Mykolayovych Bondar, on June 06, 2012.

Construction permit - The Declaration for start of construction was signed by the Director of Luhansk State Regional Laboratory of Veterinary Medicine (Dr. Valeriy Mykolayovych Bondar) and registered at GASK (State Architectural Construction Inspection in Luhansk oblast) on May 31, 2012

State Acceptance - Construction works completed, all furniture and equipment were installed. O&M training continues and ready for final inspection on February 14, 2013.

Transfer of Custody and Sustainment Memorandum of Understanding - Transfer of Custody is in process.

EDPs Permit - Permit for working with Pathogens will be obtained after signing TOC and MoU.

USG Investment - Total cost of laboratory: USD$1,746,312 (USD$1,267,124 for Design & Construction; USD$479,188 for lab equipment and furniture)

Source: https://ua.usembassy.gov/wp-content/uploads/sites/151/Kherson-DL-Fact-Sheet-Eng.pdf

Kherson Diagnostic Laboratory
Kherson Oblast Laboratory Center
3 Uvarova Str., Kherson

Fact Sheet

Technical Assistance Project - Technical Assistance Plan for designated recipients of the Ministry of Health of Ukraine. Registration card #2225-04 dated 21.05.2012.

Donor – the Department of Defense of the United States of America

Beneficiary/Executive Agent - the Ministry of Health of Ukraine

Recipient – Kherson Oblast Laboratory Center (former Kherson Oblast SES)
Address: 3 Uvarova Str., Kherson
POC: Dr. Vasyl Oleksiovych Stryapochuk, Director of the Oblast Laboratory Center

Contractor Team - Integrating Contractor: Black & Veatch. Ukrainian Subcontractors: Techno Project (Designer) & Macrochem (Construction & Equipment supply).

Design Oversight (Avtornadzor) - Vasyl Petrovych Lysenko

Construction Oversight (Technadzor) - Pavel Yakovlevich Andrievskiy

Expert Examination of Design Approval - Conceptual Design was approved by the MoH Central Regime Commission on September 23, 2011. The Working Design was approved by Kherson "Ukrbudderzhexpertise" on February 21, 2012.

Construction permit - The Declaration for start of construction was signed by the Chief Docor of Kherson Oblast SES (Vasyl Oleksiovych Striapochuk) and registered at GASK (State Architectural Construction Inspection in Kherson oblast) on April 03, 2012.

State Acceptance - "Construction Ready for Operation Declaration" was signed by the Chief Doctor (Dr. Vasyl Oleksiovych Stryapochuk) on December 25, 2012 and registered at GASK (State Architectural Construction Inspection in Kherson oblast) on December 28, 2012.

Transfer of Custody and Sustainment Memorandum of Understanding - Transfer of Custody is in process.

EDPs Permit - Permit for working with Pathogens will be obtained after signing TOC and MoU.

USG Investment - Total cost of laboratory: **USD$1,728,822** (USD$1,285,845 for Design & Construction; USD$442,977 for lab equipment and furniture)

Source: https://ua.usembassy.gov/wp-content/uploads/sites/151/130131-Kharkiv-DL-Fact-Sheet.pdf

Kharkiv Diagnostic Laboratory
Kharkiv Oblast Laboratory Center
Pomirky region, Kharkiv

Fact Sheet

Technical Assistance Project - Technical Assistance Plan for designated recipients of the Ministry of Health of Ukraine. Registration card #2225-04 dated 21.05.2012.

Donor – the Department of Defense of the United States of America

Beneficiary/Executive Agent - the Ministry of Health of Ukraine

Recipient – Kharkiv Oblast Laboratory Center (former Kharkiv Oblast SES)
    Address: Pomirky region, Kharkiv
    POC: Dr. Tatyana Mykhaylivna Kolpakova, Chief Doctor of Oblast Laboratory Center

Contractor Team - Integrating Contractor: Black & Veatch. Ukrainian Subcontractors: Techno Project (Designer) & Macrochem (Construction & Equipment supply).

Design Oversight (Avtornadzor) - Vasyl Petrovich Lysenko

Construction Oversight (Technadzor) - Elena Aleksandrovna Sobol

Expert Examination of Design Approval - The Conceptual Design was approved by MoH Central Regime Commission on September 23, 2011. The Working Design was approved by Kharkiv "Ukrbudderzhexpertise" on May 08, 2012.

Construction permit - The Declaration for start of construction was signed by the Chief Doctor of Kharkiv Oblast SES (Dr. Tatyana Mykhaylivna Kolpakova) on May 28, 2012 and registered at GASK (State Architectural Construction Inspection in Kharkiv oblast) on May 31, 2012.

State Acceptance - "Construction Ready for Operation Declaration" was signed by the Acting Chief Doctor (Dr. Lubov Stepanivna Makhoya) on December 25, 2012 and registered at GASK (State Architectural Construction Inspection in Kharkiv oblast) on December 29, 2012.

Transfer of Custody and Sustainment Memorandum of Understanding - Transfer of Custody is in process.

EDPs Permit - Permit for working with Pathogens will be obtained after signing TOC and MoU.

USG Investment - Total cost of laboratory: USD$1,638,375 (USD$1,195,398 for Design & Construction; USD$442,977 for lab equipment and furniture)

Source: https://ua.usembassy.gov/wp-content/uploads/sites/151/130202-Dnipropetrovsk-DL-Fact-Sheet.pdf

Dnipropetrovsk State Regional Diagnostic Veterinary Laboratory
(Dnipropetrovsk RDVL)
48, Kirova ave., Dnipropetrovsk

Information Summary

Technical Assistance Plan - Memorandum for technical assistance to designated recipients of the State Committee of Veterinary Medicine of Ukraine and the National Academy of Agrarian Sciences of Ukraine. Registration Card # 2225-04 on 21.05.2012.

Donor – the United States Defense Threat Reduction Agency (DTRA)

Beneficiary/Executive Agent - State Committee of Veterinary Medicine of Ukraine (currently - State Veterinary and Phytosanitary Service of Ukraine)

Recipient – Dnipropetrovsk State Regional Laboratory of Veterinary Medicine; 48, Kirova ave., Dnipropetrovsk. Malimon Oleksandr Grygorovych, Director

Contractor Team - Integrating Contractor: Black & Veatch Special Projects Corp. Ukrainian Subcontractors: Project Technical Center (Designer) & Mediamax (Construction & Equipment Supplier).

Design Oversight –Project Technical Center, Sergey Volodymyrovych Mutilin

Construction Oversight – Georgii Petrovych Granich

Design-project Expert Assessment - Draft project was approved by the Central Regime Committee of the Ministry of Health of Ukraine on March27, 2012. Working design-project was approved by the Decree of the Director of Dnipropetrovsk SRLVM on June 21, 2013

Construction permit – Declaration for construction works was signed by the Director of Dnipropetrovsk Regional State Veterinary Laboratory (Oleksandr Malimon) and registered in the State Architectural Construction Inspection in the Dnipropetrovsk region on July 19, 2012.

Operational readiness - Declaration of facility operational readiness was provided to the Director of the Dnipropetrovsk State Regional Veterinary Laboratory to sign and submit to the State Construction Inspection. Veterinary Working Group inspected the facility on May 23, 2013. The Black & Veatch has received the comments and sent the answer on July 7, 2013.

Transfer of Custody (Acceptance Act) and Memorandum of Understanding – The TOC was signed on April 17, 2013

EDPs Permit – The obtaining of the Permit for working with pathogens is in process.

Certification of Attestation / Accreditation - Certification of Attestation / Accreditation process will be started after obtaining Permit for working with Pathogens.

USG Investment - Total cost of laboratory: **$1, 810, 547 USD** ($1,298,805,19 for Design & Construction; $511,742 for lab equipment and furniture)

Dnipropetrovsk Diagnostic Laboratory
Dnipropetrovsk Oblast Laboratory Center
39/A, Filosofs'ka str., Dnipropetrovsk

Fact Sheet

Technical Assistance Project - technical assistance plan for relevant recipients of Ministry of Health of Ukraine.

Donor – the Department of Defense of USA

Beneficiary/Executive Agent - Ministry of Health of Ukraine

Recipient – Dnipropetrovsk Oblast Laboratory Center (former Dnipropetrovsk Oblast SES)
         Address: 26, Smidta /39/A, Filisofs'ka Str., Dnipropetrovsk.
         POC: Dr. Valeriy Grygorovych Kapshuk, Chief Doctor

Contractor Team - Integrating Contractor: Black & Veatch. Ukrainian Subcontractors: Dnipropetrovsk Domus-Proekt (Designer) & RK-Center (Construction) & Mediamax (Equipment supply).

Design Oversight (Avtornadzor) – Dnipropetrovsk Domus-Proekt

Construction Oversight (Technadzor) – D.V Zyrianov

Expert Examination of Design Approval - The Conceptual Design was approved by MoH Central Regime Commission on August 11, 2010. The Working Design was approved by Dnipropetrovsk "Ukrbudderzhexpertise" on December 01, 2010.

Construction permit - The Construction Permit was signed GASK (State Architectural Construction Inspection in Dnipropetrovsk oblast) on December 21, 2010.

State Acceptance – "Construction Acceptance Act" was signed by the Chief Doctor Kapshuk Valeriy Grygorovych on October 03, 2011 and registered by GASK (State Architectural Construction Inspectorate) on October 03, 2011.

Transfer of Custody and Sustainment Memorandum of Understanding – The TOC and S&T MoU was signed by the Chief Doctor, Dr. Valeriy Grygorovych Kapshuk on January 18, 2012.

EDPs Permit – The permit for working with Pathogens was issued by Regime Commission of MoH on February 15, 2012.

USG Investment - Total cost of laboratory: **USD$1,935,557** (USD$1,531,479 for Design & Construction; USD$404,078 for lab equipment and furniture)

B. Saga of Emails to Different French Politicians

EMAIL to Bruno Le Maire, Sept 2015. The content of the email is the subject of the book. I mention the Nazification of Ukraine, the murders, torture, the genocide in Donbass, the MH17 affair…

Bruno Le Maire, Minister of Economy, knew ALL the details of what was happening since September 2015

Bruno Le Maire <contact@brunolemaire.fr>
to me ▾

Tue, Sep 22, 2015, 11:09 PM   ☆   ↩   ⋮

文A French ▾   >   English ▾   Translate message

Turn off for: French ✕

Cher Monsieur,

Je vous remercie pour votre message et pour la confiance qu'il traduit.

Je suis avec une grande attention la situation en Ukraine, l'engagement de la Russie dans ce pays et la position de la France à cet égard.

N'hésitez pas à me transmettre toutes les informations que vous estimerez utiles à mon bonne compréhension de ce dossier très sensible. J'en prendrai connaissance avec le plus grand intérêt.

Bien à vous,

Bruno Le Maire

Le 31/08/2015 16:11, laurent-pellet thierry a écrit :

Formulaire de contact

civilite : mme
nom : laurent-pellet
prenom : thierry
adresse_1 : Malaya zhitomyrskaya 5 #45
adresse_2 :
cp : 1100
ville : Kiev/ Ukraine
tel_fixe :
tel_portable
email :

UKRAINE   ⁻ ₓˣ x

EMAIL TO THE PRESIDENT OF THE SENATE: To prevent the arrival of the founder of the 1st Ukrainian Nazi party in **our institutions** I called G. Larcher's secretary. An email followed to summarize the discussion and, of course, keep a written record. "Lobster-Man" F. De Rugy in the parliament, G. Larcher in the senate and the minister of foreign affairs JY. Le Drian received with great fanfare the organizer of the Maïdan and Odessa killings, Andriy Parubiy. He also did a short internship in a psychiatric hospital in his youth in Lviv, from which he escaped!

Visite de Andriy Parubiy - Suite à notre conversation téléphonique ⊃

WnV   thierry laurent ▆▆▆▆▆▆▆   Jun 11, 2018, 10:25 AM
to sp.president@senat.fr ▾

Monsieur le président du Sénat Gérard Larcher,

Je me nomme Thierry Laurent Pellet, Entrepreneur internet, j'ai vécu en Ukraine presque 10 ans, 3 à Odessa et 6 à Kiev, Malaya zhitomirskaya #5, apt 45, 50 m de Maidan. J'ai été le conseillé de Thierry Mariani que j'ai rencontré à l'assemblée nationale pour lui remettre des documents jamais publiés sur l'affaire du MH17 (émis par le safety board of Deutschland) et je l'ai renseigné sur tous les événements de la crise Ukrainienne (assassinat de journalistes et de députés de la Rada [Oles Bysina, Olga Moros, Irina Bereznaya], torture de citoyens...), et tout ceci commendité par Arseniy Avakov (ministre de l'intérieur) et Andriy Parubiy (fondateur du 1er parti néo nazi ukrainien encensant Stepan Bandera, le boucher de Treblinka et de Baby Yard et président de la Rada). Ce dernier que vous vous apprêtez à recevoir cette après midi est le team leader des snippers du Maidan (ci joint photo)et l'organisateur du massacre d'Odessa (ci joint la photo d'une femme enceinte assassinée par strangulation, en zoomant vous observerez les traces sur son cou et une batte de baseball qui ne devrait pas s'y trouver). Mr Mariani a d'ailleurs reçu une délégation de famille de victimes qui lui ont décrit des horreurs. Étant moi même en relation avec l'avocat Odessien en charge de l'affaire, Mr ▆▆▆▆▆▆▆, je suis en possession d'un ▆   UKRAINE   – ⤢ ×

NB: typo this afternoon in the screenshot.

Paruby, co-founder of the Ukrainian UNO-UPA Nazi party during a neo-Nazi meeting in the Lviv region in 1988.

Note the socialist minister, Le Drian next to a neo-Nazi at the Ministry of Foreign Affairs, this is a bit out of place, but nowadays, anything is possible since giraffes are streetlamps without bulbs...

C. Soros: Control and Influence

Soros, real name Schwartz, who is persona non grata in Russia and Hungary, founded in 1993 an NGO proselytizing globalism to establish global governance "Open Society." In a few numbers:

- A budget of 32 billion dollars

- 120 offices around the world and many more unknown

- 1300 direct employees (not counting the ancillary funded NGOs)

- Income $370 M (NGO: non-profit organization of international utility?)

- Buys the votes of 200 Euro deputies

- Control by four judges of the ECHR

- Finances African/Middle East migration in Europe and the South

- Americans in the USA…

- Finances presidential candidates (Macron, Clinton, Obama)

- Overthrows governments (Ukraine, USA, etc.)

- Etc…

Soros' Open Society Site: http://tinyurl.com/OPENSOCLOC

http://tinyurl.com/50IRFUA

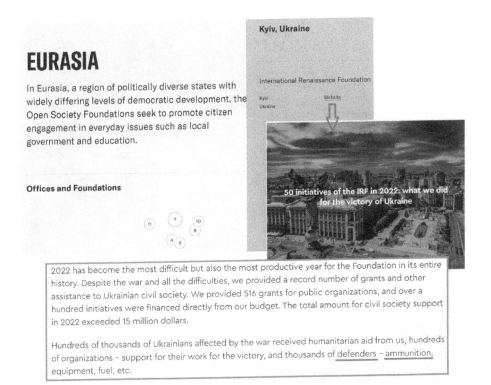

EURASIA

In Eurasia, a region of politically diverse states with widely differing levels of democratic development, the Open Society Foundations seek to promote citizen engagement in everyday issues such as local government and education.

Offices and Foundations

Kyiv, Ukraine

International Renaissance Foundation

Kyiv
Ukraine   Website

50 initiatives of the IRF in 2022: what we did for the victory of Ukraine

2022 has become the most difficult but also the most productive year for the Foundation in its entire history. Despite the war and all the difficulties, we provided a record number of grants and other assistance to Ukrainian civil society. We provided 516 grants for public organizations, and over a hundred initiatives were financed directly from our budget. The total amount for civil society support in 2022 exceeded 15 million dollars.

Hundreds of thousands of Ukrainians affected by the war received humanitarian aid from us, hundreds of organizations – support for their work for the victory, and thousands of defenders – ammunition, equipment, fuel, etc.

According to the site, Soros spent $230 million to overthrow this country. Would the NGO International Renaissance Foundation, have the right to buy weapons and ammunition to supply them to neo-Nazi organizations?

29
years
———

The Foundation has been
working on the development
of civic society in Ukraine

230+
million USD
———

The Foundation has invested
about in the development of
democracy in Ukraine in the
course of its activities

9+
thousand projects and initiatives

Have been supported by the
Foundation

400+
projects
———

Per year are supported by
the Foundation in the last
decade

253+
million hryvnias
———

The Foundation spent on the
support of civil initiatives in
2018

57
specialists

Work in the Foundation for
the development of Ukraine

INTERNATIONAL
RENAISSANCE
FOUNDATION

An example of a Polish NGO certainly working for Soros…

Opendialog www.ODFoundation.eu

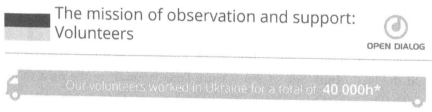

The mission of observation and support: Volunteers

OPEN DIALOG

Our volunteers worked in Ukraine for a total of **40 000h***

Volunteers
480
applied to us

Persons
54
went to Ukraine

The age of the volunteers
20 - 80
ranged between

Our volunteers
have been working
on the Maidan
76
days now**

Volunteers from
7
countries applied
to us***

We observed
the developments in
14
cities and towns****

* 54 volunteers working an average of 10 h a day for 14 days each
** From 1 January, 2014 to 7 April, 2014
*** Poland, Ukraine, Kazakhstan, Belarus, England, Canada, Latvia

**** Kiev, Lviv, Drohobych, Dnipropetrovsk, Cherkasy, Poltava, Donetsk,
Zaporizhe,Kharkov, Odessa, Sevastopol, Simpheropol, Yalta, Perevalne

Extract from the *New York Times* reporting the financing of the Hillary Rodham Clinton campaign, by the same Soros. When you give millions to a politician, what do you get in exchange?

The New York Times   **BUSINESS** | George Soros Transfers Billions to Open Society Founda... 🎁 Give this article

> Mr. Soros eventually became one of the biggest donors to Democrats, including Mrs. Clinton. During the last election cycle, Mr. Soros gave millions to super PACs that opposed Mr. Trump and supported other Democratic candidates and causes. He also bet big in the markets that Mr. Trump would lose the election, a wager that cost him about $1 billion.

D. Future of Ukraine

Here are the future borders at the end of the conflict that I projected in March 2022 with my US senior contacts in view of my ethnic knowledge and the ambient geopolitical dynamics. It was the most reasonable Balkanization solution and which would have avoided many disasters; Novorossiya had to unite with Russia.

In February 2023 we intercepted the map (below) in a Polish magazine and on TV after an interview with Duda, the president of Poland. The boundaries thus defined are quite surprising. We measure the curious progress of Romania which plans to seize Moldova which is 50% pro-Russian in terms of its population. Maia Sandu, the new post-Dodon Moldovan president (from the World Bank), imposed the Romanian language as the only national language, and Romanian senator Diana Şoşoacă submitted a legislative initiative to parliament, which provides for the annexation of certain former territories Romanians, today Ukrainians. An additional source of friction is to come with a former president of Moldova Do-don, threatening Ukraine with his intrusive desire towards Russian Transnistria. Ukraine is thus reduced to nothing by its own "friends and allies."

This new configuration would make Ukraine what it could already have been, a sort of security belt between Russia and Europe. What a waste to refuse federalization. A severe punishment that the nationalists being killed on the front line today will really appreciate. At a time when Poland has just announced that the NATO headquarters in Europe is taking place on its soil, we can measure the hegemonic desire of its government in the region: an area of Volhynia, Ukraine has been sold by Zelensky so a Polish base can be set up there. The map below is really coming together to Ukraine's detriment.

Transnistria, a pro-Russian separatist state on the border (East-oriented North-South) of Moldova, which hosts a significant military warehouse of the former USSR, is the object of all covetousness and prevents any unification of the map thus defined. Ukraine or Romania will try to bring this strip of land into their own hands if Russia gives up on conquering the Odessa region, which could be seen as a provocation. This is a new hot spot that is about to flare up because Russia will not abandon its people.

That said, isn't the great Ukrainian sellout organized by Zelensky himself by orchestrating the destruction of all the country's armed forces through his stubbornness in the Bakhmut region which has become a real butchery? Therefore, there would no longer be any resistance to the resolution of this plan... It is very plausible but at one's own risk!

E. Proposal for an End of Conflict

The Patriots International Alliance
To End the Russia-Ukraine Conflict

PRESS RELEASE

On behalf of

Global Humanitarian Crisis Prevention and Response UNIT

&

The Legacy National Security Advisory Group (US)

In the interest of global security, The Patriots International Alliance (Alliance) seeks to prevent a potential nuclear conflict associated with the war in Ukraine and, instead, promote international peace by calling for both sides – Russia and Ukraine, to promptly call for an unconditional ceasefire and make room for peace talks.

In doing so, the Alliance calls upon the President of the United States of America and the Prime Minister of Great Britain to immediately cease all forms of military aid to Ukraine and instead assist in peace negotiations between Russia and Ukraine.

The Patriots International Alliance's recommendation is based upon the following points:

1. The United States of America and the United Kingdom of Great Britain have provided military support to Ukraine based on the **false premise-** that, under President Vladimir Vladimirovich Putin, the Russian Federation has invaded a sovereign state *without* provocation.

Below, the Alliance contradicts the assertion in 1 and presents the points as to why the Russian Federation initiated the Special Military Operation (SMO) in February 2022.

   a. NATO's provocation:

NATO's intention to deliberately provoke Russia is most clearly present in the admission on behalf of Ms. Merkel and Mr. Hollande, that the Minsk agreement signed by Ukraine in 2014 was merely to buy time for Ukraine's NATO-backed militarisation.

Contrary to Ukraine, Russia has adhered to its Minsk agreement clauses.

The US and the rest of NATO expanded at least five times. This was contrary to assurances given by three US presidents and in contradiction to numerous international agreements on indivisibility so as not to strengthen the West at the expense of the East. Those agreements, stretching from 1990 to 2010, were designed to prevent the event on 24 February 2022.

Additionally, Ukraine's failed to implement Minsk I and Minsk II to which it had agreed, under the Normandy Format with Germany, France, and Russia.

Further, Ukraine sought to join NATO, at great US and NATO encouragement, even though, it was contrary to its own 1990 Declaration on State Sovereignty of Ukraine- to remain non-aligned.

In December 2021, Moscow sent Washington and NATO it's concerns over these violations of expansion to the border of the Russian Federation, but those warnings were ignored.

b. Neo-Nazi Afflictions of Ukraine:

It is well documented that the Armed Forces of Ukraine (AFU) and the associated Nazi groups of Ukraine have committed crimes against humanity, including various forms of torture of civilians, ethnic cleansing, and extra-judicial killings since before 2014.

Taken from – Antonopoulos, P. in https://infobrics.org/post/34477 - The 32nd UN Security report noted a '51% increase in Donbas casualties between February 1 and July 31, 2021, accounting for 62 killed and wounded civilians. 81% of civilians died from Ukrainian shelling, and more than 80% of hits during the reporting period led to destruction. Among the victims, a significant number were young children. The number of ceasefire violations from February 1 to July 31 was noted to have increased by 369%. With these harrowing figures, at least 3,390 confirmed civilian deaths have occurred since April 14, 2014.'

c. US Security Threat to Russia:

The Ukrainian territory is home to several US Department of Defence (DoD) - run biological laboratories, where sensitive work on enhancing the pathogenicity of microorganisms was being conducted.

Documents obtained by the Russian Federation during the SMO reveal that the engineered biological materials and other related products were being tested on the AFU members.

Further, extensive DNA sampling of ethnic Russians was also conducted under the direct orders of the US Air Force.

Ukraine was also procuring drones with the specialized ability to release bioweapons in and over the Russian territories close to Ukraine.

In light of the above clauses (1a, 1b, 1c), it is clear that the Russian Federation, through its launch of the Special Military Operation (SMO) in February 2022, has acted (*according to Article 51 of the UN Charter*), in self-defence of its territory and its people.

2. During the course of the SMO, both, the United States of America and Great Britain have severely jeopardized their own national security by:

    a. Keeping their public deliberately misinformed, disinformed, and uninformed of the true nature and objectives of the SMO.

    b. Misleading their public into **unknowingly supporting** fascism through a vicious campaign of media censorship and psyops to promote **Russophobia**.

    c. Drawing the world precariously close to a nuclear conflict.
       Britain's actions of providing Depleted Uranium shells to Ukraine and further, justifying its actions by falsely claiming that the toxicity from these shells is not an issue, despite scientific evidence to the contrary, is a blatant and daring provocation of the Russian Federation at the expense of its security.

As Defence and Intelligence Community veterans, we have served our nations in good faith and with pride and honour.

To stand by and do nothing is beyond our ethics and moral code, while our national security and, more so, the world's security is put at risk by the actions of the United States of America and Great Britain.

The Alliance, therefore, proposes the following recommendations to be adopted with immediate effect by the United States of America and Great Britain-

1. Cease all forms of support (Military and Intelligence) to Ukraine immediately.
2. Promptly recall all US and UK nationals serving in any form in the territories of Ukraine.
3. Cease all training of the AFU personnel by the United States of America and Great Britain.
4. Initiate **unconditional** ceasefire talks between the Russian Federation and Ukraine through-
    a) International Recognition of the grievances of the Russian Federation on the grounds of –

  i) Crimes committed against humanity in Donbas by the AFU and other related agencies during the last decade.
  ii) The installation of US DoD bioweapons laboratories in Ukraine as a threat to the national security of the Russian Federation.
  iii) Active intervention by the US and other NATO states in the internal politics of Ukraine to promote anti-Russian sentiments within Ukraine.
  b) Encouraging Ukraine to seek peaceful compromise with the Russian Federation to promote regional security.

Based upon the document above, and identifying the severe threat that the world faces due to the ongoing Russia-Ukraine conflict, the Alliance seeks to take necessary steps to ensure an environment for a ceasefire is created promptly and without any further delay.

SEAL of UNIT

SEAL of LNSAG

Contacts

UNIT

unit.press@ghcpru.com

LNSAG

raydilorenzo@protonmail.com